ENCYCLOPAEDIA OF INDIAN GOVERNMENT: PROGRAMMES AND POLICIES

ENCYCLOPAEDIA OF INDIAN GOVERNMENT: PROGRAMMES AND POLICIES

Vol. 5

Education: Development & Planning

Edited by

Satish Tiwari

ANMOL PUBLICATIONS PVT. LTD.

NEW DELHI - 110 002 (INDIA)

ANMOL PUBLICATIONS PVT. LTD.
4374/4B, Ansari Road, Daryaganj
New Delhi - 110 002

Encyclopaedia of Indian Government: Programmes and Policies

First Edition, 2000
ISBN 81-261-0515-1 (Set)

PRINTED IN INDIA

Published by J.L. Kumar for Anmol Publications Pvt. Ltd., New Delhi - 110 002 and Printed at Mehra Offset Press, Delhi.

Contents

Preface

Encyclopaedia of Indian Government: Programmes and Policies contains authoritative information on about fifty departmental policies and their future developmental programmes.

Organised to be completed in 40 volumes, this gigantic work covers Agriculture; Atomic Energy; Chemicals and Fertilizers; Coal; Commerce; Communication; Culture; Defence; Education; Environment and Forests; External Affairs; Finance; Food & Consumer Affairs; Food Processing Industries; Health and Family Welfare; Home Affairs and Internal Security; Human Resources; Industry; Information and Broadcasting; Labour; Law, Justice and Company Affairs; Non-conventional Energy Sources; Ocean Development; Parliamentary Affairs; Personnel, Public Grievances and Pensions; Petroleum and Natural Gas; Planning and Programme Implementation; Planning and Statistics; Posts and Telegraphs; Power; Rural Development; Science and Technology; Social Justice and Empowerment; Space; States Affairs; Steel; Steel and Mines; Sugar and Edible Oils; Surface Transport; Textiles; Tourism; Urban Development; Water Resources; Women and Child development etc.

Based on the information derived from authoritative sources, this work contains authentic facts and figures. I am deeply beholden to all the scholars whose writings are cited or substantially made use of in the present work. I am also thankful to Anmol Publications Pvt. Ltd. for undertaking publication of this encyclopaedia. I am solely responsible for shortcomings in presentation of matter.

Encyclopaedic in nature, this will prove a dependable reference work for scholars and academics besides those appearing for different competitive examinations.

—**Satish Tiwari**

1

Education and Literacy

Education was one of the goals of the India's freedom movement and Mahatma Gandhi, even while leading the epic struggle against colonial power, evolved an alternative, community based system of education. Rooted in the struggle for Independence, several articles in the Constitution of India bring into focus the general principles governing educational development in the country. At the time of Independence in 1947 India inherited an educational system which was not only quantitatively small but was also characterized by striking regional and structural imbalances. Only 14 per cent of the population was literate and only one child out of three had been enroled in primary school. The low levels of enrolment and literacy were compounded by acute regional and gender disparities. Recognizing that education is vitally linked with the totality of the development process, the reform and restructuring of the educational system was accepted as an important area of state intervention.

Accordingly, the need for a literate population and universal education for all children in the 6-14 age group was provided with a precisely defined and delineated framework in the Indian Constitution as well as in successive Five Year Plans. The Constitution makes an elaborate legislative, administrative and financial distribution of powers between the state governments and the union government. Decisions regarding the organisation and structure of education are largely the concern of the states. Within the overall policy framework, each state determines independently the educational structures to be adopted. However, the Union Government has clear responsibility regarding the quality and character of education.

The Central Advisory Board of Education (CABE), set up during the pre-Independence period in 1935, continues to play a lead role in the evolution and monitoring of educational policies and programmes, the most notable of which are the National Policy (NPE), 1986, Programme of Action (POA), 1986, and a revised NPE and POA (1992).

In addition to policy formulation, the Department of Education shares with the states the responsibility for educational planning. Till the Sixth Plan, education was taken to be a social service rather than an imput in the development process. But now education is considered pivotal in social and economic development through development of human resources.This is reflected in the National Policy on Education, 1986 and in the budgetary allocation of resources. The Eighth Plan outlay for education (Centre and states) at Rs. 19,599.7 crore is higher than the Seventh Plan expenditure of Rs. 7,633.1 crore by 2.6 times. In keeping with this set up, the Central plan outlay for education has been substantially increased from Rs. 1,541 crore in 1994-95 to Rs. 1,825 crore in 1995-96. There has also been an inter se shift in the allocation of resources within the education sector from higher education to elementary education. The outlay on elementary education is up by 24.5 per cent to Rs. 651.04 crore in 1995-96. Further the outlay consists of Rs. 409.11 crore for secondary and physical education, Rs.

245.55 crore for university and higher education, Rs. 234 crore for adult education and Rs. 253.41 crore for technical education. Plan expenditure on different sectors of education (percentage) is given in table 1.

The National Policy on Education (NPE) 1986, a landmark in the educational development of the country was reviewed by a committee under the Chairmanship of Acharya Ramamurthi in 1990. Its recommendations were considered by the Central Advisory Board of Education (CABE) Committee on Policy under the Chairmanship of Shri N.Janaradhan Reddy, then Chief Minister, Andhra Pradesh which submitted its report on 22 January 1992. The Report was considered by the CABE which recommended certain modifications. Consequently, a Revised Policy Formulations containing the modifications recommended by the CABE were tabled in the Parliament on 7 May 1992. Subsequently, a revised Programme of Action (POA) was prepared to opertionalise the policy and the revised POA, 1992 was tabled in the Parliament on 19 August 1992.

Five thrust areas viz,. adult literacy, primary education, decentralisation of management of education, vocational education and technical education, have been identified to achieve Universalisation of Elementary Education to make education relevant to the needs of the community and also to meet new challenges of liberalisation and globalisation of the economy.

Education is the lifeline of development, be it spiritual or economic, scientific or technological, national or global. In the 21st century, countries will be measured by the education and health status of their population and not by GDPs and GNPs. The foremost component of education is its definition, aims, goals and objectives translated into an effective and practical policy. Included in this policy are a national curriculum, teaching strategies and evaluation procedures for measuring stated outcomes. Hence, an education policy and curriculum is to educational institutions what a blueprint is to an architect.

The education of an individual can be divided into five stages, namely preschool, primary, secondary, tertiary and adult education. The stage of preschool education is to the nation and educational institutions what a foundation is to a building. Both require a lot of specialization, knowledge and planning. Both are areas where we cannot afford to make a single mistake, else the entire structure will come tumbling down, or, we will have a scenario as highlighted they are both invisible. Further, just as a building can only be constructed with locally available materials, so too, a successful education policy and curriculum must reflect the culture, the needs, the norms, the language, and the values of its people.

Last but not least just as the construction of a building does not start from its roof, so too, there cannot be a downward extension of the education policy and curriculum. However, an examination of our education system over the length and breadth of the country, reflects just that! CBSE, ISC and IB (International Baccalaureate diploma) have become the focus and objective of our education system with an overdose of formal learning, texbooks, an overemphasis, on English language, an inappropriate age for admissions, and proliferation of private schools and teaching shops.

There are many problems with the Ministry's perception, namely:

- The most basic issue is that the new policy on education (NPE 1992) notwithstanding, the focus of our education system is CBSE, which neither prepares the children for life nor for the existing international competitive ethos—a point that MHRD has chosen to ignore. The problems as highlighted are an outcome of the deliberate ignorance of education by the MHRD in the past:

- As per National Council of Applied Economic Research (NCAER) report, excluding drop-outs, 55 million primary school children have never stepped into a school. Not only does it burgeon child labour statistics, these children and their parents know that the existing system does not prepare their children for life. So rejection of the system through child labour, and, poverty make for an excellent scapegoat. Instead of applying itself to the curriculum issues as highlighted by the Yashpal Committee report and advise the Planning Commission to make 'Education Policy' as the springboard to success, the MHRD has chosen to indulge in populist programmes like NSPE and DPEP.
- There has been a sharp rise in our interest payments and interest rates as highlighted. But the MHRD has chosen to borrow further from commercial international banks to fund a dead end UEE programme.
- The statutory transfer and enforcement of elementary education from the Directive Principles of the Constitution to Fundamental Human Right, will in all probability backfire. Instead of decentralizing power and placing it in the hands of the people, it has the capacity to further empower and strengthen the bureaucrats.
- Further, for the past 50 years, the government has demonstrated a stubborn lack of will to implement the Directive Principles of the Constitution. What is so sacrosanct about Fundamental Rights? Do we have a democratic education policy in place? Is the infrastructure in place? Do we have the required and

trained human power, ready to take the plunge? Have the PRIs really placed the power into the hands of the 'real' people or is it still concentrated in the secretariats of the Union and State governments? Have we really reached the monitoring and supervision stage to dare statutory enforcement of primary education? Have we really dumped the frivolous and cantankerous educational issues into the Indian Ocean?

- There is a contradiction in allowing the corporate sector and private sector into primary education as well as making it free and compulsory through statutory enforcement.
- Last but not least is the issue of funding and finance. A glance at the primary education trend during the eight five year plans, and the continuous tussle at the State-level of financing primary education vs other sectors, it is a foregone conclusion that primary education will emerge a loser.

With the colossal expenditure just on incentives to attract students through midday meals, free textbooks and uniforms, and scores of other expensive programmes, a question on everybody's lips is: After all this expenditure and programmes, do the students learn anything? If so, what do they learn? Is the acquired information useful to them? Despite such heavy funding through borrowed and taxpayers' money and the numerous populist programmes, why are the dropout rates so high? What is the correcd message–privatization of primary education or free and compulsory primary education? How does the government explain 10 per cent of rural population attending private schools vs 2 per cent in 1986? Why are we spending so heavily on a dead-end adult education programme? How has the programme benefited them if during the VIII Plan unemployment and underemployment has increased while self-employment and salaried employment has declined.

If we want to outbeat the competitive ethos and emerge a winner without being a drain on the exchequer, the following suggestions need to be placed on the front burner:

- Define education, literacy and development such that the entire nation understands it, accepts it and fully embraces it.
- The focus of the education policy must shift from the 3 Rs to the 3 Hs, i.e. the head, heart and hand—an education policy towards self-reliance and self-employment. The way we have defined education, literacy and development, we are only trying to catch our shadows, knowing fully well that shadows cannot be caught.
- Justify the logic for transferring education and health to the sector—charity syndrome. Such segregation and compartmentalization only fuels deficits and inflation.
- Ours is the typical case of the candle burning upside down! It is indeed very sad that during the Ninth Plan, primary education is to be guided and pushed forward for achieving the 7 per cent growth rate against the NPE (1992) grain of separating jobs from education.

— The issue is not one of resource crunch but one of will power, imagination and magnanimity to shun the powers and material gains accrued through chairs. The issue is one of redefining our education policies, be it industry, agriculture, employment, etc. The issue is one of redefining our education policy so that rural-urban dichotomies, gender dichotomies, rich-poor dichotomies are reduced. The issue is one of having the will to implement the new policy. The issue is one of demonstrating flexibility and tolerance to other points of issue is one of shedding fear and hypocrisy.

There is a saying: "If you graduated yesterday and stop learning today, you become uneducated tomorrow". Well, education is a continuous and patient process whereby individual talents and interests are developed and fostered; thereby giving a certain sense of completeness. Education is not purely a matter of literacy, or paper qualification. It is an exercise to be dignified, clam, austere, self-controlled and above all to be humane. Pursuit of knowledge must be supplemented by bond of love and friendship. As Plato says in the Republic, "True education, whatever that may be, will have greatest tendency, to civilize and humanize".

Scraps of information is worthless; education must promote rational autonomy , it must make men cultured, humane, and receptive to beauty and truth. Tagore too has said, "We have become learned but have ceased to be human". The high-brow attitude on the lowly and deprived is unworthy of an educated person. Education become meaningless without a sense of commitment towards the other. For the Baganda villages in Uganda, to be educated implies passionate dedication to God. Education in the Sri Lankan tradition has a similar connotation. He is considered educated who strives for the Buddhistic middle path.

Plato states wuite concisely the aims of education in the Laws: "education in youth upwards... makes a man eagerly pursue the ideal perfection of citizenship..." The Hellenic education made the Greeks mentally and physically perfect. The Greeks loved to argue as much as they loved to run or wrestle; there was no dichotomy of mind and muscles. In Sparta, education comprised in moral and civic training. Respect for age was a distinctive character of Spartan youth. The relation of the young to the adult was one of extraordinary obedience. On observing the revential attitude of the youth towards age, a stranger said praising. "It is a pleasure to grow old in Sparta". The Spartan's unflinching valour, uncomplaining endurance, and unfaltering devotion to the state was due to the training and education. The Athenians too, became good mannered, artistic and graceful through their education. It made them refined and appropriate in each activity. It made them respectful towards gods and parents. Marriages arranged by the fathers were preferred to than that of Cupid because, and only because, a Greek could not be disobedient to his father. Anything that was inarstic, clumsy or awkward was offensive to the Greeks.

The Hellenic eduction system made the Greeks open-minded, single-minded, sincere, responsible and wise. The Greeks offered their physical and intellectual abilities to glorify Gods. Their love of sports was so encyclopedic and extraordinary that even the dead were honoured by arranging an athletic festival. When Achilles desired to pay the highest honour to the spirit of his dead friend, Patroclus, he organised a festival of athletic games.

The Greeks always maintained a balance between mind and body. Sane mind and sound body were skillfully blended and balanced in human personality. Aristotle advocated this balance, through his principle of 'mean' or 'middle' which implied avoiding excess and deficiency. To achieve the balance the Greeks were made to pursue literature, philosophy, science, gymnastic, music, gesture, mimicry, oratory, stories, and choral singing.

Sophistication and modern technology has made individual extremely dependent on modern gadgets. This over-dependence must be off-set by deriving joy from sky, trees, plants, animals, rivers, lakes etc., in fact the entire nature must educate us. Tagore declared, "learning to see fire air, water, land, and the whole universe as pervaded by; universal consciousness is true education".

Tagore highly extolled the ability to learn directly from nature. The role of nature in education is so unique that Froebel who gave the basic concept of kindergarten schools, compared the school with a garden, and the educator with a gardener who attends his pupil as if they were plants.

Constant touch with nature develops in the individual the ability to appreciate beauty, truth and goodness.

The current system of education can have an added filip by having in the frontline the education model of Gurudev, so that "where the mind is without fear and the heads is held high, where knowledge is free,... where the clear stream of reason has not lost its way into the dreary desert sand of dead habit, ... Into that heaven of freedom, my Father, let my country awake".

It was Netaji Subhas Chandra Bose, who, in his Haripura presidential address in February 1938 gave birth to the concept of national planning. Later, in his address delivered at the Industries Ministers' Conference in Delhi on 2 October, 1938, he outlined his concept of national planning. On 19 October, 1938, he offered the chairmanship of National Planning Committee to Jawaharlal Nehru. In October 1946, a national level Advisory Planning Board was wet up. And in 1952, the Planning Commission was formed.

Since his Haripura address, Netaji had been stressing on industrialization, employment and education as the three springboards of national reconstruction. So had Gandhij, but with a different perspective and focus,with some convergence and overlapping. While Netaji was more inclined towards self-reliance through socialism, Gandhiji was inclined towards an indigenous model of education and capitalis. Neither views prevailed. Eventually, it was industrializaton, with neither a socialist nor capitalist ideology, that monopolized the first eight five year plans, accompanied with its positive and negative outcomes.

On 16 january, 1997 the National Development Council approved the Ninth Five Year Plan (1997-2002) approach paper, targeting a seven per cent economic growth. The Plan seeks growth with equity and distributive justice while focusing on agriculture and rural development as the means to provide employment and eradicate poverty. The target for agricultural growth is 4.5 per cent. The total Plan outlay proposes a 30 per cent increase over the VIII Plan outlay.

Ever since, the Plan has attracted immense criticism. But before discussing the Ninth Plan approach to education, a quich overview of the Ninth Plan framework is required.

Interestingly, in its introductory chapter, the plan is silent on the health sector. The preoccupation is with economics and the accompanying materialistic infrastructure at the cost of human capital. By clubbing education, health, family welfare, women and child development, housing, water supply and urban development under social sector, the Plan has deliberately chosen to inculcate and further the 'dependence-on-government' syndrome.

Criticisms: In the process, the Plan has attracted much flak, and rightly so, from the nation's intelligentsia, luminaries and common people. The criticism ranges from questioning the very significalce of the Planning Commission, to its methodology, to the finances and budgets.

Just to highlight a few comments, Mr. Jagmohan, MP, compares the Plan to a loose denture with blunt and uneven teeth. Columnist Shastri finds it fundmentally antagonistic to the liberalization ideology. And Mr. B.M. Bhatial, economic analyst has termed the entire approach as cavalier. Of course, the maximum criticism it has attracted is on the budgetary support and resources. With a budgetary outlay of Rs. 8,75,000 crore, bifurcated into a capital investment of Rs. 7,60,000 crore and a budgetary support of Rs. 3,70,000 crore, everything has been left to our imagination.

On the other hand, the biggest failure of the Plan has been to deliberately miss the 'education' boat for the ninth time. It took all of 50 years of our Independence for the contry's situation to be as highlighted. Simply, because our most learned planners refused to make an integrated, indigenous education policy as the springboard of national reconstruction.

During the early phase of the Independence Movement, leaders like Gokhale, Ranade, Naoroji and others tried to bring home to the Indian elite the illiberality of the so-called liberal education offered to the elite in the country. They, however, did not reach the masses, the downtrodden and the opressed in rural areas who did not have any infrastructure to receive any kind of education. This resulted in mass illiteracy, ignorance, cultural backwardness and all the miseries associated with the lack of literacy and education. In fact, nobody except Mahatma Gandhi advocated the education of the masses in a manner conducive to national development. Perhaps Gandhiji was the first in modern India to think of the enormity of the problem in a holistic manner and offer national solutions for the removal of ignorance, illiteracy and the lack of education. One reason for the massive illiteracy, ignorance and cultural backwardness prevalent even today is this indifference (forced by education) among the educated elite of pre-and post-independence India.

Gandhiji's vision of modern India was related to his ideas about education. Whatever Gandhiji said or did was relevant to the building of an India of his dreams because he had an integrated vision. like Ivan Illich or Paulo Freire whom he anticipated by several decades, Gandhiji questioned the relevance of the colonial type of education for a free and independent India. "I would revolutionize college education and relate it to national necessities".

Even about industry-university interaction, job-degree delinking, privatization of education and such other vital topics that agitate the minds of modern educationists, Gandhiji had clear ideas. For example, he advocated self-supporting schools and industry-institution-supported colleges.

The revolutionary aspects of the Gandhian vision of education for New India were summarized by himself as follows:

— For primary education extending for seven years, taken as a whole, a vocation or vocations are the best medium for all-round development of a boy a girl, and therefore all syllabus should be woven round vocational training.

— Higher education was to be left to private enterprise and it ought to meet national requirements 'whether in the various industries, technical arts, belles-letters or fine arts'.

— University charters should be given liberally to any body of persons of proved worth and integrity, it being always understood that the universities will not cost the State anything except that it will bear the cost of running a Central Education Department.

— Education should lead to the highest development of the mind but this development can take place only through a scientific cultivation of the faculties of the mind and body at various levels.

— Education should make the educated aware of what is going on in their surroundings, and enable them to analyze and why's and the wherefore's of every thing in their immediate environment.

Gandhiji was not opposed to literacy training, physical exercises or religious instruction. But he opposed literary training without vocational training physical exercises for body beautification purposes, and relligious instruction of a narrow kind. His thrust was on vocationalization of education at school and college levels because he believed that true learning could be imparted only through DOING. Education for self-aggrandisement was, according to him, anti-social education. Only that which served society, especially the poorest of the poor, could be termed true education.

But while advocating vocationalization, Gandhiji opposed the evils of mechanization and repetitive and mononotonous work.

"By working with the machines we have ourselves become machines and have lost all sense of art and handwork", Gandhiji said. He, however, said that in order "to develop the whole personality of the students, education through manual work is essential. The true development of the mind and the heart could be achieved only through manual labour. Thus Gandhiji questioned the usefulness of liberal arts education in a country where a very large number of young people remained unemployed after obtaining higher education. As a critic of the then existing educational system in India, he pointed out that it sohould be replaced by "a more constructive and human system, which (would) be better integrated with the needs and ideals ofnational life, and better able to meet its pressing demands".

Gandhiji ideas of education were tried by free India's government for a few years. The idea of BASIC EDUCATION (Nayi taalim) was tried in the rural setting for a short period in the mid-sixties but abandoned by the political decision makers responsible for educational matters. The old system of liberal arts education got all encouragement. Craft was discontinued at the school level. And no emphasis was given to vocationalization at the higher levels. We have thus created a huge army of unemployed, under-employed and unemployable graduates. And the acquisition of a degree has come to mean a passport to a clerical or other jobs unrelated to the education and training obtained at school/college. Sometimes even post-graduates go for employment as bus conductors, office clerks and other body jobs. A good many graduates do not go for any manual job or for self-employment.

The UGC's attempts to vocationalize are confined to the additon of a vocational courses in the undergraduate programme. By merely adding a vocational subject to the list of subjects now taught at the B.A., B.Sc. B.Com. levels, the problem of non-employability of present day graduates cannot be solved to any great extent. Vocationalization has to start in school; it will help reduce the mad rush for college education in the liberal tradition and make young people more career-oriented even at a young age. Morever, the UGC has to take steps for the introduction of the Credit-and-Semester System even at the under-graduate level for reasons explained below.

Gandhiji was not a professional economist, but he held strong views on the problems that are certainly the domain of economics.

He did not deny the impact of one's surroundings and material resources upon one's character, but he did not subscribe to the Marxian view that the final causes of all social changes and political revolutions were to be sought, not in man's sould, not in man's insight ito eternal truth and justice, but in changes in the modes of production. "I believe" Gandhiji said "and I have noticed too that thought transforms man's features as well as character".

He rejected outright the sordid figure of the economic man, who was always motivated by the tinkle of gold. He did not believe that man lives by bread alone. He saw faith as the mainspring of social well–being.

Like Hawtrey and Bohson, he believed that economics could not be dissociated from ethics. In him we find a powerful denunciation of the neutrality of economics as between ends preached by Senior, Cairness and Say, and rehabilitated recently by Robbins. "True economics", he said, "never militates against the highest ethical standard just as all true ethics to be worth its name must at the same time be also good economics".

His simple way of living earned for his economic views the nickname of loin—cloth economics. It was mistakenly though that he stood for a state of wantlessness or pleaded for a low, depressed standard of living. His approach was pragmatic and realistic. How could he lead a life of ease and luxury, when the millions of India were submerged in abysmal poverty? He gave up all possessions because being in the service of the poor he though he had no claims on those "I came definitely to the conclusion" hesaid, "that if I had to serve the people in whose midst my life was cast and to whose difficulties I was witness from day to day, I must discard all wealth, all possessions....and a time came when it became a positive joy to give up those things".

He further remarked, The golden rule...is resolutely to refuse to have what millions cannot". If the need of his fellow beings for something that he possessed was greater than his, he looked upon that thing as stolen property.

The theory of trusteeship of property is a logical projection of his theory of non—possession of what others cannot afford to get. He wanted the industrialists, the landlords and the other fortunate sections of the community t act as trustees of the wealth, which they were to use for the betterment of their poorer brethren.

He was against the blind application of economic theory as developed in the West to Indian conditions. Like Justice Ranade he was for the evolution of an Indian economy suited to the peculir conditions of Indians. "Each country has its ownb economies. German text-books are different from the English. Free trade may be England's salvation. It spells our ruin." His denunciation of free trade and solicitude for Swadeshi is a re—echo of List's plea for protection.

He was no enemy of machine, but he stood against it when it evslaved man or elbowed him out of the factory. Lack of capital ckoupled with a surfeit on man—power in India and theevils of the factory system led him to advocate a decentralised economic system with its accent on small–scale and cottage industries. "The salvation of India lies in cottages," was his slogan.

In his advocacy of cooperative farming he anticipated the presentday emphasis on it in the context of our backward agriculture and food deficit. "Ifirmly believe," he wrote in the 'Harijan', "that we shall not derive the full benefits of agriculture until we take to cooperative farming. Does it not stand to reason that it is far better for hundred families in a village to cultivate their lands collectively and divide the income therefrom than to divide the land anyhow into a hundred portions."

He was not blown off his feet by the material achievements of socialism in the West. He believed in the evolution of and indigenous variety of socialism. "Let us study our eastern institutions in that spirit of enquiry and we shall evolve a truer sokcialism and a truer communism that the world has yet dreamt of". His socialism can be classed with that of the Utopian socialists, who received the undisguised contempt of Marx. He was not against communism as such. He claimed for himself the title of "a foremost communist." His communism was, however, based on non–violence and pure means to achieve it. "If communism comes without violence", he said, "would be welcome." These words ring in sharp contrast to the Communist Manifesto of 1843.

Gandhian economics, in sum, is rooted in non–violence, truth, love and self—sacrifice. It rejects coercion, regimentation, self–interest, centralisation of means of production and wealth, and above all a mad pursuit of the material goods of life.

Literacy and education

- Our system of elementary education is the second largest in the world with 151 million children enrolled in 1994-95 in the age group of 6-14 years covering about 91 per cent of the children in this age group.
- The number of primary schools increased substantially from 2.10 lakh in 1950-51 to 5.90 lakh in 1995-96. During the same period, the number of upper schools rose from 0.14 lakh to 1.71 lakh. The Gross Enrolment Ratio (GER) in the primary stage (classes I-V) increased from 42.6 per cent in 1950-51 to 104.3 per cent in 1995-96 and in the upper

primary stage (classes VI-VIII) from 12.7 per cent to 67.6 per cent. These changes have contributed in raising the overall literacy rate from 18.3 per cent in 1951 to 52.2 per cent in 1991.

- What is equally important at this stage is that concerted efforts are required for raising the GER at the primary stage in States like Bihar, Haryana and Uttar Pradesh which are having GERs of less than 90 per cent. This would help in raising the literacy levels in these States.
- The affirmative policies of the Government have helped in raising the enrolment of Scheduled Castes (SCs) and Scheduled Tribes (STs) considerably as was mentioned in the Economic Survey 1995-96. The participation of SCs and STs in now more or less primary level. Dropouts, though declining over the years, are significantly large. Gender disparities are also very conspicuous among SCs and STs.
- The total Literacy Campaign has become the principal strategy of the Naitonal Literacy Mission (NLM) in the eradication of illiteracy throughout the country. The target for achieving the total literacy is now 2005 A.D. As December 1996, 417 districts have been covered either fully or partially under the Total Literacy Campaign. Similarly, 178 districts have also been covered under the Post Literacy Campaign. Under all the schemes of NLM, 57.96 million persons have so far been made literate as per NLM norms against an enrolment of 96.80 million. The new scheme of Continuing Education for neo-literates (approved in December, 1995) is now under implementation.
- In view of the importance of the National Programme of Nutritional Support to primary education (Mid-Day Meal Programme) which was launched from 15th August, 1995 for boosting

universalisation of education and improving the nutritional level of students in primary classes (I-VI), the Central Plan allocation has been raised from about 612 crore in 1995-96 (RE) to Rs.1400 crore in 1996-97 (BE). The Central support under this programme is on the following:

— Provision of foodgrains free of cost to the implementing agencies.

— Reimbursement to District authorities for transportation cost for moving of foodgrains from Food Corporation of India's godowns to schools/villages at the rate of Rs.25 per quintal as applicable under Revamped Public Distribution System.

— Remuneration for conversion of foodgrains into cooked food as well as expenditure on construction of kitchen sheds will be eligible for coverage under the poverty alleviation schemes being administered by the Ministry of Rural Development.

- The Mid-Day Meal Programme has commenced in all the States/UTs. Seven States, namely, Gujarat, Haryana, Jammu & Kashmir, Kerala, Madhya Pradesh, Orissa and Tamil Nadu and UT of Pondicherry are serving cooked meals. In rest of the States/UTs foodgrains are being distributed.
- The District Primary Education Programme (DPEP) introduced in 1994 is the most intensive effort by the Central Government to operationalise the strategy of deccentralised planning for Universal Elementary Education (UEE) as envisaged by the National Policy on Education, 1986. This has been in operation in 59 districts of eleven States of Andhra Pradesh, Assam, Gujarat, Himachal Pradesh, Haryana, Karnataka, Kerala, Madhy Pradesh, Maharashtra, Orissa and tamil Nadu, DPEP is funded by multiple external agencies including the World Bank and the European Commission.

- The Central Plan outlay for DPEP has been raised substantially from Rs.25 crore in 1995-96 (Be) to about Rs.239 crore n 1996-97(BE).
- With a view to bringing the benefits of Techno-Economic advances and large scale investments in the Technical Education Systen to the poorest of the poor in the country, the Government has been running an institutionalised and structured scheme of Community Polytechnics functioning all over the country. This alongwith its extension centres in remote/inaccessible areas provides a delivery capacity comparable to that of the committed voluntary organisations. The network of Community Polytechnics. A large number of villagers have also been benefitted through transer of technology these institutions.
- The share of both Central and State Governments including local bodies, etc. in financing educational institutions to be quite high. It accounted for 92.9 per cent of the total income of educational institutions in 1990-91, whereas the share from fees and endowments and other sources of educational institutions declined sharply.
- While the Central Government plays an important role for overall policy directions in education and funding of centrally sponsored plan schemes, the State Governments provide most of the funding for education system. There is, therefore, an urgent need for State Governments to re-prioritise expenditure and tighten fiscal discipline. Private initative s in education may be encouraged for supplementing the public resources. Further, resources must be mobilised by revising fees and other user charges especially for higher levels of education.

For the purpose of census, a person is deemed as literate if he or she can read and write any language with understanding. In the 1991 census, the question on literacy was canvassed only for population aged seven years and above, unlike earlier censuses which took into account population of five years and above for this purpose.

The final results reveal that there has been an increase in literacy in the country. The literacy rate in the country (excluding Jammu and Kashmir) is 52.21 per cent (64.13 for males and 39.29 for females).

Kerala retained its position by being on top with a 89.81 per cent literacy rate in the country. Bihar stood at the bottom with a literacy rate of 38.48 per cent, with Rajasthan being close to it having 38.55 literacy percentage. But literacy among the women was the lowest in Rajasthan with a percentage of 20.44 as compared to 54.99 among the males.

— In 1981, census was not conducted in Assam. Based on the 1971 census and the final results of the 1991 census the population of Assam as on 1 March 1981 has been interpolated.

- The 1991 census has not yet been conducted in Jammu and Kashmir. The population figures for India include the population figure for Jammu and Kashmir projected by the Standing Committee of Experts on population projection (October 1989).
- The 1971 census was conducted with 1 April 1971 as the reference date. In both the 1961 and 1981 censuses the reference date was 1 March. The average annual exponential growth rate presented in the statement takes into account this difference. No such adjustment has been made while calculating decadal growth rate.
- In Arunachal Pradesh the census was conducted for the first time in 1961. While working out the decadal

growth, both absolute as well per cent for 1951-61, 1961 census population of Arunachal Pradesh has been excluded.

According to the 1991 Census, the national literacy rate for the population aged seven years and above, increased form 43.56 per cent in 1981 to 52.21 per cent in 1991 registering an increases by 8.65 percentage points. While the male literacy increased by 13.10 per cent, the female literacy rate increased by 6.45 per cent. The number of literates aged seven and above in 1991 at 3,593 lakh compares very well with the number of literates at 2,357 lakh in 1981. The number of illiterates in 1991 was 3,289 lakh which is a marginal increase form the 3,053 lakh in 1981. The increase in the number of literates in 1991 over 1981 was 1,236 lakh whereas the corresponding increase in the number of illiterates was 236 lakh only. Kerala (89.81 per cent) tops the literacy rate followed by Mizoram (82.27 per cent), Lakshadweep (81.78 per cent) and Chandigarh (77.81 per cent). At the end of the ladder are Bihar (38.48 per cent), Rajasthan (38.55 per cent) and Dadra and Nagar Haveli (40.71 per cent). The increase in female literacy rate has been very significant in the states/union territory–Sikkim (19.29 per cent), Lakshadweep (17.59 per cent), Nagaland (14.45 per cent), Manipur (13 per cent), Andaman and Nicobar Islands (12.26 per cent), Pondicherry (12.63 per cent), Tripura (11.65 per cent) and Kerala (10.47 per cent).

The literacy rate is above the all India level of 52.21 per cent in case of 22 states/union territories but nine states/union territories viz., Bihar, Rajasthan, Arunachal Pradesh, Madhya Pradesh, Uttar Pradesh, Andhra Pradesh, Meghalaya, Orissa and Union Territory of Dadra and Nagar haveli are still below the threshold level of literacy i.e. 50 per cent. All these states/union territories except Meghalaya are also below the all India level in case of female literacy.

Education is the key to, all processes of development especially human development. Catalytic action of education in this complex and dynamic growth process needs to be planned meticulously and executed with great sensitivity. Education is fundamental to allround development of human potential-material and spiritual. It refines sensitivities and perceptions that contribute to national cohesion, a scientific temper and independence of mind and spirit -thus furthering the goal of socialism, secularism and democracy enshrined in our Constitution.

Education develops manpower for different levels of economy and empowers the poor masses to become self-reliant enough to participate, in the process of national development. Education is thus an instrument for developing an economically prosperous society and for ensuring equity and social justice.

The education scenario at the time of independence was structurally flawed with inequities characterised by gender, social and regional imbalances. Even though the post-independence period saw significant achievements in the field of education, the structural flaws continued and, to a certain extent, got accentuated. An attempt to take a holistic view was made in 1986 through the National Policy on Education.

The National Policy on Education (NPE), 1986 is a landmark in the history of Indian education. The NPE visualised education as a dynamic, cumulative, life-long process, providing diversity of learning opportunities to all segments of society. It envisaged improvement and expansion of education in all sectors; elimination of disparities in access and stresses on improvement in the quality and relevance of education at all levels-from primary to higher education along with technical and professional education.

The National Policy on Education (NPE) also emphasised that education must play a positive and interventionist role in correcting social and regional imbalances in empowering women and in securing a rightful place for linguistic and minorities. The nation is now firmly committed to provide Education For All. Overriding priority to provide compulsory primary education, coverage of children with special needs, eradication of illiteracy, vocationalisation, education for women's equality, special focus on the education of SCs/STs and Minorities are the major strategies to achieve the national goal of Universalisation of Elementary Education (UEE).

The educationally backward areas are given special attention to remove regional disparities. Emphasis has been laid on the improvement of infrastructural facilities in the primary schools to make the school environment more attractive. Flexible and innovative programmes in the form of Non-Formal Education (NFE) have been launched to cater to school dropouts, girls, working children, etc. The National Literacy Mission (NLM) was set up to represent a national and political commitment on the need to harness all social forces to achieve the objective of eradicating illiteracy and effecting a qualitative change in the lives of the people.

It has made it possible for the country to set a target of making 100 million non-literates in the age group of 15-35 years functionally literate. Vocationalisation has been given emphasis to develop healthy attitude among students towards work and life, to enhance individual employability to reduce the mismatch of demand and supply of skilled manpower, and to provide an alternative for those intending to pursue higher education without particular interest or purpose.

Secondary education has its importance in the

national development as it provides large skilled manpower for the economy and prepares for higher, technical and professional education. It is the stage where a proper understanding of work ethos and values of a humane and composite culture is provided to future citizens of the country.

There is great demand for expansion of higher education on account of increasing expansion of primary and secondary education and rising social expectations. Consequently, emphasis has been on the removal of disparities and to equalise educational opportunities attending to the specific needs to those who have been denied equality so far. The country is passing through major economic developments with liberalisation and globalisation of the economy. The universities are also expanding their territorial boundaries through distance education. In all these areas, quality assurance has become a major focus.

Educational development is a participatory process. Education was incorporated in the Concurrent List to facilitate evolution of all India policies in the field of education. The concept of concurrency implies a meaningful partnership between the Union Government and the States. While the role and responsibility of States to provide education continues to remain essentially unchanged, the Union Government has assumed a larger responsibility to reinforce the national and integrated character of education, to look after the international aspects of Education, Culture and Human Resource Development; and, in general, to promote excellence in all sectors of education throughout the country.

Having regard to the size of the population, diversity and economic frailties the challenges are enormous. This realisation has resulted in steadily rising levels of budgetary allocations, and resource transfer for educational initiatives to the States. Given in the succeeding paras is a resume of the current state of education in some of the areas of fundamental concern.

Elementary education

The Elementary Education system in India is one of the largest in the world. There has been massive expansion of Elementary Education (EE) during the post-independence period, however, the goal of Universalisation of Elementary Education (UEE) is yet to be achieved.

Universal access, universal retention and universal achievements are broad parameters to achieve UEE. Considering the magnitude and the complexity of the problem, meticulously formulated strategies have been adopted in the form of Operation Blackboard (OB), Non-Formal Education (NFE), Teacher Education (TE). District Primary Education Programme (DPEP) to address the specific problem areas, gender and regional disparities.

Special focus has been laid on the access to education for millions of girls and working children, who cannot participate in the school system on account of socio-economic compulsions. These segments largely constitute girls, SCs/STs and the other deprived sections of the society. Unattractive school environment, unsatisfactory conditions of buildings and insufficiency of instructional material acting as major demotivating factors for enrolment and retention of children in primary schools called for a drive called Operation Blackboard for substantial improvement in the infrastructural facilities at the primary stage. The physical targets for the Eighth Plan were achieved with remarkable success. The scheme has been expanded to cover upper primary schools as well. A national evaluation of the scheme has been entrusted to NIEPA recently.

A large and systematic programme of Non-Formal Education (NFE), which is an integral component of the strategies to achieve UEE has been taken up to cover children who cannot attend formal school due to socio-economic compulsions. Girls, working children, dropouts and those belonging to SC/ST and deprived sections of the society stand to benefit from this approach. NFE has enough flexibility to provide education at their doorsteps to enable them to learn at their own pace and convenience. The major challenge is for NFE to maintain quality comparable with the formal system.

The National Programme of Nutritional Support to Primary Education is intended to boost enrolment, attendance and retention in primary schools and also to supplement nutritional requirements of children. The scheme covers the children studying in primary classes in the Government, local body and Government- aided schools throughout the country. Total beneficiaries are estimated to be 9.75 crores in nearly 6.88 lakh primary schools in the country during the period under report.

The District Primary Education Programme provides special thrust to achieve Universalisation of Primary Education (UPE) through decentralised planning and management, disaggregated target setting, community mobilisation, district and population specific planning. The programme mainly aims at providing access to primary education for all children, reducing dropout rates to less than 10 per cent, increasing level of achievements of primary students by at least 25 per cent and reducing the gap among gender social groups to less than 5 per cent catering to the needs of special target groups like tribals, SCs, women and other marginalised sections.

The Teacher Education scheme envisages setting up of DIETs in each district to provide academic and resource support to elementary education teachers and non-formal and adult education instructors. It also envisages establishment of CTEs/IASEs to organise preservice and in-service training for secondary teachers and provide extension and resource support service to secondary schools. IASEs are expected to conduct programmes for preparation of elementary teacher educators, conduct in-service training for elementary and secondary teacher educators and Principals of secondary schools; engage in advanced level fundamental and applied research especially of inter-disciplinary nature; and provide academic guidance to DIETs and support services to CTEs. 448 DIETs, 76 CTEs and 34 IASEs have been established under the scheme till the end of January 1999.

Some area-specific externally aided projects in the field of primary education are also being implemented. Shiksha Karmi Project (SKP) aims at universalisation and qualitative improvement to primary education in remote and socioeconomic backward villages of Rajasthan with focus on girls. It identifies teacher absenteeism as a major problem in primary schools and in inaccessible areas. Mobilisation and participation of the community to improve primary schools is an important feature of the project. Lok jumbish is an innovative people's movement for education. Bihar Education Project (BEP) is meant to provide education for all through people's mobilisation and participation. It is a basic education project which aims at bringing out qualitative improvement in the educational system and overall socio-cultural situation in Bihar. Although special programmes have been taken up to improve upon specific deficiencies in the educational system, no strategies can succeed in achieving UEE without specifically addressing its gender and regional dimensions. Gender disparities are conspicuous in India. Recognising this gender bias, most programmes have specific components for ameliorating the condition of the girl child.

Adult education

Literacy is an important tool for communication' learning and information. It is a virtual precondition for individual and national development. The National Literacy Mission represents a national and political commitment on the need to harness all social forces to achieve the objective of eradicating illiteracy and effecting a qualitative change in the lives of the people. It has made it possible for the country to set a target to make 100 million persons in the age group of 15 to 35 years functionally literate in the foreseeable future.

The Total Literacy Campaign (TLC) is the principal strategy adopted by NLM for eradication of illiteracy in the country. The Literacy Campaigns are area-specific, time-bound, delivered through voluntarism, cost effective and outcome- oriented.

After completion of the TLC in a distruct, Post Literacy Programme (PLP) is launched to mop up the leftover illiterates and also to consolidate the gains accrued during TLC. This enables the neo-literates to develop abilities for self-learning and skill upgradation. A total of 450 districts have been covered by TLCs. Of these, 250 districts have moved into the Post Literacy phase.

The ultimate objective is to carry forward the literacy programmes in the district to the third phase of life-long learning which is conceived under the scheme of Continuing Education. In this final phase the Centre-based approach in a revitalised and restrengthened form is brought back to the centrestage of adult education activities. The Continuing Education Centres would aim to create a learning environment in the villages and habitation which they serve. There would be opportunities here for addressing the residual non-literates and for providing neo-literates with Equivalency Programmes, Income Generation Programmes, Quality of Life Improvement Programmes, and Individual Interest Promotion Programmes.

The NLM takes special care to emphasise linkages between literacy and life and in so doing provides enhanced opportunities for skill development and improved income generation. This attempt is operationalised through the scheme of Shramik Vidyapeeths. The basic idea behind the multi -dimensional or polyvalent education approach to the education of urban working community in Shramik Vidyapeeth is to meet the various inter-related needs of target groups which mainly constitute the socially and economically deprived sections of worker communities with specifically tailored programmes. This provides knowledge and imparts vocational and technical skills in an integrated manner. The programme helps in enhancing employment opportunities and supplementing their income.

The NLM also lays emphasis on involving voluntary agencies. Several of them have been provided with assistance to take up innovative programmes on adult education in various parts of the country.

The NLM also has set up 25 State Resource Centres which provide academic input, improved training practices and opportunities for creation of imaginative literature for neo-literates. Under Adult Education Programmes 72.56 million persons have been made literate so far, 60 per cent of them are women: 22.40 per cent are SCs and 13.20 per cent belong to STs.

The NLM has a system of concurrent and external evaluation of literacy campaigns and post-literacy programmes by reputed research agencies in the field of social sciences.

According to the National Sample Survey Organisation (NSSO) the percentage of literacy has increased from 52 in 1991 to 62 in 1997 and projected at 64 for 1998.

The quantum jump of 10 percent between 1991 and 1997 and 12 per cent between 1991 and 1998 thus compares extraordinarily favourable with the decadal trends of previous years which are at an average of 8.5 per cent since Independence. The urban-rural differential in literacy rates has also shown a marked decline of 4 per cent, this is faster than in any previous decade. The rise in female literacy between 1991 and 1997 has been 11 per cent whereas the male literacy rate has risen by 9 per cent. This is a tribute to the special emphasis laid by NLM on women's participation. With annual rate of literary growth of 2 per cent revealed by NSSO survey, India could be expected to touch sustainable threshold level of 75 per cent by 2005.

Although the literacy campaigns are being implemented with varying degrees of success, it is certain that remarkable progress has been achieved. The focus is now on the four low literacy Hindi-speaking States which together account for nearly 50 per cent of the total number of illiterates in the country. Now that the process has begun in these States as well, the goal of universal literacy appears closer.

Some of the spin-offs of TLCs have been improved enrolment at primary level; social empowerment of women; improvement in immunisation and acceptance of the small family norms and organised correction of superstitions and social evils. This has generated a great demand for adult education projects throughout the country.

The National Literacy Mission has undertaken a number of new initiatives in adult education. These include rigorous system of monitoring of literacy campaigns; transparent and more effective evaluations; sensitising Panchayati Raj representatives to ensure mass participation in literacy programmes and decentralising of financial and administrative powers to State Literacy Mission Authorities.

Secondary education

Secondary Education which serves as a bridge between primary and higher education serves a step towards preparation for higher and professional education. Socio-economic imperatives and initiatives taken during the Eighth Plan to provide learning facilities to school-going children up to elementary stage, has necessitated that the perspective for Secondary Education Sector in the Ninth Plan would be, besides vocationalisation, substantial expansion of infrastructure, innovation in harnessing technology for improved teaching/ learning and quality upgradation. This visualises the maximum expansion requirements of the secondary education infrastructure during the Ninth Plan without diluting the quality.

The schemes initiated during the Eighth Plan such as Vocationalisation, Improvement of Science Education, Computer Literacy, Educational Technology, special interventions for girls, Integrated Education of Disabled Children, etc. have been made fully functional during the Ninth Plan. Besides, applications of available communication technology to promote school education at all levels and in all areas figure prominently in the deficient and remote areas. For this, open learning system (Distance Education) has been emphasised.

The key issues in Secondary Education apart from access are quality, relevance, modernisation and diversification. The norms developed by the NCERT for standards of minimum facilities for schools are being provided. The concept of Minimum Levels of Learning is being extended to the secondary stage as well. Emphasis has been laid on programme in Value Education, Population Education and various newly emerging concerns such as Human Rights, Adolescence Education. Greater diversification and flexibility, proper education materials, capacity building in the schools to gradually eliminate the domination exercised by the public examinations are some of the aspects of modernisation of curriculum. The NCERT continues to play a nodal role in evaluation of textbooks from the standpoint of national integration and incorporation of core elements outlined in the National Policy on Education (NPE). More transparency and authenticity is being visualised as a part of examination reforms.

Teacher Education is being strengthened to provide quality pre-service and in-service training to secondary school teachers to update their competency and professional skills.

The thrust on Vocational Education is continuing to meet the increasing demand of skilled manpower in the context of changing economic environment with globalisation and consequent induction of new and emerging technologies. Given the complexity and magnitude of the task a multi-pronged strategy has been adopted with multiple entry and exit options to vocational students. Almost 35 per cent of children drop out before reaching Class V and over 50 per cent reach Class VIII Finally, only about 6 per cent reach the degree level and hence, intervention at each stage in the form of vocational education is necessary to enable the potential dropouts with some skills. The programme is being strengthened and expanded.

Kendriya Vidyalayas and Navodaya Vidyalayas are promoting excellence in education with a national identity throughout the country. Navodaya Vidyalayas have an added objective to provide opportunities to talented rural children particularly girls of deprived sections of the society. These schools are intended to become pace-setters of a nationwide programme of school improvement with innovation and experimentation.

The National Open School has been providing flexible life-related education through distance education mode to deprived and socio-economically backward sections of the society in the remotest parts of the country. It designs, develops and offers flexible courses at secondary/ senior secondary stage and is equipped to meet the growing demand of those who find it difficult to attend full time school and the working people, who could not complete secondary stage. The major beneficiaries are women, SCs/STs; and other deprived sections of the society. The technological advancement has increased its potential substantially.

The National Council of Educational Research and Training (NCERT) continues to provide major resource support to school education in the form of various experimental innovative programmes; to diversify and make qualitative improvements in secondary education and also reducing the burden of school bag.

The NCERT textbooks have the unique distinction of being attractive and inexpensive. These books are widely adopted by schools throughout the country. 'Persons with Disability Act, 1995' has placed responsibility on the Government to ensure that every child with disability has access to free education until the age of 18 years. The integration of disabled children in the ongoing and evolving schemes is in progress to achieve additional coverage.

Higher education

Higher Education has a crucial role to play in the process of progress and modernisation. There has been considerable expansion of higher education with its role for economic and social development. The expansion of the system has been affecting the quality to a great extent. The Government, during the year, has tried to focus upon the initiatives to address the quality issues in higher education.

There has been consistent efforts to improve upon the salaries and service conditions of University and College teachers so as to attract talents in the teaching profession. Accordingly, the recommendations of the Fifth Central Pay Commission were extended to the University and College teachers with further improvement and modifications in the scales suggested by the committee earlier set up by the UGC for this purpose. As a result, the expenditure on account of the salaries to Central University teachers increased over Rs 300 crores during the year 1998-99. The Government also agreed to meet 80 per cent of the expenditure incurred by the State Government towards implementation of the improved pay scales, for a period of five years.

The country made significant contribution to setting up the world agenda for higher education in the twenty-first century. A high power delegation led by the Minister for Human Resource Development attended the UNESCO World Conference on Higher Education held at Paris between 5-9 October 1999. India's amendments to the World Declaration on Higher Education were highly appreciated by the Conference. One such accepted amendment. Ultimately, higher education should aim at the creation of a new society—non-violent and non-exploitative—consisting of highly cultivated, motivated and integrated individuals, inspired by love for humanity and guided by wisdom.

The Government took concrete measures to reform Higher Education and initiated steps for restructuring the UGC to achieve the purpose, during the year. A Task Force, headed by Prof. Amrik Singh submitted its report and has recommended amendments in the UGC Act so as to provide for wholetime members in the Commission, increase the penalty for running fake universities and awarding unrecognised degrees and make the laws more stringent, regulate the operation of foreign universities, encourage the setting up of self-financing institutions that could award degrees also and allow colleges and universities to determine the tuition fees within a broad policy framework and guidelines.

By the end of Ninth Plan it is expected that at the rate of 5.5 per cent compound rate of present growth there will be 8.5 per cent million students, and 10,000 colleges. Innovative initiatives have been taken up in the form of distance education to cater to the unprecedented expansion. It is expected that reforms initiated in Higher Education during the year would go a long way to meet the needs and challenges of the system in terms of quantity as well as quality.

Technical education

Technical Education which includes Management Education as well, is the main vehicle of social and economic transformation in the country. It is one of the most vital and significant components of the human resource development spectrum with great potential for adding value to products and services, for contributing to the national economy and for improving the quality of life of the common man. It has also been instrumental in making significant contribution to India's economic development by way of manpower production and relevant activities suiting to the needs of the industry and society and adapting to the vast changes in the global economy.

Background and growth

The rapid industrialisation during the post-independence period witnessed phenomenal growth of technical education facilities in the country. The first three Five Year Plans were devoted to expansion of technical education to meet the growing demands for technical personnel at Diploma, Degree and P.G. levels. From the Fourth Five Year Plan onwards, emphasis was on the improvement of quality and standards of technical education. Apart from the Government Sector, involvement of private and voluntary organisations in setting up of Technical and Management Institutes helped in the expansion of the system. From 43 Polytechnics with an intake of 3,400 students at the time of Independence, the number has grown to 1, 128 Polytechnics with the intake of 1.90 lakh students in 1997. Similarly, the number of Degree level institutions and the corresponding intake figure rose from 38 and 2940 in 1947 to 552 and 1.36 lakh in 1997. 185 institutions today conduct P.G. courses in Engineering and Technology with an annual intake capacity of 16,800. Facilities for Doctoral Studies in Engineering, Technology and Applied Sciences have also been created in a number of Technical Institutions.

This quantitative increase had its repercussion on the quality of technical education. A mushroom growth of self-financing private Engineering Colleges /Technical

Institutions in the country, particularly in the southern region was causing concern to the policy makers, throwing to the winds all norms and standards for ensuring quality technical education. Accordingly, AICTE which was an advisory body since 1945, was given statutory status with the introduction of AICTE ACT, 1987 with a view to the proper planning and co-ordinated development of technical education system throughout the country. The AICTE issued Regulations in October 1994 relating to grant of approval for starting new technical institutions, introduction of courses or programmes and approval of intake capacity of seats for the courses for programmes. These were subsequently amended in May 1997.

The technical education system was to enhance its coverage and accessibility suiting to the needs of organised as well as unorganised and rural sectors with its relevance to productivity. Several initiatives were taken to revamp the technical education system by modernising the laboratories, etc. in technical institutions, promoting industry-institution interaction, providing continuing education for upgrading the skill and knowledge of technical personnel working in industry and services sector, transfer of technology to the rural sector and setting up of Technology Development Missions to meet the emerging challenges in the field of engineering and technology with active participation of industries. A major project was undertaken with the assistance of the World Bank to upgrade the technician education system for enabling the Polytechnics to improve their capacity, quality and efficiency. The scheme of Community Polytechnics was launched that aims at sustainable community development without environmental degradation by way of science and technology applications for socio-economic uplift and improvement in the quality of life of the common man through micro-level planning and people's participation at the grassroot level. The scheme lays stress on poverty alleviation, employment generation and removal of drudgery for the women through location- culture specific non-formal need-based short term training in skill oriented technical /vocational trades.

To upgrade the Technician Education System in the Polytechnics, in the terms of capacity, quality and efficiency, a massive World Bank aided State Sector Project was launched in two phases starting 1990. The fall-out of the project created increase in women's participation in Technician Education from 12 per cent to 27 per cent through establishment of new Women's Polytechnics and Women's Wings in the existing Polytechnics. To render the benefits of techno-economic advances in Technical Education towards rural/ community development, the scheme of Community Polytechnics with Extension Centres are functioning all over the country today including hilly, desert, coastal, remote, difficult and minority concentrated areas. Meaningful and relevant Apprenticeship Training is being provided under the apprentice Act, 1961 (amended) to a large number of Engineering Degree, Diploma and 10+2 (Vocational) Pass-outs to bridge the gap between the world of Academics and the Industry and to help them achieve better employment prospects.

Development of appropriate technical manpower with assured quality in technology and management areas, was sought to be achieved through establishment of six Indian Institutes of Technology and six Indian Institutes of Management at different places in the country. Two specialised institutes with flexible academic design and non-conventional modular courses at Certificate, Diploma and Degree levels in Engineering / Technology/ Applied Sciences, viz. (i) North Eastern

Regional Institute of Science and Technology (NERIST), Itanagar, Arunachal Pradesh and (ii) Sant Longowal Institute of Engineering and Technology at Village Longowal, Sangrur, Punjab were also set up for appropriate manpower development in technical areas. An Institute for Information Technology and Management for development of specified technical manpower in the emerging area of Information technology has also been set up at Gwalior.

It may thus be seen that India has a large infrastructure of technical institutions spread all over the country which qualitatively and quantitatively can compete with the best available facilities in the world. The Indian -Institutes of Technology (IITs) are premier centres of education and training in engineering and applied sciences at under-graduate level and provide facilities for post-graduate studies and research. Indian Institutes of Management (IIMs) have been functioning as centres of excellence with the objective of providing education, training, research and consultancy in management. Indian Institute of Science, Bangalore has earned recognition as centre of research in basic and engineering sciences and allied fields. Excellence and creativity in research and development and learning programmes have characterised academic activity of the Institute. The Institute has also set up Super Computer with an Internet Hook-up.

The National Policy on Education has laid emphasis on modernisation and removal of obsolescence of laboratories and workshops of engineering colleges and polytechnics in order to enhance functional efficiency. The scheme covers IITs and Regional Engineering Colleges (RECs) and other Engineering Colleges, Technical Faculties of Universities and Polytechnics.

Priority is being given to bring industrial

commercial system and institutions closer. Technology missions in seven identified generic areas of strategic significance have been set up on the basis of their relevance to the Indian economy through IITs and IISc. These missions have earned wide acceptance and confidence among industries for development and know-how transfer of various technologies/ products by them and as such a unique example of industry-institute partnership has been established. The technical education system is vibrant even in the remote areas of North East (including Sikkim), Andaman & Nicobar Islands, Jammu & Kashmir and the Union Territories of, inter alia, Daman and Dadra & Nagar Haveli. Towards promotion of overall societal development in such areas through technological inputs, expansion of technical education facilities is always encouraged through establishment of newer technical institutions and strengthening of the existing ones through all sorts of academic, technical and managerial support, co-operation and guidance.

As such, while we have higher level technical institutions like (i) I.I.T, Guwahati, (ii) NERIST, Itanagar, (iii) R.E.C., Silchar and scores of Diploma level Polytechnics in the North East, the Union Territories of Delhi, Chandigarh and Pondicherry offer high quality technical education through Degree and higher level technical institutions as well as Diploma level Polytechnics which are there even in the other UTs of A&N Islands, Daman and Dadra & Nagar Haveli. The State of J&K does not lag too far behind with one Regional Engineering College at Srinagar, one Government College of Engineering and Technology at Jammu and a large number of Polytechnics in the State. In spite of this massive and cumulative build-up of a diverse infrastructural base, technological capability and institutional growth stand threatened from the sudden and complex change in the industrial base of the country and the advent of global competition in the wake of economic liberalisation. To face new challenges the thrust during the Ninth Plan is envisaged on the following four dimensions:

— Sustaining and consolidating the infrastructures and initiative with visible gains developed during the Eighth Plan and expanding the scope of such infrastructures for additional gains.
— Strengthening system of management and governance at all levels, networking between institutions and developing effective new linkages.
— Introducing new and innovative schemes which shall enhance the vibrancy of the system and help it conform to the emerging demands of industrial growth and societal development in terms of new technologies as well as quality enhancement.
— Expanding the research base amongst technical institutions to effectively tackle the industrial problems related to product, process and technology developments and also the manpower need.

Monitoring and evaluation

Under the scheme of Teacher Education it has been decided to undertake an assessment of the technical and infrastructural capacity of DIETs with a view to critically assessing the adequacy and quality of various training resource functions being carried out and to recommend immediate and long-term actions aiming towards strengthening of capacity of DIETs thereby enabling them to discharge their critical functions as nodal district level training institutions and as a vital link in achieving the national goal of Universalisation of Elementary Education.

The first in-depth review of District Primary

Education Programme generally commended the progress of programme implementation and has observed that the impact of DPEP on the entire Primary Education system is visible. There has been increase in enrolment in the DPEP districts, gender and social inequities have been substantially reduced and preliminary signs of increased learning achievements are in evidence.

In the scheme of Vocational Education, a network of external agencies have been used for the evaluation of the scheme on a state-wise basis.

The National Literacy Mission (NLM) has a system of concurrent evaluation by which each literacy campaign district is subject to external evaluation by the end of the Project. The NLM has identified agencies capable of undertaking external evaluation. Efforts have been made to provide substantive funding for strengthening the programme of modernisation and removal of obsolescence in order to upgrade the infrastructural facilities and thereby improving the overall quality of Technical Education all over.

2

Women Education

The National Policy for Education document recognised that the educational structure had not been able to address traditional gender imbalances on educational achievement and that women and girls continued to have low levels of literacy and be marginalised form development. The NPE document made a strong commitment to 'a well conceived edge in favour of women' as 'an act of faith and social engineering'. These commitments have been translated into concrete guidelines, and have resulted in a number of interventions which focus on the empowerment of women as the critical precondition for their participation in the educational process. The impact of these programmes is reflected in the decennial growth rate in female literacy of 9.54 per cent (Census 1991) which is significantly higher than the corresponding figure for males (7.76 per cent).

The following special provisions for women have been incorporated in the existing schemes: (i) The Operation Blackboard scheme now provides that atleast 50 per cent of the teachers recruited in the future should be women. Out of the 1,13,259 posts of the teachers filled under the OB scheme, 48.60 per cent are by women; (ii) An innovative approach taken up in Rajasthan to improve access to education is the Shiksha Karmi Project.

It envisaged substitution of the primary school teacher in single teacher schools by a team of two locally resident educational workers called Shiksha Karmis, of whom 10.2 per cent are women; (iii) Under the scheme of Non-Formal Education, 90 per cent assistance is given for NFE centres exclusively for girls. The scheme has recently been revised so as to provide more facilities for educating girls by increasing the ratio of NFE Centres exclusively for girls from 25 per cent to 40 per cent of the total; (iv) Efforts are being made to ensure that at least one third of the students in each Navodaya Vidyalaya are girls. In Navodaya Vidayalayas and Kendriya Vidyalayas, free education is imparted to girls up to class XII; (v) Free education is provided to girls upto class VIII in Punjab (Government schoold), Manipur, Rajasthan (Government schools), UP, Delhi, Meghalaya and Chandigarh and upto secondaryd stage in Andhra Pradesh, Assam, Bihar (Government schools), Himachal Pradesh (Government schools), Karnataka., Tamilnadu (Government schools), Mizoram and Lakshadweep and upto senior secondary stage Class XII in the states of Arunachal Pradesh, Goa, J&K, Kerala, Sikkin (Government schools), Tripura, West Bengal, A&N Islands, D&N Haveli, Daman and Diu, Pondicherry, Gujarat and Madhya Pradesh; (vi) Under the Centrally-sponsored programme at +2 level vocational programmes with emphasis on enterpreneurhsip are being designed to cater to the needs of girls who drop out of schools. Efforts are also on to consciously encourage participation of girls in the nontraditional and emergent technologies; (vii) Womwn's education at the university and college levels have been diversified and reoriented in tune with the changing requirement of society, industry and trade. The number of women enrolled in institutions of higher education increased from 40,00 in 1950-51 to about 16,64,000 in 1993-94, an increase of more than 41 times over the 43 year period; (viii) The enrolment of women students at the beginning of the year 1993-94 was 15.90 lakh as against 15.12 lakh in the previous year. At the post-graduate level the enrolment of women was 34.09 per cent of the total enrolment; (ix) The UGC has been providing assistance to universties for undertaking research projects in women's studies; a number of research projects have been approved for assistance. Also assistance has been provided to 22 universities and 11 colleges for setting up women's studies/cells. The UGC has also created * and (x) The participation of women in technical and professional streams has also showna marked increase from a little over 6,000 in 1950-51 to 1.46 lakh in 1986-87, an increase of 23 times. There was also noticeable growth in the number of women students in the engineering an technology streams (in IITs and Polytechics). As against 40 women students in 1950-51 (0.3 per cent) it rose to 16.67 thousand in 1986-87 (7.7 per cent) and 78.3 thousand in 1993-94 (13.1 per cent).

Mahila Samakhya Programme (Education for Women's Equality) is a Dutch assisted project which is spread over 14 districts of Uttar Pradesh, Karnataka, Gujarat and Andhra Pradesh. Mahila Samakhya is a women's empowerment project which does not aim at service delivery but seeks to bring about a change in women's perception about themselves and that of society in regard to women's traditional roles. It endeavours to create an environment for women to seek knowledge and information in order to make informed choices and create circumstances in which women can learn at their own pace and rhythm. The centrality of education in the struggle to achieve equality is an important focus of Mahila Samakhya.

The Cabinet has approved the continuation and expansion of the Mahila Samkhya Project during 1992-97.

The total outlay over 1992-97 is Rs. 51.29 crore. Like in other spheres, Indian women have proved their great potential as successful entrepreneurs. Some of Indian women entrepreneurs today lead the biggest shi-pping companies, trading and export houses, brewing industry, plastic & electronics establishment. Garment and handicrafts exports are primarily in the hands of women entrepreneurs. However, such achievement by about 100,000 women entrepreneurs in India touches just the fringe of vast future potential promised to Indian women.

Out of the total 761 million people in India, female comprise 360.74 million representing 47.7% of the total population. There are 99.4 million women workforce (representing 28% of the female population), but as per 1981 census, there are only 150,000 self-employed women accounting for only 5.2% of the total self-employed persons in the country. Majority of them are engaged in the unorganised sectors like agriculture, agrobased industries handicrafts, handlooms, and cottage based industries. Participation of women as industrial entrepreneurs, however, is comparatively a recent phenomena commencing from 70s onwards According to an estimate among 1.6 million SSI entrepreneurs in India during 1986-87, the total number of women entrepreneurs does not exceed 100,000.

Table 1

India women's status in entrepreneurial terms

Item	*Percentage*
Women % to total population	47.7
Women % to total Workplace	36.4
Women % to total Unemployed	40.0
Women % to total Self-employed	5.2
Women % to total SSI Entrepreneurs	7.5

In late 70s, it became conspicuous that women offer great potential as entrepreneurs. Accordingly, besides encouraging more women to join regular EFP, a number of special programmes and strategies were thought out to ensure women to take up entrepreneurship as their career.

During 1978-87, Small Industry Development Organisation (SIDO) with its network of Small Industries Service Institutes (SISI) spread throughout the country conducted 248 Courses exclusively for women benefitting 8,904 potential women entrepreneurs.

During 1986, Industrial Development Bank of India (IDBI) launched a special Scheme for Women Entrepreneurs according to which the training support and counselling is offered in a package. The scheme emphasized the need to set up modern small scale units in electronics engineering, plastic and chemicals, etc. consistent with the knowledge, skills and personal background of trainees further suggests to include women entrepreneurs so far as possible and provide long lead time and the post-training escort services by the conducting agency until the projects taken up by women entrepreneurs generally reach their break-even stage. The success rate under this scheme has crossed the 50% mark of the national averag. Further, a this helped several new voluntary organisations in acquiring and improving their competencies and infrastructural facilities for conducting effective EDPs for Women. In September, 1986 the Government of India set up a National Level Standing Committee for Women Entrepreneurs under the Chairmanship of the Minister of State for Youth Affairs, Sports, Women & Child Development. The Standing Committee made suitable recommendations & suggestions to the Government regarding the problem of entrepreneurship amongst women.

In view of the growing importance of women entrepreneurship, several nationalised banks opened special Cells for women entrepreneurs. Many State Financial Corporation have also developed special schemes for assisting the women entrepreneurs. Several entrepreneurs associations are very active in promoting and supporting the cause of entrepreneurship development. Most of them are now having a separate Women's Wing.

Only about a few year ago, an women entrepreneur, in India was visualised as a maker of pickles, papads, masala (spices) and other such household goods. But the recent EDPs have helped them in organising enterprises of complex type, bigger in size, with sophisticated technology involving higher managerial abilities. As such, the number of women entrepreneurs is increasing very fast. In order to further accelerate the process, it may be necessary to develop more man-power undertaking training and support to women entrepreneurs. Presently, two National Institutions, NIESBUD and EDII are organising half-a-dozen trainers training programme producing not more than 150 trainers in a year. To this even another 100 are added by other newly established institutions such as ICEW in Ahmedabad and IED in Lucknow hardly meeting the 50% of the total requirement.

Usually, it has been observed in the West that economic independence to women will increase the incidence of breaking of 'family tie'. Economic prosperity through entrepreneurial pursuits by Indian women has proved just the contrary. More often, women entrepreneurs have succeed in evolving other family members such as husband, father, mother etc. into her entrepreneurial folds. This is supported by the fact that majority of successful women entrepreneurs were married (85.5%), mostly between the age 36-45 year

(56.2%) and most of them (81.7%) had children of about the age of 10 years. These empirical evidences raises a great of early entrepreneurisation of the whole society by promoting entrepreneurisation of the whole society by promoting entrepreneurship amongst women. Through women participation, the movement is bound to add momentum.

Grouping of women has increased their awareness and eliminated exploitation by the middleman, in the case of 'active' groups. In many trades like weaving, processing food items...giving women access to finance through revolving funds and cheap credit has resulted in women directly procuring raw materials and producing and marketing goods without having to depend on the middleman for raw materials to process on measly daily wages, that too at disadvantageously lower levels for women. Incomes have also increased in the process. Studies by the Self Employed Women's Associaton (SEWA), Ahmedabad on the DWCRA groups helped by them in respect of crafts women and gum collectors clearly show that these groups have strengthened women's economic position, increased their bargaining powers, self sufficiency and thereby social status. Women are held in esteen now and men have become more cooperative on the domestic front and even help women in fuel and fodder collection. Women n turn feel more confident and have a sense of belonging. These self helf groups are a new source of social security with the crumbling of the joint family system. Other field level experiences and studies have clearly shown that despite all its limitations, the group strategy has empowered women to approach functionaries and banks to their advantage.

Given the potential power of groups, it serves us well to increase their cover. The government has sincerely tried to generate formation of informal groups.

But this is a time consuming process requiring a high degree of social awareness of the local area. Finally, the regions which have highly successful groups are those with highly committed Gram Sevikas and Project Officers. Such functionaries who are invaluabel assets are however not too large in numbers. The government's efforts therefore need to be supplemented to a far larger extent than at present. In the current context, this could best be handled through involvement of local and Non—Government Organisations in a big way. Intervention by Non Governmental Organisations with a feel for the people and their problems, in some areas, has brought about very successful and functional groups.

This brings us to the next related issue—Committed Non Governmental and Voluntary Organisations are not in abundance and involvement of greater numbers of committed people is essential.

Education is understood as an ongoing process of learning and empowerment which transcends mere literacy. The programme, which is not constrained by present agenda or predetermined targets, responds and designs interventions to meet the articulated needs of rural poor women. The *sangha* (village level women's collective) is the nodal point around which the programme revolves.

The process of mobilising and organising women is facilitated by a *Sahayogini* (a cluster coordinator in charge of 10 villages). She is a crucial link between the village sangha and the district implementation unit of the programme. The latter provides resource support and inputs to meet the needs of the women.

The district units in turn are supported by a State Office which ensures a facilitative environment and brings in necessary resource inputs for the programme.

At the state level, an autonomous registered society as an empowered body has been set up to oversee the programme. At the national level the programme is coordinated by a Project Director. A National Resource Group, an advisory body of eminent women activists, academics, development workers and bureaucrats, supports the programme bringing in new concepts, experiences and advises on programme policies and strategies.

Mahila Samakhya has expanded its coverage to 40 districts and over 6,876 villages in the States of Uttar Pradesh, Karnataka, Gujarat, Andhra Pradesh, Bihar, Madhya Pradesh and Assam. During 1998 the programme was expanded into a new State, i.e., Kerala where it would cover two districts. The effectiveness of the MS strategy in mobilising women for education has resulted in it being adopted by other basic education projects. Through the International Development Agency assisted UP Basic Education Project, six districts have been additionally covered in Uttar Pradesh. The programme is being implemented in seven districts of Bihar as part of the Bihar Education Project and in three districts each of Madhya Pradesh and Assam the programme is supported by the District Primary Education Programme.

The sangha, which is a nodal point of the programme, has emerged as an effective women's collective at the village level. The *sanghas* address a wide range of issues relating to their livelihood, education, health, to accessing resources among others. At the village level, sanghas have carved out a niche for themselves by actively participating in village affairs and are recognised by the communities as a force to reckon with.

Adult and children's education continue to be of

central concern to the sanghas. Sanghas have taken an active lead in enrolling children primarily girls in the village schools. Monitoring the functioning of schools and encouraging parents to send their children to school has become part of sangha agenda. Campaigns, Melas, Participatory Rural Appraisals have been some of the strategies through which issues of girls education have been brought centre-stage. In all the States, strategies for a functional convergence with the DPEP programme are being undertaken.

Non-formal education centres for drop-outs of school girls continue to grow in numbers bearing testimony to the growing importance of girl child education within the programme as well as with the *sanghas*. The Mahila Shikshana Kendras (16 in number) are a unique residential learning opportunity for adolescent girls and young women. The curriculum based on a holistic approach includes imparting basic literacy, life skills, and a preparation to play a leadership role in the development of their communities. The Mahila Shikshan Kendra is evolving as an innovative strategy to address the learning needs of adolescents and young women.

Adult literacy is being addressed in a variety of ways. In some States like Andhra Pradesh, Mahila Samakhya has actively converged with the TLC launched in Mahabubnagar district. In the other States, literacy centres/camps continue to be quite popular. Efforts are on to collate and prepare gender-sensitive learning materials. Legal and environmental literacy needs are also being integrated in the learning materials.

Under the Mahila Samakhya programme, health education has received considerable attention primarily because it is of great concern and interest for the sanghas. Baroda Unit of MS in Gujarat has opened two Jasod

Health Centres in which use of herbal medicines, home-made remedies are propagated. Baroda Unit has also initiated necessary plantation of medicinal plants as part of dealing with health problems as well as economic development programme in collaboration with State Forest Department.

As the sanghas have become stronger, demands for economic programmes have been on the rise. Thrift and credit has picked up as a vibrant activity in all the States leading to training in numeracy and book keeping. In States like Gujarat and Karnataka, linkages with National Bank for Agriculture and Rural Development (NABARD) are being established to meet the growing credit needs of sanghas. In Baroda district, District Rural Development Agency (DRDA) training on file making and flour mills are organised and in Rajkot, Training Rural Youth for Self Employment (TRYSEM) training was organised in 19 villages. In Mahabubnagar district in Andhra Pradesh, MS is implementing the watershed programme in eight villages with a focus on enabling sanghas to demand and establish a more transparent system of functioning. In all the States sanghas' access to various government schemes like Development of Women and Children in Rural Areas (DWCRA), TRYSEM, DRDA, etc. has increased substantially.

3

Education, Awareness and Information

The Department of Education, one of the four Constituent Departments of the Ministry of Human Resource Development, is under the overall charge of the Minister of Human Resource Development who is assisted by a Minister of State. The Secretariat of the Department is headed by a Secretary, who is also assisted by an Additional Secretary. The Department is organised into Bureaux, Divisions, Branches, Desks, Sections and Units. Each Bureau is under the charge of a Joint Secretary/Joint Educational Adviser assisted by Divisional Heads. The set-up of the Department is shown in the organisational chart appended to this report.

Subordinate offices/autonomous organisations

The Department has a number of Subordinate Offices / Autonomous Organisations including Central Universities, Institutes of Technology and other Institutions of Higher Learning and Research.

The Subordinate Offices are:

— The Directorate of Adult Education (DAB), New Delhi

— The Central Hindi Directorate (CHD), New Delhi

— The Commission for Scientific and Technical Terminology (CSTT), New Delhi
— The Central Institute of Indian Languages (CIIL), Mysore.

The important Autonomous Organisations are:

— The University Grants Commission (UGC), New Delhi, a national level organisation responsible for coordination and maintenance of standard in the area of Higher Education.
— The All India Council for Technical Education (AICTE), New Delhi, responsible for coordination and maintenance of standards in the area of Technical Education.
— The National Council for Teacher Education (NCTE), New Delhi, responsible for maintenance of standards and for development of Teacher Education.
— The National Council of Educational Research and Training (NCERT), New Delhi, a national level resource institution in the School Education sector.
— The National Institute of Educational Planning and Administration (NIEPA), New Delhi, a national level resource institution, specialising in educational planning and administration.
— The National Council for Promotion of Urdu Language, New Delhi.
— The National Council for Promotion of Sindhi Language, Vadodara.
— Rashtriya Sanskrit Sansthan.

Important organisations/institutions in various sectors of education are given below.

Elementary education

National Bal Bhavan, New Delhi has been contributing

towards promotion of creative activity among children in the age group 5-16 years. The National Bal Bhavan also provides general guidance, training facility and transfer of information to state and district Bal Bhavans in the country.

School education

— The Kendriya Vidyalaya Sangatban (KVS), New Delhi administers schools for the children of transferable Central Government employees.

— The Navodaya Vidyalaya Samiti, New Delhi administers schools for talented rural children.

— The Central Board of Secondary Education (CBSE), New Delhi affiliates schools and conducts examinations in Secondary Education sector.

— National Open School (NOS), New Delhi provides education through an open learning system at the school stage.

Higher education and research

— Indian Institute of Advanced Study (IIAS), Shimla

— Indian Council of Social Science Research (ICSSR), New Delhi

— Indian Council of Historical Research (ICHR), New Delhi

— Indian Council of Philosophical Research (ICPR), New Delhi

— The National Council of Rural Institutes (NCRI), Hyderabad

Central universities

— Aligarh Muslim University, Aligarh

— Banaras Hindu University, Varanasi

— University of Delhi, Delhi

— University of Hyderabad, Hyderabad

— Jamia Millia Islamia, New Delhi
— Jawaharlal Nehru University, New Delhi
— North Eastern Hill University, Shillong
— Pondicherry University, Pondicherry
— Visva Bharati, Santiniketan
— Nagaland University, Kohima
— Tezpur University, Tezpur
— Assam University, Silchar
— Indira Gandhi National Open University, New Delhi
— Babasaheb Bhimarao Ambedkar University, Lucknow
— Mahatma Gandhi Antarrashtriya Hindi Vishwavidyalaya, Wardha
— Maulana Azad National Urdu University, Hyderabad

Technical education

— Indian Institute of Science, Bangalore Indian School of Mines, Dhanbad
— National Institute of Training in Industrial Engineering, Mumbai
— National Institute of Foundry and Forge Technology, Ranchi
— School of Planning and Architecture, New Delhi
— Administrative Staff College of India, Hyderabad
— Indian Institutes of Management at Ahmedabad, Bangalore, Calcutta, Lucknow, Calicut and Indore.
— Indian Institutes of Technology (IITs) at Mumbai, Delhi, Guwahati, Kanpur, Kharagpur and Chennai
— Regional Engineering Colleges (RECs) (17 in number)
— Indian Institute of Information Technology and Management (IIITM), Gwalior

Adult education

— Directorate of Adult Education, New Delhi:

— Functions of the Department

Languages

— The Kendriya Hindi Shikshan Mandal, Agra

— Central Institute of Indian Languages, Mysore

— Central Institute of English and Foreign Languages, Hyderabad

— The Rashtriya Sanskrit Sansthan

— Maharishi Sandeepani Rashtriya Veda Vidya Pratishthan, Ujjain

Book promotion

The National Book Trust, New Delhi, an apex body caters to the needs of all segments of the society by publishing works of fiction and nonfiction on a variety of subjects in Indian languages including books for children and post-literacy reading material for neo-literates at moderate prices.

Functions of the department

Education is a concurrent subject. Concurrency implies a meaningful partnership between the Union Government and the States. The National Policy on Education (NPE), 1986 clearly defines the roles of the Union Government and the States.

The Union Government has assumed a larger responsibility to reinforce the national and integrative character of education, to maintain quality and standards, to study and monitor the educational requirements of the country as a whole in regard to manpower for development, to cater to the needs of research and advanced study, to look after the international aspects of Education, Culture and Human Resource Development and, in general, to promote excellence at all levels of the educational pyramid throughout the country.

The Department has been closely interacting with States and Union Territories to fulfil the role perceived by the NPE. The Department has also been striving to achieve the objective of development of human potential in the education sector through a countrywide network of field organisations, academic institutions, etc.

Progressive use of Hindi

The Department of Education is equipped with sufficient staff for implementation of Official Language Policy of the Union Government and Official Language Act framed thereunder. The Official Language Act, 1963 is being implemented in the Department, an Official Language Implementation Committee has been set up under the chairmanship of the Joint Secretary (Languages). The Committee in its meetings held from time to time considers the problems faced in the acceleration of the use of Hindi in the Department and suggests measures to solve the same. The Committee also reviews in its meetings the progress made in the use of Hindi in the offices and autonomous bodies under this Department. The difficulties faced by each Department are also looked into in these meetings. As a result thereof, all notifications, resolutions, general orders, circulars, memoranda, advertisements, etc. are issued bilingually. All name plates, notice boards, rubber stamps, seals, letter heads, etc. are prepared both in Hindi and English languages. The communications received in Hindi are replied to in Hindi. The Performance Budget and Annual Administrative Report of the Department are prepared both in Hindi and English. As more than 80 per cent staff members in the Department possess working knowledge of Hindi, the Department has, therefore, been notified under Rule 10(4) by the Department of Official Language. The staff members who do not have working knowledge of Hindi are being deputed for training in Hindi in batches. Similarly, the employees who do not possess knowledge of Hindi typing and stenography are also imparted training.

All possible efforts are being made in the Department for accelerated use of Hindi in official business. In the month of September, a Hindi Fortnight is held and a number of competitions are conducted during that period. A Hindi Advisory Committee has also been set up under the chairmanship of Minister for Human Resource Development and the meetings thereof are held from time to time.

Vigilance activities

The vigilance set-up of the Department is under the overall supervision of the Secretary who, in turn, is assisted by a Chief Vigilance Officer of the rank of Joint Secretary, an Under Secretary and other subordinate staff.

During the period under report, sustained efforts were continued to tone up the administration and to maintain discipline amongst the staff members of the Department, both at the headquarters and in the subordinate offices.

Efforts were also continued to simplify the procedures so as to minimise the scope of corruption. A close watch was maintained over the persons of doubtful integrity, The staff posted to sensitive posts were transferred to other Sections/ Divisions periodically on rotational basis. Disciplinary proceedings against five officials were concluded and appropriate orders were passed in two cases. Inquiry reports in three cases are under examination and submission to disciplinary authorities. Disciplinary proceedings against six officials including one gazetted officer are still in progress. Preliminary inquiry against two complaint cases pertaining to the Department of Education has been completed and the cases have been closed on the advice of the Central Vigilance Commission. Of the 89 Autonomous Organisations and one Public Sector Undertaking under the administrative control of the Department, 53 Organisations have so far accepted the advisory jurisdiction of the Central Vigilance Commission. Of them, 27 Organisations have appointed the Chief Vigilance Officer with the prior approval of the Central Vigilance commission.

A specific Grievance Redressal Machinery functions under a Joint Secretary nominated as the Director of Grievances in the Department. The Director of Grievances is accessible to the staff as well as the members of public and to listen to their problems. In order to ensure the implementation of the policy of the Government regarding redressal of Public Grievances in its totality, 40 Autonomous Organisations out of a total number of 89 have created their Public Grievance Redressal Machinery and have in turn designated officers as Director of Grievances. Efforts were also made to persuade the remaining four organisations to set up Machinery for Redressal of Public Grievances. Overall emphasis continued to be laid on the observance of discipline and punctuality in the Department.

Professional development

Training updates knowledge, sharpens skill and techniques and improves performance. The main objective of the Training Cell of the Department is to coordinate/ monitor various training programmes for professional development of staff working in the Department of Education. The Training Cell assists in deputing the officials for training in India as well as abroad. During 1998, the Cell scrutinized and forwarded 98 nominations for various training programmes—83 in India and 15 abroad. Out of these nominations, 65 were accepted by various institutions including five for training abroad.

Information and facilitation centre

A NICNET-based Information and Facilitation Centre which was set up in June 1997, caters to the queries of the visitors visiting the Ministry of Human Resource Development. The main objective of the Centre is to provide information to NGOs, Indian students and foreign students visiting India for higher studies.

Office council

Under the Scheme of Joint Consultative Machinery of the Government, the Department has its Office Council having representatives of various Staff Associations. The Office Council of the Department is very vigilant and takes keen interest in service matters, promotional prospects, motivational aspects, improving working conditions and welfare activities of the officials of the Department. The Office Council has always been extending cooperation to the Administration. The meetings of the Council are arranged periodically under the chairmanship of Joint Secretary (Admn).

Publications

The Publication Unit is the nodal unit for coordination, compilation of bilingual (English and Hindi) Annual Report of the Department and brings out the Report every year. Besides this, the printing jobs of the Department, viz. Performance Budget, Demands for Grants, Directory of Recipients of National Award to Teachers, and other publications of the Department are a regular feature.

Computerised management information system

Computerised Management Information System (CMIS) Unit was established by the Department for taking care of computerisation needs of the Department. The Unit is continuously providing their support since its establishment. The Unit is also assisting in finalisation of hardware requirements, building up of skilled manpower and handling various requirements of the Department through computers.

Identification of areas for computerisation and to conduct feasibility studies for the development of computer-based management information system: analysis, design and development of software for the implementation of the management information system; maintenance of software packages as per varying needs of the users in the Department; act as a resource unit and provide training to the officials of the Department to develop local know-how for day-to-day processing of information, design and develop database methodologies and build an effective educational information system and liaison with the National Informatics Centre (NIC).

To enhance the technical skill of officials in the Department, 40 members of the staff of the Department of Education were trained in usage of computer application software like DOS, Windows 95, MS-Office, Library Information System, etc. To provide E-mail facility, Internet accessibility and sharing of information among the officers of the Department, a Local Area Network (LAN) is established with the help of NIC.

The Unit is also handling software development projects of various divisions of the Department of Education. The important publications /projects/ database/reports, inter alia, generated through data processing during the year under report are:

— Selected Educational Statistics

— Education in India Series Volumes I, II and IV

— Computerisation of International Standard Book Numbering System (ISBN)

— Database for National Programme on Nutritional

Support to Primary Education Computerisation of work relating to Cash Section like pay billing, arrears, etc.

— Budgetary proposals of the Department

— Database on Parliament Questions

— Installation of software and hardware.

Education, awareness and information

The process of group formation could take the following from: The starting point should be the settingup of local 'Skill Exchanges'. Women possessing various skills like craftwork, tailoring, toy making etc. could register themselves for employment. Their motivation to work would be spontaneous as registration is a voluntary act. Also many of the skilled labourers would belong to the poorer sections though not necessatily below the poverty line. There is a strong justification for this, because as gender experts have pointed out, when we talk of the poverty line we talk in aggregates i.e. of a family as a whole being below or above it. While this is absolutely logical in the aggregate sense, it overlooks the inequities in intra household distribution of income and consumption, since women may not have access to a large part of the spouse's income but they may be responsible i seeing that all the children and family member are well fed. So technically though the family may be slightly above poverty line, most of its members may be living in below poverty line conditions. Merely picking up women without skills or motivation from the list of 'Below Poverty Line' families has resulted in many cases in total waste of effort.

From these skill exchanges, Non Governmental local organisations could group women by homogeneity of skills and location for functional success. Such groups of motivated and simimlarly skilled women may perform better and result in faster may perform better and result in faster spread of groups through 'Demonstration Effect'. Further, in due course some of the more successful of these groups could themselves become local voluntary organisations and help in formation of groups in their neighbourhoods.

The government would have to play the role of overseer and facilitator in this entire process—a role that it is most competent to play. The government should first group its activities for a coordinated delivery system of services at the local level. District level teams could be formed with personnel drawn from various departments like health, education etc.—not the higher planning oriented personnel but middle and lower level implementing functionaries. These teams could cater to various blocks for referral services and problem solving through nodal local organisations or group leaders. The Indira Mahila Yojana is a step forward in this direction.

The above system could be tried out along with the existing system which boils down to government gram sevikas exploring possibilities of setting up groups, then motivating the women, selecting an activity for them, arranging for training in some cases and so on without ultimate guarantee of the sustainibility of the group.

Once economic empowerment is achieved it would have major implications on the overall empowerment of women. Intra family relationships and domestic work culture would dnage resulting in social empowerment and a more equitable participation of women in decisions concerning the family. Leadership and active participation in group culture would improve political acumen and eventually help successful political empowerment. Political empowerment in turn would result in more representiative planning for women and a strengthening and sustaining of the process of overall empowerment of women.

Priority is accorded by the Ministry of Environment and Forests to promote evironmental education, create environmental awareness among various age groups and to disseminate information through Environmental Information System (ENVIS) network to all concerned. Special emphasis is given to non-formal environmental education through seminars/symposia/workshops, training programmes, eco-camps, audio-visual shows etc. The Ministry has been organising a National Environment Awareness Campaign (NEAC) since July 1986. As a part of this Capaign, 19 Novmber to 18 December every year is observed as the National Environment Month. Students/youth, techers, women, tribals, administrators, professionals, legislators, industrial workers, Armed Forces and the general public are covered under this Campaign. During 1994-95 about 2,200 organisations have been granted financial assistance by the Ministry to organise various activities for creating environmental awareness. The Ministry also provides financial support for setting up eco-clubs at schools and for production on films on environment.

A new scheme "Paryavaran Vahini" has been launched during 1992-93 to create environmental awareness and to ensure active public participations by involving the local people in activities relating to environmental protection. Parayavaran Vahinis are proposed to be constituted in 183 selected districts all over the country which have high incidence of pollution and density of tribal and forest population. The Vahinis also play a watch dog role by reporting instances of environmental pollution, deforestation, poaching, etc. They function under the charge of District Collectors with active cooperation of the state/union territory governments. this scheme is entirely financed by the Ministry of Environment and Forests.

The National Museum of Natural History (NMNH) set up in New Delhi in 1978, is concerned with the promotion of non-formal education in the area of environment and conservation. Besides permanent exhibit galleries on various aspects of environment, the museum also conducts temporary exhibitions and a large number of educational programmes and activities for school children, college youth and the general public. A Regional Museum of Natural History has been established at Mysore and two more and planned at Bhopal and Bhubaneswar.

The Indian Council for Forestry Research and Education is the focal point for forestry education and extension developmnet in the country. Indira Gandhi National Forest Academy, Dehra Dun imparts in-service professional training to Indian Forest Service (IFS) professionals. State forest service colleges provide training to the officers of the State Forest Service (SFS). The Indian Plywood Industries Research and Training Institute, Bangalore organises short-term courses in the area of wood science. The Indian Institute of Forest Management, Bhopal, also provides training in forest management and allied subjects to persons from the Indian Forest Service, forest development corporations and forest related industries to develop forestry management skills. The Wildlife Institute of India, Dehra Dun conducts various programmes to provide in-service training in wildlife management for forest officers, wildlife ecologists and other professionals.

Environmental Information System (ENVIS) has been set up by the Ministry in 1982 as a decentralised information system network for collection, storage, retrieval and dissemination of environmental information to decision makers, policy planners, scientists, engineers, environmentalists, research workers and the general public all over the country. Besides the Focal Point in the Ministry, the ENVIS network presently consists of 20 subject oriented centres known as ENVIS centres, set up in various institutions/organisations of the country on priority areas of environment such as environmentally sound and appropriate technology, bio-degradation of wastes, desertification, estuary, mangroves, corals and lagoons, media and environment, environmental education, solid wastes disposal, animal ecology, Himalayan ecology, etc. The Focal Point brings out a quarterly abstracting journal "Paryavaran Abstracts" containing information about environmental research in the Indian context.

ENVIS has been designated as National Focal Point (NFP) and Regional Service Centre (RSC) for South Asia sub-regional countries by INFORTERRA (an international referral system for sources of information on environment) of United Nations Environment Programme (UNEP). As NEP, ENVIS updated more than 250 Indian Potential Sources in the International Directory of UNEP for providing information in the field of environment and its related areas.

The Ministry functions as a nodal agency for United Nations Environment Programme (UNEP), South Asia Cooperation Environment Programme (SACEP) and International Centre for Integrated Mountain and Development (ICIMOD) and various international agencies, regional bodies and multilateral institutions. In coordinates all bilateral cooperation in the field of invironment. India has such cooperation programmes with the Netherlands, Norway, Sweden, Denmark, Great Britain, USA, the Russian Federation, Canada, Japan and FRG in addition to forestry programmes with external assistance.

India is signatory to the following important international treaties/agreements in the field of environment:

(i) International Convention for the regulation of Whaling; (ii) International Plant Protection Convention; (iii) The Antarctic Treaty; (iv) Conventon on Wetlands of internatonal importance especially as waterfowl habitat; (v) International Convention on international trade in endangered species of wild flora and fauna; (vi) Protocol of 1978 relating to the international convention for the prevention of pollution from ships, 1973; (vii) Vienna Convention for the protection of the ozone layer; (viii) Convention on Migratory Species; (ix) Basel Convention on trans-boundary movement of hazardous substances; (x) Framework Convention on climatic change; (xi) convention on conservation of bio-diversity; (xii) Montreal Protocol on the substances that deplete the ozone layer and (xiii) International Convention for Combating Desertification.

Instituted in 1987, the Indira Gandhi Prayavaran Puraskar, consisting of a cash component of rupees one lakh, a silver trophy and a citation, is awarded every year to an organisation and to an individual for significant contributions in the field of environment.

The Indira Priyadarshini Vrikshamitra Awards have been constituted by the Ministry of Environment and Forests in 1986 to recognise outstanding contributions of individuals and organisations in the field of afforestation and wastelands development. Ten awards are given every year to individuals, educational institutes, Panchayats, voluntary agencies and government agencies. Each award carries a medallion, a citation and a cash component of Rs. 50,000.

The Maha Vriksha Puraskar, instituted by the NAEB during 1993-94 will be given every year to individuals/ organisations for trees of notified species having the largest girth and height and in good health and vigour. These awards would consist of a cash prize of Rs. 25,000, a plaque and a citation.

Since 1991, national awards are being presented every year to eligible industries in recognition of their contributions to the prevention and control of evnvironmental pollution.

In order to have more national generalisation, the past performance can be reviewed separately for two categories, i.e., (i) those efforts related to income generation and self-employment and (ii) others related to self-employment-cum-entrepreneurship category.

The first category covers the programmes/schemes under KVIC, TRYSEM, SEEUY and some other institutions exclusively devoted for self-employment. During 1985-86, KVIC, provided employment opportunities to 39.8 lakh persons whose earning amounted to Rs. 349.53 crores. In the total employment under KVIC Programme the share of SC/ST was about 29% and women's participation about 46%. Under TRYSEM Scheme 200,650 youths were to be trained during 1985-86. Out of this, 56,500 youth were trained and 41.845 were reported taking up self-employment.

The second category by and large, refers to SSI entrepreneurs. Under Indian context the two strategies, i.e., developing entrepreneurship and small industries are interwoven. Between 1973-74 and 1986-87, the number SSIs increased by over three folds generation by about two and half times. It is difficult to assess as to how much oif it is the outcome of planned efforts. But programme wise SIDO conducted more than 1638 EDPs and trained 50,130 potential entrepreneurs during 1978-88. During 1970-86 they conducted 287 programme specially for 6,757 engineer entrepreneurs. IDBI sponsored 550 EDPs benefiting 15,369 entrepreneurs. 6 Since its inception NSTEDB sponsored 147 EDPs benefitting 3,090 potential science & technology entrepreneurs. 7 SBI conducted 125 EDPs during 1978-87 and trained 2,939 persons with success rate of 33 percent. NIESBUD masseurs sponsored 42 EDPs benefitting 1125 potential entrepreneurs. Besides such national bodies large number of programmes were conducted locally by other governmental and non-governmental organisations which have not been recorded systematically. As per one estimate about 1,250 full EDPs of 6 weeks duration are conducted every year benefitting more than 40,000 potential entrepreneurs.

Since entrepreneurship development presently pursued by variety of organisations/agencies with different types of approaches/strategies and also with varying degrees of resources for varied target groups, their rate of success (in terms of the ration of number of entrepreneurs who actually set up their enterprises to the number of persons trained/promoted) naturally show a very wide range of variation (8% of 80%). Recently nationwide study by NIESBUD, however, reported 27.8% success rate as national average since there are experiences of higher rates of success there seems to be enough scope for further improvement in all aspects of EDPs starting from Identification & Selection of Potential Entrepreneurs; and Quality & Content of Training; Support Services; and Availability/accessibility to infrastructural facility.

There are very few, if any, published documents presenting quantitative and qualitative evaluation of EDPs. In the absence of uniform data for all reported programmes, it may be useful to consider cost of emploment generation from the typical programmes separately.

The cost of conducting full entrepreneurship development programmes include cost of initial campaign, identification & selection, 4-6 weeks training, and follow-up for about 4-6 months after the completion of training.

These can be estimated from the existing pattern of expenditure. SISIs are conducting integrated EDP with an expenditure of Rs. 56,000/- for TCOs and other voluntary organisations who conduct EDPs sponsored by IDBI and other financial institutions; NSTEDB & NIESBUD, the cost comes in between Rs. 70-80 thousand. Under difficult areas and for special schemes such as women entrepreneurship the coast goes upto Rs. 100,000/-. Considerig 30% as success rate and on an average 30 participants per programme the cost for promoting entrepreneurship comes in between Rs. 6000/- and Rs. 11,000/- (without establishment cost) per entrepreneurs who sets up an enterprise with an investment between few thousand to 35 lakhs. SBI Evaluation Study (1986) 10 further help us understand the pattern and size of investment and return by entrepreneurs promoted through such EDPs. The overall average investment by them was reported as Rs. 3.55 lakhs. To be more precise maximum, i.e., 57.4% invested between 2-5 lakhs; and followed by those 27.9% who invested between 1-2 lakhs; and 8% invested upto Rs. 25,000/- and only 6% invested over Rs. 10 lakhs. In terms of benefits, out of such promoted entrepreneurs 83% sampled units reported making on an average a net profit of Rs. 48,200/- (about 4000/- per month) during 1985.

Another study that provided detailed information about cost/benefit refers to Assam Experiment-Self-Employment through entrepreneurship Motivation Training Centres during 1973-76. With the total expenditure of Rs. 17.96 lack that included the cost of training of officers, all recurring and non-recurring expenditrue of 6 EMTCs in Assam 534 units started functioning (another 593 received financial sanction but not considered for calculating benefits here) and accordingly the cost for promoting each succeessful entrepreneur was reported having net profit between Rs. 300/- to Rs. 1500/- per month (during mid seventies). Further the total amount raised and invested by these entrepreneurs in the area amount raised and invested by these entrepreneurs in the area amounted to Rs. 1.2 crores to which Govt. contributed only 12.26 lakhs as seed money. The evauation study further revealed that more than 90% units thus established provided employment to 1-2 persons besides the self-employed owner.

Another valuable and more recent information related to cost-benefit of a typical entrepreneurship development programme for self-employment (in SBI sector) is available with Rural Development Self-emploment Training Institute (RUDSETI), Gurgaon which has been set up jointly by a Trust and two nationalised banks since 1984. RUDSETI trained 1,832 candidates and 1127 of them have already set up their enterprises, the total of cost on selection, two weeks training counselling and support activities comes to Rs. 795/- per successful self-employed entrepreneurs (this does not include the establishment cost). In addition, the bank financing to these entrepreneurs on an average was reported as Ps. 18,214/- per self-employed person, enterprises set up by these entrepreneurs represented 'business' enterprises 28.7% followed by 'industries' 19.6% and 11.6% 'service units'. It was further revealed that 68% of thus promoted entrepreneurs have started earning net profit between Rs. 500/- to Rs. 1500/- per month.

Entrepreneurship development in Gujarat started in April, 1970 as a jointly sponsored programme by Gujarat Industrial Investent Corporation (GIIC), Gujarat State Financial Corporation (GSFC), and later on by Gujarat Small Industries Corporation (GSIC). Initially the programme started at the 4 centres of Ahmedabad, Baroda, Godhra and Surat. But soon the activites were extended to 15 other Centres in the State to include participants under the entrepreneurship development, educated unemployed and engineer entrepreneur schemes. These institutions were committed to help the trainees and they constituted an Advisory Board to supervise and guide the implementation of the programme. The administrative matters were entrused to the Managing Director of GIIC.

As there was no permanent faculty, a full-time project leader was employed to provide individual attention, guidance and encouragement to each of the trainees. The training was scheduled for 90 days, and 50 trainees were selected on the basis of their experience, definite idea of the product, family support, business and manufacturing experience, degree of discontent with present status and motivation for higher economic achievement. Later on a test for entrepreneurship identification developed by the Behavioural Science Centre, Delhi,was used to select the trainees. The training programme included motivation laboratory process, management and organisational techniques, financial accounting, cost analysis, purchase and sales techniques, labour relations and labour laws, taxation laws, licensing policy, state facilites and general knowledge.

The training was not the end in itself. Rather, the project leader assisted the trainees even after the training was over, to prepare the project, and also provided counselling in setting up the enterprise.

The achievement of this project in terms of setting up of enterprises was very encouraging, the approach was pragmatic and the selection concentrated on person with experience rather than on education or unemployment. The main feature of the programme was the close links between the various developmental agencies, which ensured that loans were sanctioned, machinery ordered and raw materials arranged at an appropriate time and place.

In SIET, members from various disciplines had been working towards entrepreneurial development. Initially, it was thought that the answer to entrepreneurial development lay in that discipline alone. The development group, being economists, believed that potential surveys, industrial profiles and easy accessibility of resources would do the trick. The management group was certain that a person without management techniques and experience could not succeed in his business. Later realisation of the necessity of technical and commercial information for the guidance of entrepreneurs led to the establishment of a Documentation Centre. When all these groups joined hands, they realised that their combined impact would be far greater than individual effort. SIET learnt the importance of motivational training, growth centres, technology, marketing network, institution building and coordination for mobilising resources and energies.

The SIET Integrated Model for Entrepreneurial Development was evolved with the following 5 features (Akhouri):

- Specialised Agency to initiate support to potential entrepreneurs;
- Inter-disciplinary approach for counselling and training;
- Strong information support;
- Training as an important input for Entrepreneurial development among first generation entrepreneurs;
- Institutional financing.

This classical model was tried in many parts of India and offered rich experiences particularly in the states of J&K, Assam, Karnataka and Andhra Pradesh.

In 1970 about 15,000 educated persons were unemployed in the state. To tackle the unemployment problem, the State Government set up a Department of Employment. The officers of this department were assisted by Officers of various other departments at the district level. All such officers attended a 15 day workshop at SIET to orient them to the implementation of the SIET integrated model for developing self-employment in J&K. The same officers went back and conducted training programmes and organised after training support in their respective areas. As a result, 575 units came into being within a year, indicating the effectiveness of the model for promoting entrepreneurship.

A more comprehensive trial to the SIET integrated model was planned in the State of Assam. On the initiative of the Chief Minister himself, the Planning Board, Government of Assam, began the self-employment programme for the educated unemployed youth in May, 1973.

Accordingly, a group of 26 officers drawn from various departments were trained for 21 days by SIET faculty in areas like the socio-psychological aspects of development of entrepreneurship, economic aspects of self-employment and management aspects of small enterprises.

Six Entrepreneurial Motivation Training Centres (EMTC) were established in six districts by the end of October 1973. According to the Action Plan, the team made intensive efforts to draw the attention of the unemployed educated youth the selected trainees in batches of 40 through written tests and personal interviews. Preliminary motivation training for 15 days was given to selected prospective entrepreneurs, with the objective to develop entrepreneurship and to strengthen the motive self-employment.

After preliminary training, the prospective

entrepreneurs were helped in selecting the entreprise for themselves. This was followed by market survey and preparation of the projkect. In case enterprise training was needed, the EUMTC helped the candidate to arrange necessary inputs like finance, land, building machinery and equipment, raw materials, power, skilled persons, etc. The responsibility to EMTC did not end here, but went further in helping the entrepreneurs in establishing their units, marketing their goods/services and finally repaying the credit, and if needed offered assistance for further expansion of the enterprise. The Assam experiment had an in-built programme of evaluation at the end of every year by SIET, with a view to constantly improving the programme.

The achievement of these six EMTCs during November 5, 1973 July 1974 has in many respects exceeded those several other programmes going on in some developed parts of the country.

The Karnataka Government launched a massive self-employment programme in April 1974 to meet the challenges of sudden growth of unemployment during the period 1962-72, 4000 persons were trained in self-employment under this programme.

The important features of the programme were systematic selection of prospective entrepreneurs and a well-knit package of inputs for the training programme. The strategy to develop entrepreneurship among self-employed persons comprised of the following major aspects:

(a) Acquainting the entrepreneurs with the various tools and techniques required for weighing alternatives and conflicting claims which arise when starting a new enterprise;

(b) Overcoming their hesitation in starting the enterprise; and

(c) Developing an entrepreneurial spirit with a will to take moderate risk in competing with others.

A team was formed to explore the various entrepreneurial opportunities in and around Bangalore and to find the possibilities of establishing ancillaries for the Electricity Boards, Karnataka State Road Transport Corporation, Mysore Iron and Steel Works, etc. The above efforts yielded opportunities for 25 ancillaries with Karnataka State Electricity Board, 45 with Karnataka State Road Transport Corporation and 30 with Mysore Iron and Steel Works Ltd.

The Karnataka State Financial Corporation agreed to finance the projects and the Karnataka State Industries Small Corporation agreed to allot sheds to the selected entrepreneurs.

A well conceived idea in the programme was to develop functional industrial estates around industries like bicycle manufacturing, making of Kannada typewriters, etc. Each estate was to comprise of 20-30 small sub-units manufacturing components with a mother unit assembling the financial products.

Similar explorations were made with HAL, HMT Watch Factory, etc. An attempt was also made to identify industrial and business opportunities at various centres in Karnataka and for this the total support and participation of official from various industries in Karnataka was ensured. The officials were given 15 days orientation training at the SIET Institute in Hyderabad. During training they were encouraged to prepare an action plan for their respective district. This action plan aimed at providing basic guidelines for the industries officers who were expected to conduct a survey of their districts, identify the entrepreneurs and guide them in the selection of enterprise. The experiences generated in this programme were used in similar programmes conducted by the Karnataka State, and those in other parts of the country.

With the objective of providing technical skills to rural youth, to enable them to take up self-employment in the fields of agriculture and allied activities, industries, services and business activities, this Scheme was launched on 15th August, 1979. The Sixth Plan aimed to train 2 lakh rural youth every year at the rate of 40 youths per block per annum 9.4 lakhs youths were actually trained during the Sixth Plan and 4.64 lakh youth (49.4%) were self-employed. The target group comprised rural youth between the ages of 18-35 for families living below of the poverty line. A minimum of 30% of the trained youth, who belong Scheduled Caste and Scheduled Tribe communities, and a minimum of $33^{1/3}$% of the rural youth trained, should be women.

The Seeuy scheme was introduced in 1983 to provide self-employment to education unemployed youth. The scheme provided for the granting of loans up to a maximum of Rs. 25,000 (since revised) to educated youth residing in areas other than cities with a population of 10 lakhs or ore, and with no other source of finance for self-employment. The implementation of the scheme was entrusted to the District Industries Centres under the guidance of the Development Commissioner for Small Scale Industries. Government assistance in the form of an outright capital sub-city of 25% of the loans taken by entrepreneurs from the banks, was envisaged and Rs. 25 crores were allocated for the programme during 1984-85.

The Maharashtra State Small Scale Industries Development Corporation (MSSIDC) initiated the entrepreneurship development programme in 1974, based on the Gujarat experiences. The MSSIDC designed the programme to correspond to the needs of the participants. Participants were selected from economically and socially backward districts, with their development as the main social objective of the programme. A series of Entrepreneurial Development Clinics were organised in several backward district of the state. The duration of the programme varies between nine and twelve days, of which five days were devoted to motivation development and the rest to enterprise building.

The experiment demonstrated convincingly that even in the backward districts there was tremendous entrepreneurial potential that can be tapped, and induced into the industrial field. Encouraged by the initial success, the programme was considerably refined and implemented in 5 more districts of Maharashtra, under the auspices of four nationalised banks during the year 1966-67. Since then, the state continues to accumulate experiences and build on it in an effort to promote entrepreneurship in the state.

The Xavier Institute of Social Service, Ranchi, Bihar is engaged in development of tribal entrepreneurship since early 1970 through its extension wing "Vikas Maitri". An earlier attempt by the orgnisation was the development of the tribal economy, with the help of rural youth volunteers trained by the Institute. The first batch of 20 potential entrepreneurs were trained over 4 months.

The strategy for tribal entrepreneurs consisted of a media campaign to attract he prospective entrepreneurs from remote tribal village and semi urban areas. The Institute used a modified selection strategy consisting of background information of the candidate, written test, followed by an interview for final selection. The training involved mainly two components; i.e., practical shop floor training and theoretical training. Candidates were placed for 2 months in different units and enterprises as per their choice of trade. Most of the enterprises set up by the tribal entrepreneurs were small shops and business. The evaluation of this programme brought into focus an emerging profile of successful tribal entrepreneurs.

Another significant effort by XISS is in the area training village entrepreneurs. The programme consist of training college youth for self-employment as tailors, carpenters, watch repairers, grocers, cycle repairers, petty traders and photographers. The "intervention" was basically in the form of a residents training programme at Ranchi, lasting six months, during which 30 candidates (boys & girls) at a time, were placed as apprentices with practicing small entrepreneurs in town, to learn the skills of the trade they intended to adopt. They (were also taught the skills of management as relevant to tiny establishments. They were asked to conduct a market survey in the place where they intended to set up their business, draw up a project proposal, which was submitted to nationalise banks or other governmental financial organisations. On completion of the programme, the candidates were helped by the staff of Xavier Institute (four full-timers) as well as the Vikas Maitri, in obtaining finance & setting up their units till they reached the take-off stage.

On an average between 50 and 60 per cent of the candidates completing the course, succeeded in setting up their enterprises.

SEWA which is the abbreviated version of "Self-Employed Women Association means" "service" in sevral Indian languages. It is a registered trade union and functioned as the Women's Wing of the Textile Labour Association till April, 1981. It is now an autonomous union. Gandhian philosophy is the source of SEWA, and they work with the group leaders and members in organising the various trade groups, and in tackling the problems of their respective groups.

Each member of SEWA gets the services of three organisations-the SEWA Union, the Sewa Bank, and the SEWA Mahila Trust. The union provides the necessary structure for organising the trade groups and for engaging in the struggle against vested interests. The Bank provides the banking and credit facilities and the Mahila Trust extents the facilities for legal aid, social security, productivity training and education.

Creating banking and credit facilities for the poor self-employed women were among the first development efforts spearheaded by SEWA. The Mahila Sahakari Bank (Women's Co-operative Bank), was registered in 1974, and is the only one of its kind in the country. The SEWA Bank has belied all the reservation of the organised banking structure against extending credit to poor, illiterate, self-employed women and has become a viable financial unit with share capital and deposits from its members. The SEWA Bank also shattered the myth of loan repayments from poor women being almost impossible. In fact SEWA's experience with banking and credit to its members has proved it to be a vital input in helping poor women in their struggle to be self-reliant, in freeing them from the clutches of money-lenders.

In the year 1975, a group from the faculty of the Indian Institute of Management, Ahmedabad decided to experiment with a strategy through which people could utilize local resources, value these resources and retain the added value so as to increase their earnings, and finally improve their standard of living.

This project demonstrated the need to continuously work with the new emerging class of rural entrepreneurs if entrepreneurship has to be developed. This project pointed out that those interested in developing entrepreneurship among rural people should be willing to work actively with them, should be patient, and should be able to play the role of an agency that can cater to the social, economic and technical dependencies for the rural people.

The National Science and Technology Entrepreneurship Development Board (NSTEDB) was established in January 1982 to look into the question of unemployment and under employment among science and technology graduates and diploma holders in the country. As a consequence, the Board has undertaken a number of initiatives and formulated innovative plans to promote science and technology entrepreneurship in the country. One of the important initiatives by the Board is the establishment of Science and Technology Entrepreneurs (STEPs). This is to enable science and technology graduates emerging from academic institutions to experiment with new products and processes on a pilot basis on the one hand, and to convert them into entrepreneurial ventures on the other hand. The STEP could be considered a nursery industrial estate which accepts potential entrepreneurs with S&T background into its fold and transforms them into confident entrepreneurs within a period of 2 to 3 years. In order to evolve a workable STEP model, the Board, in collaboration with Department of Science & Technology, organised a number of workshops. In addition, an expert committee was constituted, and its deliberations have resulted in a model could be the forerunner to a series of future STEPs. As a result of various measures taken by the NSTEDB, STEPs have been established at some institutions like Birla Institute of Technology, Ranchi; C.C. Shroff Research Institute, Bombay; Jadavpur University, Calcutta and S.J. College of Engineering, Mysore.

The functioning of the STEP is based on the assumption that the financial institutions would provide 'money capital', and the universities and laboratories would bring in 'knowledge capital'. An amalgam of the two would give birth to scientist-entrepreneurs dedicated to the production of improved and quality goods.

Developing Women Entrepreneurship in India to harness the growth potential of unemployed women is widely acknowledged emphasis has been laid recently on inducing entrepreneurship through training conducted some training and development organisations. SIDO with its network of 26 SISI's, has trained, through its Entrepreneurship Development Programme for women during the period 1977-78 to 1985-86, about 8100 women entrepreneurs all over the country. These training programmes are extended to rural/tribal women, extension workers and semi-literate/matriculate women. Efforts are being made to link to training programmes with planning. This includes minimum cost of establishing production unit/enterprieses, avenues for procurement of the raw materials and marketing of finished goods, scope for cooperatives and arrangements for getting institutional finance. The ficilities extended include accommodation, stipends, etc. in Some of the programmes mobile workshops have been included to enable rural women to take up training. A number of polytechnics and hostel facilities for women are also being provided.

Encouraged by the policy statement of the Centre and State Government, several training organisations have started imparting training to women entrepreneurs. NIESBUD took the initiative to formulate a model syllabus for the women entrepreneurship development programme. To meet the encouraging demand of resources persons for entrepreneurial training for women, a few training organisations have already started EDP training for trainees. An assessment of economic activities generated by women in India led to the establishment

shment of the Women's Development Corporation at the state level. The Department of Women and Child Development under the Ministry of Human Resource Development will extend financial assistance to these Corporations to the extent of 49% of their paid-up capital. Marketing facilities through tie-up arrangements with the state level marketing organisation will also be promoted. Besides this, the Corporation aims to develop and strengthen women's cooperatives and arrange for training of beneficiaries in the concerned trade through existing institutions like Women Polytechnics and Industrial Training Institutes. Presently such Corporations are functioning in Punjab and Gujarat only.

Growing awareness of the need to bring the women entrepreneur into the main stream of national economic development led to the formulation of the National Level Standing Committee on Women Entrepreneurs in 1986, under the Chairmanship of Minister of State for Youth Affairs, Sports, Women and Child Development, Government of India. The Committee was constituted with a view to put forward recommendations on policy, programmes and other measures to be initiated for stimulating, helping and assisting women entrepreneurs in the field of industry and in particular, small industry. The Committee in its first meeting highlighted the need for training facilities and coordination requirements, publicity and dissemination of information to women entrepreneurs, laws/legislations to guard against discrimination of women, additional fiscal and financial incentives, sales and marketing support, etc. To expedite the process a sub-committee was formed to look into a) fiscal and financial incentives including marketing, b) training and c) publicity.

The Industrial Development Bank of India has formulated a special scheme to provide training and extension service support to women entrepreneurs through comprehensive packages suited to their skills and socio-economic status and to extend financial assistance on concessional terms to enable women entrepreneurs to set up industrial units in the small scale sector.

Several voluntary organisations like NAYE, New Delhi, FICCI and FASSI started a Women's Wing and took up the task of promoting entrepreneurship among the women by following the normal EFP. In Bangalore another NGO, AWAKE started developing women as entrepreneurs by attempting several innovative methods. The movement has now spread all over the country and a large number of organisations have started conducting women entrepreneurship development programmes.

The Entrepreneurship Development Institute of India is involved in promoting entrepreneurship through research, training and consultancy. With accumulated experiences over a period of time, the institute has evolved a package for developing entrepreneurship which consists of identification and selection process begins with initial screening of those responding to the media campaign. Entreprenerial trails of the candidate are assessed in the second stage, while at the third stage the candidates are interviewed for an overall assessment of suitability to undertake manufacturing activities and need for training. The institute advocates a training model of a six weeks full day programme (150 hours) for freshers and unemployed, and 3 months evenings. For a mixed group of working and non-working persons (about 180 hours). The training input aims at developing competence among selected entrepreneurs in the area of enterprise building and enterprise management, besides imparting behaviour inputs necessary for an entrepreneurial career. Practical trainings for a period of 15 days to 2 months (part-time) at a manufacturing unit related to a product chosen by the participant is an important phase of the training programme. Follow-up to the training streches from 6 months to one year. The institute seeks the follow-up by the same organisation that is involved in training and selection.

The National Institute for Entrepreneurship and Small Business Development (NIESBUD) scanned the experience gathered by various organisations and with the help of experts from all over the country, evolved a model syllabus to conduct entrepreneurship development training programmes (EDTP) for different target groups, such as general entrepreneurs, science & technology entrepreneurs, women entrepreneurs, educated unemployed youth, ex-servicemen, entrepreneurs and physically handicapped entrepreneurs. This was released in November, 1985. The NIESBUD model clearly identified four essential subject areas to be covered under each EDTP Programme. They are: Entrepreneurship Quality/ Moltivation Development; Enterprise Launching and Resourcing; Enterprise Management and Entre-preneurship Discipline/Social Responsibility. The model has been quite comprehensive and suggests the minimum requirements for any EDTP. Besides, it also provides for modification to suit the local needs and situation. The model has been widely adopted and its six-week programme is becoming very popular throughout the country.

Entrepreneurial Education : The growing importance of entrepreneurship has been widely perceived in India. The realisation of these facts have been reflected in National Policy on Education (1986) where under Clause 6.10 under "Technical and Management Vocation", it is stated that "to encourage students to consider self-employment as a career option, training in entre-preneurship will be provided through modular and optional courses in degree and diploma programmes". In order to operationlise this policy guidance there was a need to take positive steps to design a variety of course and evolve the mechanism to implement them.

There was a need to evolve courses to meet atleast the demands of the following types:

- Courses to create awareness among students about entrepreneurship as a possible career opportunity.
- Courses to prepare students to launch themselves as entrepreneurs.
- Courses to provide insight entrepreneurship development process for conducting researches or offering consultancy/industrial extension services best suited for promoting entrepreneurship in the country.

For the purpose of crating awareness among the students about the entrepreneurship as a possible career opportunity, NIESBUD in collaboration with NCERT developed curriculum, for 10+2 vocational school education system. This has been adopted through out the country and for that purpose more 500 teachers have been trained and the other is on to train many more teachers for teaching materials including text book and publications are also required and these materials should again be produced for regional languages. For the second, i.e., Course to prepare students to launch themselves as an entrepreneur under the banner of NSTED the course curriculum have been developed and teaching has started in several technical and engineering institutions. More than 25 regional engineering and technical colleges have already set up the Centre of Entrepreneurship which also undertakes the work of technical colleges have already set up the Centre of Entrepreneurship which also undertakes the work of teaching entrepreneurship to the students doing graduate courses.

The third type is relevant since university-educated persons are going to be employed in several support agencies as extension personnel. Further, they may be required for teaching and training entrepreneurship as a subject in degree or diploma courses. The efforts is on to introduce entrepreneurship teaching in the university education system. The University Grants Commission is proposing to set up more than 50 small business centres in respective universities so that both the teaching as well as training in the area of small business can be initiated. Suited to these 3 types, entrepreneurship course to be designed and adopted as a compulsory subject/optional courses to various degree and diploma curriculum; or a separate post-graduate degree and diploma courses in entrepreneurship.

Besides such courses in higher education, it may also be necessary to introduce entrepreneurial curriculum to school education system. Some efforts in this direction have been initiated and it remain a live issue to consider how best an effective design can be provided to introduce entrepreneurship teaching in the school education system.

Education and productivity growth

There is, of course, another aspect of the growth story. It is believed that efficiency and productivity increases wuld follow liberalization to such an extent that it would be possible to grow at a much higher rate without substantially increasing investment. Dismantling of irritating and irrational controls is, of course, welcome and may contribute to efficiency increases as evidence from China shows. But the greatest increases in productivity come from investments in physical and human capital. Education training, research and innovations are the key to productivity increases. Free markets may 'allow' people to compete. But it is education and training which 'enables' them to compete.

And it is here that the greatest pitfall lies. What the Ninth Plan and the budgets should do is to take up education and training as priority areas of development in the next five years. The one lesson that East Asia teaches to other developing countries is that the critical difference in productivity growth can be made by education, alone. East Asia, which is poor in natural resources grew fast primarily because of its emphasis on human resources. As Vivekananda, in his characteristic style, had observed, "it is not money which makes man, it is man who makes money". Economic growth, the creation of wealth, depends on the renewable and augmentable resource which does not show diminishing returns: human resource. Once again, the time has come to emphasize the task of 'man—making' in India.

Almost exclusive emphasis on physical capital and anear neglect of human capital formation has been a major drawback of Indian plan models and strategies. Human resources development, however, seems to hold the key to economic development and is not a peripheral social sector activity. The mistake that our earlier plans made seems to continue even today despite the vast new lilterature on growth and development which has come out in thelast ten years. A classic example here is the concept of 'rural development'—a head under which thousands of crores of rupees is spent every year to increase physical capital in rural areas. There would be a revolutionary change if a small percentage of this amount is used for building human capital in rural areas and in developing research and dissemination centres across rural India for appropriate adaptation and spread of scientific and local knowledge and skills. The focus for rural development programe should be to remove the poverty of knowledge and abilities rather than material proverty. The limited budegerary resources ought to be used not to continue to provide help to the poor but to help the poor to enabel them to help temselves.

The policy-makers should give up their obsession with high growth rates. High growth rates in the present juncture would lead to substantial erosion of self-reliance. A slower growth and a policy towards capability enhancement and not populist subsidies is what the budgets and the paln should aim at. A slower gorwth which is more widespread and a result of our own efforts and resources is preferable to higher growth based on foreign debt and capital. It is also more feasible and sustainable.

Tribal development

The total Scheduled Tribe population in India, as per 1991 census, is about eight per cent of the entire population in the country. Of this, aboupt 55 per cent Scheduled Tribe population are concentrated in central region; roughly 28.14 per cent in western religion, 12.02 per cent in north eastern region; 4.22 per cent in southern region; and the remaining in other regions. Since Independence, the Government of India continued to emphasize the programmes and schemes for raising the socio-economic levels of the tribal people. One of the main tasks of planning was to identify and remove the large disparities that existed in the country across regions and social groups. A number of Departments and Ministries in the Union and State governments had been entrusted with the task of implementing the constitutional provisions to ensure speedy development of the Scheduled Tribes. The financial allocation for their development had also been increased. Yet, why is there no perceptible improvement in their condition? Is there something wrong with the policy and planning as also the implementation?

As for the general policy approach to tribal development, it is pertinent to go back to the statements made by Dr. Rajendra Prasad and Jawaharlal Nehru, and the proposals of the Planning Commission for the Second Five Year Plan. They constitute, as a matter of fact, the policy statements towards tribal development.

Dr. Rajendra Prasad, the first President of India, indicated that "there should be no idea of forcing anything on the tribals either by way of religion, language, or, even mode of living and customs. Facilities for education and for general improvement in their economic life should be provided for them, and it should be left to them to choose whether they would like to be assimilated with, and absorbed by the surrounding society, or would like to maintain their own separate tribal existence."

"They are our own people and our work does not end with the opening of so many schools, and so many dispensaries and hospitals. Of course, we want schools, hospitals, and roads and all that, but to stop there is rather a dead way of looking at things, what we ought to do is to develop a sense of oneness with these people, a sense of unity and understanding. We must approach the tribal people with affection and friendliness and come to them as a liberating force. If they feel you have come to impose yourselves upon them, or, that we go to them in order to try and change their methods of living, to take away their land to encourage our businessmen to exploit them, then the fault is ours, for is ours, for it only means that our approach to the tribal people is wholly wrong."

The Working Group on development of Scheduled Castes and Scheduled Tribes during the VII Plan laid down that every State should prepare project report on every weaker tribe formulated by inter-disciplinary teams having social scientists and representatives of voluntary organisations in addition to administrators.

Any scheme of economic development among primitive tribes, should be undertaken after careful consideration and screening with a view to selecting only those which have relevance and suitability from the point of view of their acceptability, traditions, skills and environment.

After listing out these economic schemes, the initial approach should be to saturate each tribal group with them. The saturation approach might help these groups a great deal. The genetic approach to go into the causes of the declining population trend of some of the tribal groups might also be useful.

As far as the official machinery was concerned, the State government should make sure that it consisted of the component, empathetic and dedicated persons who should be well-rewarded as they had to serve in difficult terrains, and inhospitable areas. It was suggested that in addition to paying them handsome special allowances, they should also be allowed to retain official residence for their families at the previous place of posting. The construction of staff quarters in these areas should receive top priority. It had also been suggested that the project administrator of Integrated Tribal Development Project should be placed in over-all charge of the micro-projects for primative tribal groups.

It is a matter of concern that the detailed project reports which were required to be prepared in respect of 77 primitive tribal groups have not been done. The Government of India had been making available to the State governments financial assistance on cent per cent basis for development of primitive tribal groups since 1975-76. The State were required to gear their machinery appropriately and adequately to take up relevant programmes for these groups.

The Working Group recommended the following special measures for the development of primitive tribes:

- The saturation approach towards the economic development of the entire group with individual family as the base should be adopted. Familywise economic development plans and programmes should be formulated while adopting a holistic approach to their development;
- Special measures should be taken for improving education, health, nutrition, drinking water supply, transport and communication;
- The nearest ITDP project administrator should be declared as the direct supervisory officer of the project for primitive groups. The Project Implementation Committee of ITDP may also function as the Project Implementation Committee of the Primitive Tribes Projects with induction of one or more heads of the traditional institutions of these groups as member in the Project Implementation Committee;
- The block having primitive tribes should be included under the Integrated Child Development Services on a priority basis;
- A complete ban on purchase and settlement of land and other with outsiders in the area should be imposed. Special attention should be paid to protective and non-exploitative measures, and a special watch be kept on flow of foreign funds into the area.

In all programmes for these groups, the leaders and functionaries of the traditional tribal institutions must be actively involved at formulation, implementation, field visits and review states.

An innovative project called "Lok Jumbish": People's movement for Education for All; with assistance from Swedish International Development Authority (SIDA) has been undertaken in Rajasthan. The basic objective of the project is to achieve education for all by the year 2000 through peoples' mobilisation and their participation. Government of India approved the first phase of the project for a period of two years, 1992-94 to cover 25 blocks spread over several districts with an estimated cost of Rs. 18 crore to be shared by SIDA, Government of India, Government of Rajasthan in the ratio of 3:2:1. The phase -I concluded on 30 June 1994.

During the fijrst phase the target for project coverage was achieved (25 blocks) and project interventions were made in several components of primary education like teachers training, minimum levels of learning, opening of new schools, non-formal education centres etc.

The second phase of Lok Jumbish project will be implemented between 1994-97. In this phase the project would be extended to 50 blocks. An outlay of Rs. 80 crore has been envisaged for phase II sharable between SIDA, Government of India and Government of Rajasthan in 3:2:1: basic respectively.

Scheduled castes and scheduled tribes have been identified and specified on the basis of the criterion of extreme social, educational and economic backwardness. Their population according to 1991 Census is 13.82 crore and 6.8 crore forming 16.33 per cent and 8.01 per cent respectively of the total population of the country. Since Independence number of steps have been taken by the Government to strengthen the educational base of scheduled castes and scheduled tribes. The Department of Education, Ministry of Human Resource Development lays special emphasis on the education of these communities in all its programmes.

The National Policy on Education enunciated lays special emphasis on removal of disparities and equalization of educational opportunities by attending to the special needs of those who have been denied equality so far. Some of the important programmes of the Department of Education are: (i) Reservation of seats for SCs/STs in Central government institutions of higher education including IITs, regional engineering colleges, central universities, Kendriya Vidyalayas, Navodaya Vidyalayas etc; (ii) Remedial and special coaching for SCs/STs. The Indian Institutes of Technology have a Scheme under which SC/ST students who have marginally failed in the entrance examination to IITs are provided training for one year and are then admitted to first year of B.Tech course. IITs also provide remedial coaching to SC/ST students during the course to help them to follow the lession in the class; (III) Provision of Junior Reseacrh Fellowships, Senior Research Fellowships, Research Associateships and Teacher Fellowships by the University Grants Commission, exclusively for the students belonging to SC/ST; (iv) Instruction to state/UTs to provide priortity in opening schools, NFE Centres, Adult Education Centres, implementation of Operation Blackboard etc., in areas of concentration of scheduled * tribes; (v) Preparation of textbooks primers etc., in tribal languages through Central Institute of Indian Languages (CIIL) Mysore, NCERT etc. The CIIL has been working on using tribal languages for teaching purposes in most of the states/union territories. It has also developed bilingual education model under which primers in tribal languages and bridge materials to translate them to state language.

Minorities education

In pursuance of the revised Programme of Action (POA) 1992, two new Central schemes i.e. (i) Scheme of Area Intensive Programme for Educationally Backward Minorities and (ii) scheme of Financial Assistance for Modernisation of Madrasa Education were launched during 1993-94.

The basic objective of the scheme of Area Intensive Programme for Educationally Backward Minorities is to provide basic educational infrastructure and facilities in areas of concentration of educationally backward minorities which do not have adequate provision for elementary and secondary schools. Under the scheme cent per cent assistance is given for (i) establishment of new primary and upper primary schools, non-formal education centres where such a need is felt and viable on the basis of a school mapping exercise; (ii) strengthening of educational infrastructure and physical facilities in the primary and upper primary schools; and (iii) opening of multi-stream residential higher secondary schools for girls where science, commerce, humanities and vocational courses are taught to the educationally backward minorities.

The scheme of Financial Assistance for Modernisation of Madrasa Education is being implemented with a view to encouraging traditional institutions like Madrasas and Maktabs to introduce science, mathematics, social studies, Hindi and English in their curriculum. Under the scheme, cent per cent assistance is given to such institutions for appointment of qualified teachers for teaching the new subjects to be introduced.

The University Grants Commision introduced in 1984 a coaching scheme to prepare students belonging to educationally backward minorities for various competitive examinations. As part of implementation of the 15-Point Programme, by the end of financial year 1990-91 all the 41 minority concentration districts had been covered by community polytechnics or their extension centres. NCERT has been organising seminars and training programmes for principals/teachers of minority managed schools, in subject areas of English, science, mathematics, vocationalisation of education and educational evaluation. Department of Education have prepared and circulated to state governments policy norms and principles for recognisation of minority managed educational instutions to facilitate expenditious clearance of applications from minority educational institutions for recognition.

Subsequently, the Scheduled Areas and Scheduled Tribes Commission of 1960-61 known as the U.N. Dhebar Commission in their report adopted a similar view and divided the problem of the Scheduled Tribes into two parts, viz (i) protectionist, and (ii) developmental.

The Constitution of India aimed to give them protection against exploitation in general, and particularly in regard to their interest in land and forest, and to save them from exploitation by money-lenders, and unscrupulous contractors. It provided for protection of all tribals living scattered, and residing in other parts not declared as Scheduled Areas through general legislation. Protection also implied prohibition of bonded labour, and adequate alternative credit through simple procedure.

Developmental aspect involved four-fold development, viz (i) economic, (ii) educational, (iii) health, (vi) communication through Tribal Development Block. Economic development involved agriculture, forest, animal husbandry, and cottage industry. Educational development involved vocational and technical education, girl's education and stoppage of waste and stagnation. Development of health required provision of drinking water facilities; and communication required breaking of barrier through roads and flow of idea into the tribal areas.

The Scheduled Areas and Scheduled Tribes Commission of 1960-61 mentioned in their report about the four different layers among the tribals.

"Amongst the tribals we have been able to notice four different layers....we feel that at base of these four layers is the class of tribals which is in an extremely underdeveloped stage: and at the topmost level amongst the tribals is a layer that can very well afford to forgo any further help. We feel that this lowest layer needs the utmost consideration at the hands of the government. We would recommend that it should be made the special concern of the State governments, and special responsibility should be laid upon the chief executive offers concerned with the task of implementing policies for protection as well as development to see that is done. We feel strongly that the Deputy Commissioners and Community Development authorities should see that this nonvocal section is especially looked after. It will be necessary for the purpose to find out in each area the tribes that are in that stage."

Even after more than three and a half decades since the report of the Dhebar Commission (1961), the condition of these tribes have hardly changed.

On the basis of field visits among the Mikir (Assam); the Kharia, Sauria Paharia (Bihar); an in-depth study of the Lepchas (West Bengal: Darjeeling); reports about the Andamanese, the Sentinelese, the Onges, the Jarawas, one can emphatically say that their lot has remained much the same. The Dhebar Commission report also mentions that in the northern districts of West Bengal, the Lepchas, Bhutias and Mechs are the principal tribes. "The Lepchas are economically the weaker section and need more attention."

According to Jawaharlal Nehru, avenues of tribal

development should be pursued within the broad framework of the following fundamental principles:

- People should develop along the lines of their own genius and we should avoid imposing anything on them. We should try to encourage in every way their own traditional arts and cultures.
- Tribal rights in land and forest should be respected.
- We should try to train and build up a team of their own people to do the work of development and administration. Some technical personnel from outside will be needed in the beginning. But we should avoid introducing too many outsiders into tribal territory.
- We should not over-administer those areas or overwhelm them with a multiplicity of schemes. We should rather work through, and not in rivalry to their own cultural and social institutions.
- We should judge results, not by statistics, or the amount of money spent, but by the quality of human character that is involved.

The proposals of the Planning Commission for the Second Five Year Plan also emphasized that the tribals themselves must play their part in schemes of their own development:

"Welfare programmes for the tribal people have to be based on respect and understanding of their culture and traditions, and an appreciation of the social psychological and economic problems with which they are faced. In their implementation, the confidence of the people, and in particular, the understanding and goodwill of the elders of the tribal communities are of the highest importance. It is necessary that the welfare extension workers should be found as far as possible from amongst the educated youths in tribal communities.

In the adoption of new techniques, tribal leadership has a major role. Tribal people have to be assisted largely through their own institutions. Details of development programmes should be formulated in consultation with members of Advisory councils, leaders of tribal opinion, and institutions engaged in the study of tribal problems. The tribal people feel that these programmes area response to their own urge for better standards of living and the development of their own culture. If the programmes are implemented with popular support, they will give the tribal people a sense of partnership and integration with the nation as a whole."

These statement of the national leaders and the Planning Commission briefly set out the schemes of tribal development.

The overall policy approach towards the tribals had been (i) isolationist, (ii) assimilative, and (iii) integrationist. The first approach is: 'let them choose their own way, let them remain isolated, touch them not.'

The second approach is 'to absorb them and assimilate them.' The third approach is 'to integrate them into the national mainstream, let them develop a sense of oneness with other people, a sense of unity and understanding.'

Tribal development

The VII Plan proposed to have cent per cent coverage of tribal population under tribal sub-plan. Its benefits were also expected to be extend to the scattered tribal population not covered by any specific project through family-oriented programmes.

The plan proposal suggested that while allocating Special Central Assistance (SCA), care need to be taken to earmark beneficiaries and amounts to utilized for

Scheduled Tribes within the identified tribal units like ITDP, MADA pockets, primitive tribe projects and clusters on the one hand and the rest of the scattered tribal population on the other. But, for want of adequate and reliable data about the primitive tribes, scattered tribal groups, rationalization of allocation of special Central assistance seemed to difficult.

However, since there are four sources of financing tribal sub-plan programmes, viz—(i) SCA (Special Central Assistance), (ii) State Plan Funds, (iii) Centrally-Sponsored Schemes, (iv) Institutional finance; over-all rationalization in the allocation of resources for tribal development could be possible provided adequate data about the tribal population at various levels of development were available, and determined admi-nistrative action was initiated by:

- taking up family beneficiary programme through raising the productivity level of the beneficiary families in the field of agriculture, horticulture, animal husbandry; small-scale industries, etc.;
- elimination of exploitation of the tribals in the sphere of alienation of land, money-lending, debt bondage, forest, etc.
- human resource development through education and training programme;
- infrastructure development;
- development of vulnerable tribal areas and groups like forest villagers, displaced and migrant tribals including women; and
- upgradation of environment of tribal areas.

The Employment-orientation Programme was proposed to diversify the occupation of Scheduled Tribes who were primarily agricultural labour, through different types of income generating schemes. The main thrust was on the development of skills of tribals in their traditional and other trades and crafts.

West Bengal example: The West Bengal Scheduled Castes and Scheduled Tribes Development and Finance Corporation had been set up to give margin money loan linked with bank loan and government subsidy to provide various packages of schemes to Scheduled Caste and Scheduled Tribe target group families to assist to cross the poverty line.

The Tribal Development Co-operative Corporation (TCCC) and (LAMPS) (Large Agricultural Multipurpose Societies) are mainly involved in providing crop loans from co-operative banks.

The Training-cum-Production Centres (TCPC) were run departmentally to provide training in traditional traces and some new trades like textile, leather, carpentry, sericulture, tailoring, knitting and other handicrafts, and miscellaneous trades to the Scheduled Caste and Scheduled Tribe population. Ex-trainees were provided with one-time grant linked with bank loan to establish in trade.

The story of the tribals is much worse. They are living in the resource rich areas of this county. Most of the minerals and forest products come from this area. But thanks to the way our industrialisation is going on, they do not get any employment. They lose their territory because of industrialization. At the same time, their source of income from the forests has declined. They are raising the question of equity in modern development activities. These are the hunger prone areas. To make these areas free from hunger is not an easy task. Providing food at reduced price through the public distribution system (PDS) is a step in the right direction. The PD system must take their culture into account.

They eat millet and mahua which should be provided by the PDS in the tribal belt.

Area planning is necessary with the help of foresters, agriculturists and social workers who can plan such a manner as to liberate these areas from hunger. They are questioning the concept of modern education and health services. New educational and health technology has to be developed to suit their needs. That is why planning at micro level linking with national objective has to be worked out.

The Ninth Plan document reflects the social, cultural and economic needs of these communities. In developing a proper economic, educational strategy one has to see that the benefits are going to reach them. The present government is backed by popular support from these communities. The government has to satisfy their material needs which can sustain the democratic system. That will prove a point that planning is an instrument of social integration by allocating resources in agriculture, primary and vocational education, primary health services, and help in developing intermediate technology which will help these communities. The approach paper to the Ninth Plan has brought a lot of fresh thinking. It has brought back the role of planning to the centre of activities once more. It has provided space for the State in the era of market economy, that the State has constitutional obligation to the vast masses who are pauperized in the process of liberalization. In providing both economic and social security, the State has to strengthen the public distribution system,, education and health services by providing more resources to agriculture, rural development, primary education and primary health services. Let us hope that the spirit of the approach paper becomes a reality.

Special Development Programmes for Scheduled

Tribes living outside the ITDP should also be taken up. Not merely economic support but also social support is required to be given to the weaker tribes. Voluntary agencies should be encourage to take up work to improve and change their socio-cultural conditions and to stop conversion among them.

Need-based and appropriate type of village industries, such as basket making for packaging oranges and other fruit like guava, plum, peach, etc. and for packaging tea which grow in the north-east, and Darjeeling areas need to be developed.

Tribal technology and craft in Darjeeling region such as devices for irrigation and drinking water on bamboo pillars and tree trunk by connecting split up bamboo pieces from the hilly source of water to their villages and orchards need to be improved and properly exploited for the optimum use of water resources. The scheme of orange production should be taken up as intensively and extensively as the apple production in Kashmir Valley and Himachal Pradesh to boost the tribal economy.

Institutional finance, and the co-operative sector should be encouraged; voluntary organizations and other such agencies should also be encouraged and taken into confidence in all programmes and schemes of socio-cultural and economic development of the tribal communities.

Programmes of socio-economic and cultural improvement should go together. In this direction, the cluster approach, mutual competitive approach and family-oriented beneficiary approach need to be vigorously pursued. The smaller and weaker tribes should be encouraged to develop mutual support and competitive growth approach among the tribal groups of the same economic level.

Programmes of tribal development for the betterment of weaker and primitive tribes are laudable in premise. What is required is vigorous implementation through determined administrative action for which constant monitoring and evaluation would be necessary. This should be the responsibility of the State governments. The role of voluntary organizations, and Tribal Council would also be crucial, and must receive due emphasis and importance. At the same time, the realization must grow among the tribal groups that self-support is crucial to all socio-economic and cultural developments, all outside supports were meant only to strengthen it.

One of the most urgent and crucial tasks was the identification of the primitive tribal groups. The VI Plan emphasized the identification of these groups and then taking up unique programmes for each group relevant to its ecosystem. The Working Group on tribal development for the Sixth Plan admitted that in planning for tribal development, the basic handicap was the lack of basic statistical data relating to the Scheduled Tribes.

The Dhebar Commission also mentioned that many tribals in order to circumvent the provisions of the Act related to land, changed their names and adopted non-tribal names. Mundas changed to Mahadeo Pal because Mahadeo Pal is not a Scheduled Tribe. This change of name resulted in the parting of lands by the tribals.

In Darjeeling areas, the Bhutias took advantage of the Alienation Act and got lands from poorer sections of the tribals, i.e. Lepchas, at very nominal prices.

Article 350A of the Constitution lays down that adequate facilities for instruction in the mother tongue at the primary stage of education shall be endeavoured to be provided. To protect and promote tribal language and culture and to search out talent, tribal language must be promoted as medium of instruction at the primary level. The Central Institute of Indian Language, Mysore, NCERT, and State Tribal Research Institutes have been making their contributions in the preparation of textbooks and teaching aid and materials.

The Dhebar Commission also mentioned that the tribals and their leaders emphasized that the instruction in primary schools be imparted to them through their mother tongue. Teachers from amongst them, or tribal dialect-knowing teachers may be appointed. Boys and girls may be taught in their mother tongue up to the primary stage. In Sikkim, Lepcha language is being taught up to the primary stage.

A recent report of the Planning Commission also mentions that 'a policy decision had to be taken in regard to adoption of tribal language as medium of instruction at the primary stage', and suggested that the efforts of various agencies in this direction might be coordinated.

Another important aspect involving the improvement of life of the weaker tribe is education. While the overall situation in the field of tribal education improved as the literacy percentage went up from 11.3 in 1971 to 16.35 in 1981, and 23.03 in 1991, yet the general awareness of the tribal community to protect itself from economic and exploitative onslaught from outside has not improved much.

Formal and non-formal education, forest education, and vocational courses need to get due emphasis. Teacher should be recruited from amongst the tribals so as to engender confidence among the children and make the school functional, and minimize absenteeism among teachers. As the Christian missionaries have done for the spread of education in the north-eastern States, so should the voluntary organisations be encouraged to do among the tribal people.

A few years ago, the Ministry of Education at the Centre set up a committee consisting of social scientists, educationists and administrators et al to examine the relevance of educational curricula and contents to the tribal context and make appropriate recommendations. What happened to the Committee is not known. The committee should be revived to take up its work urgently.

The VII Plan emphasized that education in tribal areas be given highest priority; and scheduled Tribe boys in large number be placed on vocational courses; non-enrolment and drop-outs be reduced; low literacy areas and low literacy groups among Scheduled Tribes be identified; and residential schools be opened in such areas.

Surprisingly, an element of exploitation entered into the tribal areas through educational institutions permitted to be run by non-government outside agencies. Permission to such new schools to be opened may not be granted, no foreign funds be allowed to flow to educational institutions in these areas whether through foreign agencies or voluntary organizations within the country, unless a specific clearance had been obtained.

Hostel facilities at primary, middle and secondary levels both for boys and girls, sports facilities and encouragement to various aspects of tribal culture in the sphere of art, music, painting and dance be provided. Institutions like Lalit Kala Akademi, Sahitya Akademi, Sangeet Natak Akademi, besides, Tribal Research Institutes should undertake to encourage these.

Farmer's education

The Deptt. of Fertilizer (DOF) in the Ministry of Chemicals & Fertilizers is inter-alia entrusted with the responsibility of planning of fertilizer production, arrangements for movement and distribution of Ferti-lizers in terms of allocations made by the Deptt. of Agri-culture & cooperation, arrangement of subsidy for indigenous and imported fertilizers including determina-tion of rentention price and cost of imported fertilisers and administrative responsibility for public enterprises and cooperatives under the control of the Department.

The following Public Sector Undertakings (PSUs) and Cooperative under the Department of Fertilisers are carrying out agricultural extension work with emphasis on education of farmers in scientific application of fertilisers:

Besides, some of these PSUs/Cooperatives have also implemented Fertiliser Education Projects with foreign assistance.

Explaining the role of DOF as also its PSUs/ Cooperatives in regard to educating the farmers, the Department in a note stated:

> "It is submitted that while it will be ensured that the undertakings under the admin-istrative control of this Department lay greater emphasis on Farmers Education Programmes, the Undertakings can at best play a supplementary role in the promotion of agricultural education and extension. Agricultural Extension and Farmers Education Programmes are the primary concern of the Department of Agriculture in the State Governments. The Ministry of Agriculture has a nodal responsibility in this domain at the level of the Central Government. This Department will endeavour to assist the State Governments. Ministry of Agriculture in the Government of India and

> the agricultural universities and research institutions in creating greater awareness about the balanced used of fertilisers for sustained agricultural growth and productivity amelioration".

The promotional activities undertaken by the PSUs/ Cooperatives include Farmer's Meetings, Demonstration, Crop Melas, Soil Testing etc. The following statement shows number of activities undertaken by PSUs/Cooperatives during 1994-95:

During the course of examination of some of the PSUs on the subject *viz.* NFL, MFL, FACT, RCF, PPCL and PPL, the Committee pointed out the taking into the size and volume of business the promotional activities undertaken by their PSUs were too meagre. The Committee further pointed out that NFL which was being the largest producer of Nitrogenous Fertilisers in the country and wanted to know whether a PSU of the stature of NFL should not play a leading role in extending more and more help to farmers. NFL in a written note stated:

> "NFL played the role of leader, especially in the matter of providing Farm Advisory Services, facilities of farm equipments & welfare activities, in their home market comprising the State of Punjab, Haryana, Himachal Pradesh, Jammu and Kashmir and Madhya Pradesh, besides the UTs of Delhi and Chandigarh. The company has two major Urea Expansions in hand at Vijaipur in Madhya Pradesh and Nangal in Punjab. Bulk of the additional production obtained from these new expansions shall flow to the States of Andhra Pradesh, Bihar, Orissa and West Bengal from Vijaipur and Uttar Pradesh from Panipat. The Company is in the process of preparing appropriate plans to undertake Farmers Education Programmes in a befitting manner in the new territories".

In reply to another query about removing the present imbalance in use of NPK fertilizers in the country and undertaking more and more promotional activities to educate the farmers, NFL in a written note stated:

> "Much though per bag cost of fertilizer material plays a crucial role in the decision making process at the level of the farmers, efforts of NFL staff in the field are always oriented towards educating farmers that cheaper alternatives available to the farmers in the market are not always in the best interest of production and productivity. A pointed effort is also made to contain the growing luxury consumption of Nitrogen *vis-a-vis* Phosphates at the farmers level because of the comparative cheaper per bag price of Nitrogenous Fertiliser".

During the course of evidence of the representative of MFL, the Committee pointed out that MFL was a Urea and Complex fertilizers producing company and as such it was more important for MFL to impart education to farmers emphasising the need for using balanced use of fertilisers, CMD, MFL stated:

> "We recognised the importance of farmer's education had extension efforts and within our limited means we are Providing it".

When asked further whether promotional programmes undertaken by MFL should not be substantially enhanced terms, number and amount in coming years in view of the present imbalance in use of NPK fertilisers in the country, MFL in a written note informed:

> "Yes, but it should be done by both Industry and Central and state Govts. Further, unless efforts are taken to arrest the widening price gap between Urea and 'P' & 'K' fertilisers, any number of programmes implemented will not bear results. As long as Urea price is low on account of huge subsidy and the prices of 'P' & 'K' sources are

> raising every season due to factors outside the control of the industry, farmers will·be tempted to use more Urea than to apply all the NPK materials, Hence, the imbalance in NPK consumption will continue to be there. However, MFL has been consistently making efforts by organising many Educational programmes to improve balance fertiliser use and also Biofertiliser use for all crops".

On the same subject CMD, FACT, also stated during evidence:

> "The real matter of concern is what the Chairman has pointed out, that is the imbalance. At this rate, our Mother Earth will become not good for cultivation if this imbalance continues. We have been noticing this at least for the last two years and are trying to propagate more of nitrogen in the southern States and more of phosphates in the northern States. For example, the Indo-Ganges belt has now gone in more for urea because of its cheapness but it is not good at all in the longer run.
>
> Similarly, another problem is that at least seventy to seventy-five per cent fertiliser is phosphatic and it is getting sold in the southern States and the urea has to come in from the factories in the southern States as well as from North. So, the only way to get over this is to educate the farmer properly. We have realized this and our thrust now would be to bring down the imbalance by education the farmer more. After all, the decision is resting with the farmer, he being the land owner. They should know what would be good for the soil. This is a national question. Though we have a surplus situation on the foodgrains front, the imbalance in the fertilizer will not help in the future years. So, we understand our responsibility in this and we give more thrust to it".

Asked about the views of PPL in regard to adequacy of their promotional activities, PPL in a note stated:

> "We agree that substantional educational programmes to spend a large amount on these activities due to fund constraints should be substantially enhanced. However PPL can not afford to spend a large amount on these activities".

Regarding the imbalance use of fertilisers. PPL informed the Committee:

> "The imbalance in fertilisers in not only due to inadequate attention to education of the farmers in regard to optimal dosage of different fertilizers nutrients farmers but there are other reasons too. Another such reason is that the phosphatic have fertilisers become very expensive for farmers".

During the course of examination of Department of Fertilisers, the Committee pointed out that the promotional activities undertaken by PSUs are too less and should be suitably enhanced keeping in view the imbalance in use of fertilisers. The Secretary, Fertilisers informed the Committee:

> "Fertilisers play a very very important role in ensuring the productivity in agriculture. Productivity in agriculture is crucial for the development of the nation and its industry. It goes hand in hand with rural credit mechanism, agricultural prices and other inputs. Actually in this country about 143 million hectares of land are under cultivation. Out of this, about 64 million hectares are under irrigation. High yielding varieties of seeds are covering about 74 million hectares. The cultivating families are around 90 million and there is a large number of small and marginal farmers. Our endeavour from the Department of Fertilizer has been always to ensure that the production, the indigenous capability of fertilizers, the strength of

> the country is built, so that we are self-reliant in fertilisers especially in the nitrogen phosphate for which we had to depend on important raw materials. We are making all efforts towards that. We are aware that apart from the manufacturing role although this subject is with the Department of Agriculture it is equally our responsibility from the point of view of fertiliser promotion to play an active role on fertiliser education and to make the farmers conscious in the use of balance fertilisers. Our companies are engaged in commercial production".

As regards for correcting the imbalance in use of fertilisers the Secretary, Fertilisers further informed:

> "We are very clear about balanced use of fertiliser. Now, the farmer's purchasing power is to be increased. In a way, the small farmers are also entrepreneurs and they are engaged in the business of producing agricultural produce. What he wants is only some money as advance".

He further added:

> "We fully share this concern but it is necessary to point out that this imbalance is arising as a result of the wide disparity in the nutrient prices and that is the only way to correct it. Fertiliser extension and farmers education have only a supplementary role here. It can assist in the education of the farmers but then the logic that is before the farmers is that of the relative prices of the different nutrients".

The Committe further pointed out that presently targets etc. relating to promotional activities did not form part of Memorandum of Understanding signed by vari-ous PSUs with the Ministry and enquired whether the Government would consider to incorporate promotional activities/ farmers educational programmes in MOUs from now onwards. The Secretary, Fertiliser stated before the Committee:

"On the question of MOU, I would like to make a submission. MOU is provided by the Department of Public Enterprises; it is purely on commercial terms; there is no provision in the MOU for other things. What we are doing is, we are getting the direction and guidance of this Committee. We will be issuing advice to all the companies and we will be discussing it. This is my first task. They must start in a larger way. They must come and play a part in PSUs and Cooperatives".

The Committee further pointed out that even the annual targets were not fixed for the providing activities to be undertaken by various PSUs/Cooperatives. The DOF in a note stated:

"PSUs/Cooperatives under the administrative control of this Department have been advised to set targets for the promotional activities to be undertaken by them under the Farmers Education Programme at the beginning of every financial year keeping in view their specific commercial interests and the requirement of their marketing zones. They have also been advised to get these schemes and the targets for different activities approved by their respective Board of Directors before the beginning of every financial year".

From the further details furnished to the Committee it was noted that the instructions to various PSUs/ Cooperatives were issued on 27th February, 1996.

Research studies have pointed out a two—way relationship between education and other investments to improve agricultural productivity. Education—in the wide sense of the term primary education, literacy as well as extensional deucation and training—is a prerequisite qqqfor introducing modern methods of farming relying on fertilizers and new varieties of seeds.

Four basic stages of agricultural technology have been identified by Maureen Woodhall in a book on

Education and Development and they are: (a) traditional farming depending on father to son tradition; (b) use of a single modern input like fertilizer, seed; (c) Several complementary inputs simultaneously; and (d) full irrigation—based farming. Each stage calls for different levels of education to farmers commencing from literacy, maintenance skills, rudimentary knowledge of chemistry and biology and ability to calculate the effects of changes in crops, climate and so on.

It is through adequately qeqducated farmers who constitute local resources and by making available such local resources for improving agricultural productivity that the Ninth Plan target of 4.5 per cent rate of growth in agriculture can be achieved. In such an approach, requirements for improving agricultural productivity and rural development converge and it is this model of rural development through local resource mobilizaton which is the crying need of the hour. With the present level of educational backwardness, it may be difficult to achieve the agricultural growth target. But with adequate human resource development, it will be possible to achieve to goal.

Education appears to be a prerequisite to increase the yield from other types of agricultural investment, Formal education of farmers also improves the effectiveness of agricultural productivity. The extension services will become more effective if farmers have a basic level of education. This raises the question of whether the formal and non—formal education including agricultural extension are substitutes for each other.

Tamil Nadu experience: In this connnection, it is worth referring to Tamil Nadu's effort to raise productivty through investment in human resources. In 1994—95, a sum of Rs. 76 crore was allotted for human resource development to upgrade the knowledge and skill of the persons engaged in the development of agriculture, fisheries, agricultural engineering, forestry, etc. For agricultural productivity improvement through broad—based extension activities, Rs. 41.81 crore was set apart in the State budget.

There can be productivity and social change simultaneously in the rural sector. For gaining an insight into this aspect one can look at theories of social and institutional transformation as an integrated process of economic development as Schumpeter, Adam Smith, Veblen,Max Weber have advocated. Farmer education should be regarded as one link in an integrated system of generating and transferring knowledge. Other links are research and the production system like industry, services, etc. A good system of communication will serve as an intemediary.

For quite some time now Tamil Nadu has been following though not explicitly the above model. It has been called knowledge, attitude, performance and practice (KAPP) model resulting in considerable improvement in productivity in al crops (e.g. rice productivity improved from 1,306 Kg in the fifties to 3,116 Kg in the nineties).

The local needs can be carefully identified and resources can be mobilized both locally and from various sources. On the basis of the local needs a plan will have to be carefully drawn up for this purpose. There are income generating shcemes through self—employment and wage—employment and both of them should take note of the local resource endowment and the over all development strategy. At present, it is not done adequately because of the absence of local planning. Efforts should be made to get the best out of such schemes through the development of human resources and better linkage with all development schemes.

During the course of the evidence of the representatives of PSUs, Committe pointed out that the expenditure incurred by most of the PSUs/Cooperative (except IFFCO & KRIBHCO) was too meagre. Asked about the reasons/difficulty in not enhancing their budgets the CMD, NFL admitted before the Committee:

> "Sir, to be frank, the type of things which perhaps the hon. Chairman has in his mind, to that magnitude we are not going into the details".

When pointed out further that the expenditure on promotional activities should bear some relation with the turnover/profits of the respective PSUs, the witness stated :—

> "We agree that as useful Members of the society, particularly the companies which are under the Government need to do something for the welfare of the farmers in order to improve, what is called, the use of fertilizers or efficient use of fertilizers. There is nothing wrong if a Central Government undertaking spends a part of its profit for this purpose. It may not be possible for the loss making companies to do so but the profit making compaines should take interest for the development of the farmers".

In this connection CMD, MFL submitted that MFL had suffered due to less demand of its products Viz. P & K fertilizers after their decontrol in 1992. He however stated that inspite of losses they were spending on promotional activities. He added :—

> "We recognised the improtance of farmer's education and extension efforts and within our limited means we are providing it. We are also supplementing our own production because our production facilities are limited. We are supplementing it by trading activity in potassic fertilizers. We are importing MOP, a part of which we are utilizing in the manufacture of complex

> grade fertilizers or 17:17:17. It is higly rated in the Southern region, which is the traditional marketing zone. In addition to that, we are also selling MOP for direct application".

The witness further informed that there was need for common approach particularly the organisations dealing in complex fertilizers. Elaborating it further, he stated:

> "Every company likes to sell one's own product. In the field of fertilizer marketing we have seen a lot of duplication of resources & duplication of efforts. To avoid this type of wastage, they decide to explore the commonality of interest so that effort is not duplicated. The resources so econo-mised can be put to fertilizer promotion effort. But, then it seems that this might not be feasible because everybody is trying to promote his own product in no preference to others' products. Some kind of propaganda is necessary. People have to be told why Vijay brand which is produced by MFL is preferable to others. Then, in that case the development of a common strategy becomes very difficult. There should be some self-abnegation on the part of the competitors so that they may work together for a common cause".

CMD, FACT elaborating the views of his company for allocating more funds for promotional activities stated:

> "From next year onwards, we will allocate more money in the Budget so that the programmes can be done with more emphasis. This is all the more needed because they will be given further impetus".

•In reply to a further query the witness stated:

> "Sir, it is fact that there is a commonality of interest insofar as the producers of potassium and phosphatic fertilizers are concerned. But , it is also a fact there is a lot of competition, today when there is a demand compression. Not everybody is

able to place ones production in the market to the extent one would like to. Therefore, there is a lo of competition and everyone is stepping on each other's toes. So far, we had thought of some kind of synergy and exploitation of the synergy in this area and we had a wide ranging interaction with the Fertiliser Association of India. It was found that the commonalities can be exploited only to a very limited extent. However, in compliance of the direction of this Committee–you would recall that in the earlier meeting of the Committee–you had instructed about adopting coordinated approach in the promotion of fertilizers in education and extension effort".

When asked about the steps taken by PPL in raising in quantam funds for promotional activities. CMD PPL stated:

> "For 1995-96, we have provided Rs. 41 lakhs for promotional activities. And carlier, it was Rs. 30 lakh. So, we are slowly increasing it year after. That is still not sufficient. We are concentrating in the eastern part of our country, that is in states like Orissa, W. Bengal and Bihar. But we have not spent much amount. There is a justification for spending much more. We have constraints due to non-availability of funds".

However the CMD, PPL submitted before the Committee that funds for promotional activities should be pooled together and should be monitored through one agency in a given area or State which would avoid duplicity of efforts in regard to undertaking promotional activities.

He submitted:

> "However, for all the promotional activities and farmers' education, there can be a Central nodal agency which can be provided funds for promotional activities to avoid overlapping of same activities. For example, the total sale of

> fertilizers may be 15 million tonnes of nutrients. One that, Government levy cess of five to ten rupees PMT and distribute State-wise on the basis of needs. Otherwise, on the other hand each losing company may also not give any attention to promotional aspect whereas cash-rich company may not give attention to these activities because they are more concerned as to how to make more and more profits. Companies are paying less attention to promotional schemes whereas it is very very important from country's point of view".

He Further added:

> "The funds so collected should be allotted to an agency in that particular State so that they carry out the promotional activities in one or ⱡwo States. There are 13-15 companies which are manufacturing phosphatic fertilizers. That is the way how we can improve balanced fertilizer application. I can tel lyou very frankly that such approach has never been followed.
>
> PPL wants to improve the promotional activities and farmers' education in Orissa, Bihar and Bengal. We are ready to spend Rs. 1 crore in a year. But my suggestion is that it should be through a consolidated fund. That fund should be utilised for the country as a whole. Otherwise, the same activities will be done by everybody. For example, I am also distributing the pamphlets to the farmers about how much quantity they sould use. The same thing is done by others. This overlapping can be reduced if it is done by one organisation".

During the course of evidence of representatives of DOF the Committee pointed out that he amount spent by PSUs for promotional activities was too low which was even agreed to by MDs of NFL, RCF, FACT and PPL. Asked whether it did not call for higher allocation, the Secretary, Fertilizers stated:

"I am very clear in may mind that the public sector companies have a social obligation. The Committee on Public Undertakings of the Par-liament have made it very clear that these companies have a social obligation and they have so discharge it. So, a good investment is to invest in the human beings. Seventy five per cent of our farmers are marginal farmers with less than 2 hectares of land holding. They are able to cul-tivate barely enough for themselves.

I am equally clear that the Goverment must make arrangements for creating awareness. Education is the basic thing. There is no question of saying that these companies should not invest more in this field. They will have to do it and the Board will have to tell them about it. I cannot fix a percentage for them because they are autonomous. We are certainly going to benefit from your guidance on this and we will definitely give them a clear view. As far as I am concerned, in the quarterly review meeting, I will take up this issue.

The Ministry of Agriculture must play the lead role in it. I will request the agriculture sector to play the leadership role by coming into this field. The private sector companies also must play a very significant role because marketing is for everybody. We are giving a lot of support to the fertilizer companies. Therefore, the least that they can do is to give some allocation and increase their budgets for this purpose. If they do not do it they will be out of business".

When asked about the view of the DOF for fixing some percentage of turnover or profits, DOF in a written note stated:

"Although there can thus be no linkage between the turn over or profits of a PSU/Cooperative with the expenditure on Farmers Education Programme, the Department is aware of the need for PSUs to increase their allocation in this regard".

The Committee further wanted to know whether DOF ever asked PSUs to raise funds for promotional activities. The Secretary, Fertilizer stated:

> "I will have a dialogue with them. We will issue a direction from the Government that they have to increase the allocation. But they have to consider it in their Board Meetings. We will review it in the quarterly review meeting".

Subsequently in a written note furnished to the Committee, DOF stated:

> "They have advised companies to pay more attention to promotional activities involving agricultural extension programmes. The response to our advice for greater emphasis on extension and farmers education is excepted to be reflected in the outlay for these activities in 1996-97. The instructions sent to CMD's/MD's of PSUs and cooperative on 27.2.1996 inter-alia include that the Government has decided to accept the above recommendation of the Standing Committee. You are therefore, advised to:
>
> — fix specific target for the above mentioned promotional activities like educating the farmers about the need for balanced application of fertilizer nutrients, Farmers Meetings Demonstrations, Crop Melas, Soil Testing, Farmers Training, Seminars and any other activities compatible with the specific marketing needs and the requirements of your Boards of Directors before the beginning of each financial year under intimation to this Department;
>
> — Send a half yearly progress report enumerating the actual achievements against these targets by 31st October of each year and the final report within one month of the close of each financial year to this Department;

— review the budget provision for promotional activities for 1996-97 to ensure that the financial provisions are commensurate with the physical targets".

In reply to a further query the Secretary, Fertilizers informed the Committee that in addition to Cooperatives/PSUs he was in touch with private sector companies for asking them to undertake activities for educating the farmers and related matters.

Vidyalaya: Types and Other Issues

In order to provide good quality modern education to the talented children predominantly from the rural areas, Government of India launched in 1985-86 a scheme to establish Navodaya Vidyalaya on an average one in each * admission to Navodaya Vidyalayas is at the level of class VI based on an admission test conducted by NCERT. The medium of test is the mother tongue or regional language of the children. The test is largely nonverbal in nature, class neutral and so designed as to ensure that the talented children from the rural areas are able to compete without suffering any disadvantage.

The Vidyalayas are fully residential and c0-educational in which addmission to the children from urban areas is generally restricted to 25 per cent of the seats. Efforts ae made to ensure that atleast one third of the students in each Vidyalaya are girls. Reservation of seats in favour of children belonging to SCs and STs is provided in proportion of their population in the concerned district provided that in no district such reservation is less than the national level.

The Vidyalayas provide education in the streams of Humanities, Commerce, Science and Vocational upto +2 level and are affiliated to CBSE. There are at present 359 sanctioned Vidyalayas in the country operating in 30 states/UTs.

The scheme for establishment of Central Schools was approved by the Government of India in 1962 and its implementation was started by the Ministry of Education in 1963 when 20 regimental schools run by the Ministry of Defence were taken over and converted into Central Schools or Kendriya Vidyalayas. Later on the Kendriya Vidyalaya Sangathan, an autonomous body was set up by the Ministry of Education and was registered as a Society in December 1965. The main objectives of Kendriya Vidyalayas are: (i) to cater to the educational needs of the children of transferable Central Government employees including Defence and paramilitary personnel by providing a common programme of education; (ii) to pursue excellence and set pace in the field of school education; (iii) to initiate and promote experimentation and innovativeness in education in collaboration with other bodies like the CBSE and NCERT etc. and (iv) to develop the spirit of national and create a sense of 'Indianess' among children.

During the academic year 1994-95 there were 818 Kendriya Vidyalayas with a student population of approximately seven lakh. There are two Vidyalayas abroad one each in Kathmandu and Moscow. The number of staff sanctioned as on 30 April 1994 was 42,950. During the academic session 1995-96, 21 Kendriya Vidyalayas have been sanctioned out of which two are in defence, 16 in civil and three in public sectors.

Kendriya Vidyalayas are opened in Defence establishments on the recommendation of the Ministry of Defence and in the civil sector on the recommendation of the various ministries/departments employees welfare associations. The sponsoring agency has to provide a piece of land measuring 15 acre for the construction of permanent building for Kendriya Vidyalaya. The Kendriya Vidyalays are opened in the campuses of public sector undertakings if they are ready to bear all the recurring and non recurring expenditure on the proposed Kendriya Vidyalaya. The children of the employees of such undertakings get priority in admission in Kendriya Vidyalayas However, for admission in Kendriya Vidyalayas under civil and defence sectors the transferable Central Government employees including defence personnel get the priority. The reservation of 15 per cent and 7.5 per cent of fresh admissions is available in all Kendriya Vidyalayas for the children of SC and ST respectively.

All kendriya Vidyalayas follow the same textbooks and medium of instruction which is in Hindi and English, the ultimate object being to enable pupils to achieve proficiency in both the languages. The Kendriya Vidyalayas are having classes Ist to XIIth. Introductory computer science has been introduced as an elective subject in Kendriya Vidyalayas from this year for the XIIth class students.

The first "Education for All" project in India, the Bihar Education Project (BEP) is in operation in Bihar since 1991-92. Its basic objective is to bring about quality improvement in the elementary education system in the state. With an estimated outlay of Rs. 360 crore, it envisages to cover 150 blocks spread over 20 districts over the project period spanning 1991-96. UNICEF would contribute Rs. 180 crore, the Government of India Rs. 120 crore and the Government of Bihar Rs. 60 crore. Participatory planning and community participation are the important characteristics of the project which lays special emphasis on the education of SC/ST and the women. A state level registered society has been set up for its planning and implementation. As of now, seven districts of Ranchi, West Champaran, Rohtas, Muzaffarpur, Sitamarhi, Chatra and East Singhboom are covered. The

Unicef cooperation in May 1993 noted the major impact the project ;has had on the attitudes in Bihar towards education at political, administrative and community level. The project has also played a major role in mobilising greater national and international interest in basic education. * The UNICEF-Government of India Joint review in July 1994 noted certain positive features such as Mahila Samakhaya, management structures, village education committees and non-formal education through NGOs. The review, inter alia recommended consolidation of the programme and strong linkages between BEP and the education system in Bihar. Against the total releases of Rs. 84 crore so far, the total expenditure including supplies is Rs. 48 crore.

The National Book Trust (NBT) India, an autonomous organisation established in 1957 by the Government of India discharges these functions: (i) publishing; (ii) promotion of books and book-reading; (iii) promotion of Indian books abroad; (iv) assistance to authors and publishers and (v) promotion of children's literature.

NBT publishes general reading material for all segments of society and for all age groups, including books for children and post-literacy reading material for neoliterates. Moderately priced books, fiction and non-fiction in English, Hindi and 11 other major Indian languages viz., Assanese Bangla, Gujrati, Kannada, Malayalam, Marathi, Oriya, Punjabi, Tamil, Telugu and Urdu and also in Konkani, Nepali, Manipuri and Sindhi are brought out under different series. Five hundred and eighty four titles were brought out during 1994-95 including reprints and enrolled 91 new bookdellers as registered dealers of its publications, raising their total number to 460. The gross value of books sold was Rs. 250 lakh.

During 1994-95, three book fairs in Nagpur, Jalandhar and Goa and 124 exhibitions all over the country were organised. Every alternate year, NBT organises the New Delhi World Book Fair which is the largest in Asia and Africas. The next World Book Fair will be held in February 1996 at New Delhi. To help the book industry grow, NBT organises seminars and workshops in the country and every year from November 14-20 National Book Week is celebrated. On the demand of readers for the availability of books on a permanent basis, NBT has decided to launch pilot project to construst 12 book stalls in Delhi and five in states of the Hindi speaking region.

NBT participated in international book fairs and made arrangements for special exhibitions for display of select titles brought out by Indian publishers in China, Germany, Italy, Male, Nepal, South Africa and Sri Lanka.

NBT gives financial assistance to authors and publishers for bringing out reasonably priced books for higher education. Under its scheme, for the subsidised publication of books only such books are subsidised for which a definite need is felt and which relate to subject areas where books of an acceptable standard are either not available or so highly priced as to be beyond the means of students. So far NBT has subsidised the publication of 830 titles, including 13 in 1994-95 mostly in English.

NBT has established the National Centre for Children Literature to monitor, coordinate plan and aid the publication of children's literature in various Indian languages. The Centre organises workshops and exhibitions and promotes the habit of reading at school level by encouraging the setting up of Reader's Clubs. It is also compling a catalogue of select books for children published in Indian languages.

Under the present policy, as announced by the Ministry of Commerce for the period April 1992 to 31 March 1997, as amended upto 31 march 1995 any person/organisation is free to import all categories of books including journals, magazines and newspapers under open general licence except in case of children's literature.

Copyright protection governed by the Indian Copyright Act, 1957 and has been amended from time to time was last amended in 1994 as Copyright (Amendment) Act, 1994 came into force on 10 May 1995. A notification in this regard was published in the Official Gazette, extra-ordinary dated 5 May 1995. Consequential amendments in the Copyright Rules, 1958 necessitated by the amendments to the Copyright Act, have also been notified simultaneously in the same issue of the gazette as mentioned above.

The copyright office was established in January 1958 in pursuance of Section 9 of the Copyright Act, 1957. The Act, inter alia provides for registration of copyright under six different categories, viz., (a) Literary works other than computer programmes, tables and compilations including computer data bases and dramatic works, (b) musical works, (c) artistic works, (d) cinematograph films, (e) sound recordings and (f) computer programmes, tables, compilations including computer data bases. Further, the Act also provides for registering changes in the particulars entered in the Register of Copyright, issue of certified copies of extracts from the Register of Copyright as also of the public documents in the custody of the Registrar of Copyright besides facilitating inspection of the Register of Copyright/Index by the interested persons.

The Copyright Board, a quasi-judicial body, was constituted initially in September 1958. The jurisdiction of the Board extends to the whole of India. It hears cases regaring rectification of copyright registration, disputes in respect of assignment of copyright appeal against the Registrar of Copyright and granting of licences in certain specified works and other miscellancous matters instituted before it under the Copyright Act, 1957. The Secretariat to the Board is provided by the Copyright Office.

The International Standard Books Numbers (ISBN) System aims at boosting the export of indigenous publications at the international business areas. It is an international system by which a distinct identifying number is assigned to each book. In addition to the book trade, the system is very helpful to the libraries and information systems and to research scholars. From 1 January 1985 to 31 March 1995, 2,672 big and small publishers and authors have become the members of the System.

The Department of education funds several scholarship/fellowship programmes for Indian students for school and higher education. They include the National Scholarship Scheme, a scheme of scholarships to help students of non-Hindi speaking states studying Hindi, research scholarships for Indian classical languages and scholarships to enable talented rural children to continue secondary education. These programmes are administered through the state governments. A new programme of prestigious fellowships for post-graduate studies in India and abroad,named Jawaharlal Nehru Fellowship, has recently been introduced which is now administered by Jawaharlal Nehru Memorial Fund, Teen Murti House, New Delhi.

Scholarships for advanced or specialised studies are offered under the provisions of cultural programme, bilateral agreements, Commonwealth scholarships/fellowships plan and ad hoc scholarship offers received from different countries. These scholarships are mostly for Ph.D (Doctoral) and post-doctoral specialisation for which the minimum eligibility countries like Germany, France, Ireland, Korea (South), Australia, UK, Japan, China, Austria, Norway, Italy, israel, Spain, Czech., Mexico, Egypt and Indonesia.

The Computer Literacy and Studies in Schools (CLASS) and is being implemented as a Centrally-sponsored scheme from 1993-94. To be eligible for assistance under the modified scheme, the following conditions are to be satisfied by the states/UTs: (a) The coverage of the scheme for new schools will be restricted to senior secondary schools; (b) In selected schools, instructions in computer literacy will be compulsory for all students of classes XI and XII, these instructions will be part of the school time-table with the evaluation in the subject taking place with/without formal examination; and (c) infrastructure such as a pucca room with electricity and other fittings will have to be made in the schools to be covered under the project initially by the state government concerned.

The National Steering Committee under the Chairmanship of Education Secretary is responsible for monitoring and supervision etc. At state/UT levels, Cells have been set up, which are to discharge the dual responsibility of monitoring and actual implementation of the scheme in the schools and of releasing the funds to the implementing agencies. The National Informatics Centre (NIC) which was assigned the responsibility of identifying vendors for hardware had short-listed the names of two vendors which have been circulated to the states/UTs/autonomous body institutes concerned. On the recommendation of National Steering Committee the guidelines for selection of Implementing Agencies as well as course material to be adopted have also been circulated to all concerned. Rupees 146 crore has been provided for implementing the scheme during the Eighth Plan. This amount is for maintaining 2,598 schools already covered under the old scheme as well as for including 1,320 additional schools during the Eighth Plan.Two hundred and eighteen additional schools were covered during 1993-94 and 449. During 1995-95, it isproposed to cover 500 additional schools.

The Government encourages development of all Indian languages including classical, modern and tribal. Its policy lays emphasis on training of teachers in relation to adoption of the three-language formula and production of university-level textbooks with ta view to facilitating media switch over from English to regional languages. In order to assist non-Hindi speaking states/ union territories to effectively implement the three-language formula, support for provision on facilities for provision on facilities for teaching of Hindi in these states/union territories is provided by sanctioning financial assistance for appointment of Hindi teachers in schools and for establishment of Hindi teachers training colleges in these states/union territories, under a Centrally-sponsored scheme. The grant-in-aid is provided mainly to assist the consolidation and further development of Hindi teacher training colleges in non-Hindi speaking states/union territories and to a limited extent, to assist the setting up of a new institution in such areas which are in need of such assistance. Assistance is also given to voluntary organisations for enabling them to hold Hindi teaching classes, conducting research on methodology of its teaching and providing Hindi books to various organisations. Various schemes are in operation to promote and develop tribal, calssical, modern Indian languages and prepare and publish books, dictionaries, research and instructional material besides training of teachers in Hindi. Through the kendriya Hindi Sansthan, Agra the Government of India promotes development of improved mentodology for teaching Hindi to the non-Hindi speaking students. A full-fledged academic course for teaching Hindi to foreigners is being conducted by the Sansthan under the scheme 'Propagation of Hindi Abroad'. Central Hindi Directorate runs programmes relating to pruchase and publication of books and their free distribution to non-Hindi speaking states and to the Indian missions. The Directorate also brings out Hindi journals like UNESCO DOOT, Bhasha and Sahityamala. It is also implementing a scheme of teaching Hindi through correspondence courses in the media of English, Tamil, Malayalam and Bengali.

The Commission for Scientific and Technical Terminology, New Delhi, prepares and publishes definitional dictionaries and terminology in various disciplines and Pan-Indian terminology. Hindi-English glossaries in Basic sciences, humanities, social sciences, university level textbooks in agriculture and engineering and other subjects are also published. Fifty scholarships are awarded every year to foreign students for studying Hindi in Kendriya Hindi Sansthan, Agra.

4

Culture, Values and Education

Education about India's common cultural heritage has been identified in National Policy on Education as one of the core areas under the national system of education. While spelling out the cultural perspective in education, the policy has stressed on the need to bridge the schism between the formal system of education and India's rich and varied cultural traditions. It has called for enriching the curricula and processes of education in as many manifestations as possible and laid considerable emphasis on value education by highlighting the need to make education a forceful tool for cultivation of social and moral values.

Within these overall objectives, a Centrally-sponsored scheme of Assistance for Strengthening Culture and Values in Education has been designed for providing assistance to Government agencies, educational institutions, Panchayat Raj institutions, registered societies, public trusts and non-profit making companies. The scheme has two broad components (i) strengthening cultural and value education inputs in the school and non-formal education system and (ii) strengthening the in-service training of art, craft, music and dance teachers. A total grant of Rs. 98 lakh has been approved for sanction to 33 organisations during 1994-95.

National Open School (NOS) was established in November 1989 as an autonomous organisation with the objective to provide quality education through distance education mode upto secondary stage for the school dropouts and children who cannot attend formal schools. This school is vested with the authority to examine and certify students registered with it upto pre-degree level courses. The certificates issued by this school are recognised for admissions for pursuing higher education and also for employment. The students have the freedom to choose the set of subjects according to their needs, interests and abilities and are also encouraged to choose vocational subjects in combination with academic subjects. The marginalised groups, viz., rural youth, girls and women, SC and ST, handicapped, ex-servicemen are given priority by NOS.

The NOS provides student support services through a network of study centres known as accredited institutions (AIs) for academic courses and accredited vocational institutions (AVIs) for*. As on 31 March 1994, 306 AIs were functioning under NOS.

The number of students enrolled by the National Open School during the years 1992-93, 1993-94 and 1994-95 for its secondary and senior secondary courses was:

Year	Secondary	SeniorSecondary
1992-93	31,375	20,932
1993-94	35,098	25,777
1994-95	36,766	29,054

It is proposed to extend the open learning facilities in a phased manner at the secondary level in all parts of the country. In order to facilitate setting up of state open schools, the NOS provides consultancy services to the state goverments and serves as an agency for effective dissemination of information related to distance education and open learning.

The National Council of Educational Research and Training (NCERT) was established in September 1961 in New Delhi as an autonomous body. Qualitative improvement and excellence in school education and teacher education are some of its major objectives. They maintain effective liason with state education authorities for providing academic inputs to school education system.

The NCERT develops curricula, syllabi and prepares textbooks for classes I-XII which form the basis for prescription of schemes of studies by Central Boaard of Secondary Education (CBSE) for the schools affiliated to the Board. It also develops instructional material for childhood education and training packages for teacher educators and supervisory personnel. It provides technical assistance for national population education programmes designed to introduce population education in the formal education system. NCERT also provides its expertise to states/UTs. It also designs courses and material, generates software systems and sets up resource centres for computer literacy and studies in school project. NCERT organises Jawaharlal Nehru National Science Exhibition every year in which a large number of school students from all over the country participate. The Council produces science kits for the use of school students. It prepares comprehensive guidelines for curriculum evaluation and school industry linkages as well as for pre-service education of teachers on vocationalisation of education. Training courses for the officials involved in the Integrated Education Programme for Disabled Children are also conducted.

The NCERT is providing very useful assistance to the Department of Education in implementing the

District Primary Education Projects (DPEPs) in several states towards fulfilment of the recommendations made in Education For All (EFA) Summit of nine high population countries held in New Delhiin December 1993. One of the major projects entrusted to the NCERT is the Sixth All India Educational Survey which the Council is implementing in collaboration with the National Informatics Centre (NIC).

The objective of inculcating the message of small family norms and other population related issues in the minds of school and college students and the clientele of adult and non-formal education is being achieved through National Population Education Project.This project is now being implemented through school and non-formal education, higher education and adult education.

Since its inception in 1980, NPEP has done much towards achieving its main objective of institutionalising population education through the school education system. During the second cycle (1986-1990) the main focus was on consolidation of the project's multidimensional activities and further expansion of its network. During the third cycle, special attention was paid to girls and SCs/STs through various curricular activities with an emphasis on community participation. The process of interweaving population education elements into the syllabi, textbooks and of instructional and training materials will continue.

One of the main factors responsible for slow pace of growth of enrolment of adolescent girls of rural, tribal and other remote areas is the traditional social inhibitions against their movement outside the family precincts. Moreover the high/higher secondary schools in schools in such places are sparsely located. In order to actualise the recommendation in POA 1992 for formulating a special enabling plan to ensure increased enrolment of girls in secondary education and the NPE directive for encouraging NGO participation in education, the scheme for strengthening of boarding and hostel facilities for girl students of secondary/higher secondary schools was launched in 1993-94 with the objective of providing the following types of assistance to the existing hostels run by the NGOs: (i) Non-recurring assistance as non-time grant for provision of essential furniture, utensils and meeting basic recreational needs at the rate of Rs. 1,500 per boarder: and (ii) recurring assistance for food, emoluments of cook and bearer at the rate of Rs. 5,000 per annum per boarder.

In keeping with the National Policy on Education (NPE), 1986 (as updated in 1992) and its Programme of Action (POA), a new initiative to achieve Universalisation of Elementary Education (UEE) has been evolved titled, "District Primary Education Programme (DPEP)". It seeks to operationalise the strategy for UEE as enunciated in the POA, through decentralised planning and disaggregated target setting.

The DPEP is a beachhead for effecting improvements and full-scale development of the entire elementary education sector. Its fundemental principle is capacity-building at national, state and local levels and to evolve strategies which are replicable and sustainable. The DPEP, approved as a Centrally-sponsored scheme, is a major and multi-faceted programme seeking to overhaul the primary education system in the country. Infact, it is envisaged that DPEP will be transformed to a National Mission for Elementary Education, thus meeting a major commitment of POA 1992.

The objectives of the programme are: (i) to reduce diference in enrolment, dropout and learning achievement among gender and social groups to less than five per cent; (ii) to reduce overall primary dropout rates for all students to less than 10 per cent; (iii) to raise average achievement levels by at least 25 per cent over measured baseline levels and ensuring achievement of basic literacy and numerous competencies, by all primary school children; (iv) to provide, according to national norms, access for all children, to primary education classes (I-IV), wherever possible, or its equivalent non-formal education. The programme would also strengthen the capacity of national, state and district institutions and organisations for the planning, management and evaluation of primary education.

The coverage of the programme will be gradually extended to all the districts which satisfy one of the twin criteria, viz., (a) educationally backward districts with female literacy below the national average and (b) districts where TLCs have been successful, leading to enhanced demand for elementary education.

The programme which lays greater emphasis on participatory processes for planning and management, has a marked gender focus and seeks to enhance school effectiveness through inputs in teachers' training and decentralised management. DPEP lays great emmphasis on people's participation and mobilisation of communities to assist in programme implementation. VECs play a key role in the implementation of the programme at the village level.

As of now the programme is being implemented in 42 districts of Madhya Pradesh, Assam, Karnataka, Haryana, Maharashtra, Tamil Nadu and Kerala. The planning process has been initiated in five districts each in Andhra Pradesh and West Bengal where it would be funded by ODA. Nineteen districts of Madhya Pradesh are funded by European Community's Programme assistance while the remaining 23 districts are funded by

IDA. The Financing Agreement with European Community has been signed for an amount of ECU 150 millon (Rs. 585 crore). First tranche of 19.37 ECUs have already been credited to the Government of India's accounts.

The revised Programme of Action 1992 of the NPE, 1986 resolves to ensure free and compulsory education of satisfactory quality to all children upto 14 years before we enter the 21st century. Various Centrally-sponsored schemes in the elementary education sector have been initiated to supplement the efforts of states for achieving this target.

In order to opertionalise the revised policy of the government, the following three sub-schemes are proposed under Operation Blackboard during the Eighth Plan: (i) Continuation of the on-going scheme to cover all the remaining schools identified in the Seventh Plan; (ii) expanding the scope of the scheme to provide three rooms and the three teachers in primary schools with provision for about 50 per cent women teachers in primary schools as mandatory for all states/UTs; and (iii) extending the scope of the scheme to upper primary schools.

To achieve the goal of Universalisation of Elementary Education, the Non-formal Education Programme had been put into operation in 1979-80 to provide education of a quality comparable to formal system to children who do not/cannot attend school, school dropouts, girls who cannot attend whole day schools and working children. This scheme was reorganised and expanded in 1987-88 and again in 1993. Under the scheme assitance is given to the states/union territories in the ratio of 60:40 and 90:10 for running general co-educational and girls centres respectively. Hundred per cent assistance is given to voluntary agencies for running non-formal education centres and undertaking experimental and innovative projects. Presently, 2.61 lakh centres have been sanctioned for imparting education to about 65 lakh children. About one lakh centres are exclusively for girls. The programme of NPE would continue in the Eighth Plan as per the revised pattern.

In pursuance to the provisions of NPE on teacher education a Centrally-sponsored scheme of Restructuring and Reorganisation of Teachers Education was launched in 1987-88. So far 394 DIETs, 85 CTEs/IASEs have been established throughout the country to impart good quality of preservice and in-service training to teachers.

In elementary education the focus has been shifted from enrolment per se to retention and achievement. The Minimum Levels of Learning programme answers the third dimension of Universalisation of Elementary Education, namely, universal achievement. Laying down competency to be mastered by all children in the country at a particular grade, the programme envisages a package of quality improvement. It incorporates curricular revision, teacher orientation and improved pedagogy to handle multi-grade situations.

In the first phase, 18 projects were taken up and after working in 4,000 schools, the programme is being upscaled through the institutional mechanism of DIETs and SCERTs in about 12 states. After this period of initiation, the programme would be extended and expanded to cover the entire school system by 2000 AD. Currently, about 100 DIETs have been oriented in the comprehensive strategy.

Education should be looked upon as a national investment in the development of human resources. Educational development, however, must be based upon national priorities, national ethos and an international outlook. Perhaps with the exception of China, no other country in the world has got such a massive structure for higher education as India has. And the demand for education in India is expanding at an exponential rate because of the rapidly increasing population and the huge plans for socio-economic development launched by successive governments based on the principles of equality and social justice.

The magnitude of the growth of higher education in free India can be gauged better when we look at the status of education during the British period. Even as late as 1947, the number of students in colleges and universities could be counted in their thousands as against today's millions in the institutions of higher learning. The number today is about six million by 2010 A.D. Where the number of the universities in India stood at 20 in 1947, the number today is 220 (including deemed-to-be universities), an eleven-fold increase in fifty years. No other country has witnessed such a phenomenal growth. But based on population and based on the type of educational system prevalent today, India needs at least a thousand universities and a hundred thousand colleges (as against today's 8000 odd-colleges). The student population in the higher education sector alone in India is greater than the total population of Sweden or Switzerland or the Netherlands.

Growth and accountability

This problem of number ought to make our educational experts and planners think and act in a manner that is different from that in countries with small populations and high resoureces.

Education has to be looked upon as a national investment. The question of accountability needs very special attention from planners and funding agencies in India because the inputs are huge but the output is low. State and central government agencies, planning boards, private and public management, philanthropists, student, teachers, administrative staff and the general public ought to be concerned about returns on investment, not only on monetary considerations but certainly on the scale of human resource development. Otherwise, all that is investment will not only not generate excellence but create mediocrity and even patently dangerous intellectual evil.

The question of quantity versus quality assumes national importance in contemporary India because of goals of education in pre-Independence India were different. The British rulers did not finance higher education in any big manner but there was ample governmental policy support to individuals and trusts, religious and social groups for organizing, maintaining and developing colleges. The objectives of higher education during the British period were very limited and they mostly served the Macaulayan vision of creating "a class of people Indian in blood and colour but English in tastes, manners and intellect". In other words, the educated class had to think British rather than Indian and cater to the economic and political needs of governance in a country where the large majority of the governed were culturally far removed from the governors.

For higher education, the British establish three universities in the big cities of Calcutta, Bombay and Madras which were the provincial capitals of three British provinces directly under the responsibility first of the East India Company and then of Britsh Crown. The three universities were established in 1857 after the model of the London University. The responsibility of expanding higher education was lwft with the colleges affiliated to each university and they were run by private management.

The elilte in pre-Independence India were exposed to the liberal traditions, legal principles and the history of democratic and egalitarian movements in the West, particularly Europe through the syllabi prescribed for higher education. The economic aspect of life in India, the political imperatives that led to suppression of democratic aspirations of the people and the large-scale drains of wealth from the country did not receive any attention in the syllabi. This resulted in the creation of a very huge number of educated young people who lost touch with the reality of Indian political, economic and social life, particularly in the rural areas.

Higher education is imparted through 197 universities in the country. Of these, there are 12 Central universities and the remaining are functioning under the state Acts. Total number of colleges in the country is 8,210. Besides, there are 34 institutions declared as deemed-to-be-universities under the University Grant Commission Act, 1956. The enrolment of students is 50.07 lakh while the number of teachers is 2.86 lakh.

Indian Council of Historical Research, New Delhi, set up in 1972, enunciates and implements a national policy on historical research and encourages scientific writing of history. It operates research projects, financial research projects by individual scholars, awards fellowships and undertakes publication and translation work.

Indian Council of Philosophical Research, which started functioning from 1981 with offices in New Delhi and Lucknow, reviews the progress, sponsors or assists projects and programmes of research in philosophy, gives financial assistance to institutions and individuals to conduct research in philosophy and allied disciplines.

Indian Institute of Advanced Study, Shimla, set up in 1965, is a residential centre for advanced research on humanities, social sciences and natural sciences. It is a community of scholars engaged on exploring new frontiers of knowledges aimed at conceptual development and offering interdisciplinary perspectives on question of contemporary relevance.

Indian Council of Social Science Research, New Delhi, is an autonomous body for promoting and coordinating social science research. Its main functions are to review the progress of social science research, give advice on research activities in government or outside, sponsor research programmes and give grants to institutions and individuals for research in social sciences.

Coordination and determination of standard of higher education, a subject of the Union List and as a special responsibility of the Central government is discharged mainly through University Grants Commission (UGC). The UGC was established in 1956 under an Act of Parliament to take measures for promotion and coordination of university education and determination and maintenence of standards in teaching, examination and research in universities. To fulfil its objectives the Commission can enquire, among other things, into financial needs of universities, allocate and disburse grants to them, establish and maintain common services and facilities; recommend measures for improvement of university education and give advice on allocation of grants and establishment of new universities. UGC has approved 111 colleges for autonomous status, 23 in Andhra Pradesh, 44 in Tamil Nadu, 30 in Madhya Pradesh, five each in Rajasthan and Orissa, two each in Gujarat and Uttar Pradesh.

Indira Gandhi National Open University (IGNOU) was established by an Act of Parliament in September 1985 for the introduction and promotion of open university and distance education system in the educational pattern of the country and for the coordination and determination of standards in such systems. The major objectives of the University include widening access to higher education to larger segments of the population, organising programmes of continuing education and initiating special programmes of higher education for specific targets group like women, people lliving in backward regions, hilly areas, etc.

The IGNOU provides an innovative system of university level education, flexible and open in regard to methods and pace of learning, combination of courses, eligibility for enrolment, age of entry, methods of evaluation, etc. The University has adopted an integrated multi-media instructional strategy consisting of printed materials and audio-video aids, supported by counselling sessions at a network of study centres throughout the country. It conducts both continous evaluation as well as term-end examinations.

The IGNOU introduced its academic programmes in 1987 and has so far launched 58 programmes. These include a certificate course in guidance for primary school teachers, food and nutrition in seven languages and rural development, the preparatory programmes for the bachelor's degree, diploma programme in management, rural development, higher education, distance education, creative writing in English and Hindi, computers in office management and operations management, the bachelor's degree programmes in arts/science/commerce and library and information sciences as well as the master's degree in business administration and distance education.

The total number of students registered for various programmes of study during 1995 is over 91,000. The University has established an extensive students support services network consisting of 16 regional centres and 244 study centres situated in different parts of the country. A Distance Education Council (DEC) established bythe University as a statutory authority is an apex body for coordination and determination of standards in distance education.

Doordarshan commenced telecast of IGNOU'S programmes in May 1991 while the Bombay and Hyderabad stations of All India Radio started broadcasting selected audio programmes of the IGNOU from early 1992. At present there are six other open universities in the country viz., B.R. Ambedkar Open University in Hyderabad (Andhra Pradesh), Kota Open University, Kota (Rajasthan), Nalanda Open University (Bihar); Yashwant Rao Chavan Maharashtra Open University, Nasik (Maharashtra), Madhya Pradesh Bhoj Open University, Bhopal (Madhya Pradesh) and Ambedkar Open University, Ahamadabad (Gujarat).

The National Literacy Mission (NLM) which was launched in 1988 with the objective of imparting functional literacy to 800 lakh adult illiterates in the age-group of 15-35 by 1995 now aims to impart functional literacy to 100 million adult illiterates in the age group of 15-35 (including age-group of 9-14 where NFE is not in operation) by 1997. The implementation of programmes under the NLM has showed that eradiction of illiteracy is not a uptopian idea but is possible, feasible and achievable. The most important development that has taken place under the NLM is the near ascendancy of the campaign mode in the adult education programmes in the country.

On the heels of success of Ernakulam and Kerala experiments for achieving full literacy, these campaigns for total literacy have generated certain characteristic feature which make them unique and distinguished them from other programmes. They are area-specific, time-bound, volunteer-based, cost-effective and outcome-oriented. Total Literacy Campaigns have been launched in 336 districts of the country covering over 81 lakh illiterate persons and 134 districts have commenced post literacy campaigns to consolidate the gains of literacy. It is proposed to cover 345 districts by TLC campaigns by the end of the Eighth Plan period. The focus of the campaign is now on the four major Hindi dpeaking states of Bihar, madhya Pradesh, Rajasthan and Uttar Pradesh where bulk of the illiterate populations resides.

The National Policy on Education, 1986 accorded high priority to vocationalisation of education at the secondary stage. The NPE as revised in 1992, set the target of achieving diversion of 10 per cent of the students at the +2 level to the vocational stream by 1995 and 25 per cent by 2000 AD. Accordingly, a Centrally-sponsored scheme of Vocationalisation of Secondary Education was launched in February 1988 with these objectives: Providing diversification of educational opportunities so as to enhance individual employability; reducing mismatch between demand and supply of skilled manpower and providing an alternative for those pursing higher education without particular interest or purpose.

Under the scheme, substantial financial assistance is provided to states/UTs for introduction of vocational courses in classes XI and XII of the school system. Its components include; (i) creation of separate management structure at the Directorate/SCERT/district and school levels for planning and monitoring of the programme; (ii) strengthening of the technical support system for research, development of curriculum/instructional material/textbooks, training of teachers, etc,; (iii) conducting of district vocational surveys for assesment of labour market demand and (iv) provision of basic facilities for practical training in the school itself. So far all states/UTs except Lakshadweep have joined the programme. In all 18,055 vocational sections have been sanctioned in 6,280 schools all over the country thereby creating capacity for diversion of about nine lakh students to the vocational stream which is 11.46 per cent of the enrolment at the +2 stage.

A Centrally-sponsored scheme of pre-vocational education was launched in 1993-94 with the objective of imparting simple marketable skills to the students of classes IX and X. So far assistance has been provided to nine states/UTs for introduction of pre-vocational cources in 428 schools.

Assistance is also-provided to non-governmental organisations for conducting innovative and non-formal programmes of vocational education. So far 37 such organisations have been assisted under the scheme.

A joint Council for Vocational Education (JCVE) was set up in April 1990 for policyformulation and coordination at the national level. A standing committee of JCVE was also set up in April 1990 to follow up on the decisions taken by JCVE and a Central Institute of Vocational Educational (CIVE) was set up at Bhopal in July 1993 to provide technixcal and academic support to the programme. About 18 vocational courses have been introduced in six major areas i.e. agriculture, business and commerce, engineering and technlogy, health and paramedical, home science, humanities and others while 60 vocational courses have been notified under the Apprenticeship Act.

Collaborative arrangements have also been made with some government departments, undertakings like Ministry of Railways, Ministry of Health, GIC, LIC, etc. Currently the emphasis the quality of the programme States have thus been advised to strengthen the management structure at various levels, induct experts to infuse professionalism in programme, introduce need-based courses and to strenghten linkages with the industry on the job and apprenticeship training. An amount of Rs. 410 crore has been earmarked for the Vocational Education Programme during the Eighth Plan period. The budget estimate for 1995-96 is Rs. 82 crore.

While those shouting from the roof-tops about the escalating pollution and energy shortages talk of economics and budgetary provisions for more resources, none seem to bother about the basic malady of indicipline that is at the root of most of our environmental ills. Whether it is energy-efficiency, conservation or preventive maintenance of gadgets and vehicles, the crux is the discipline of the working populations. Since environment not only has no political and geographical barriers, it has also no distinction between the rich and the poor; the socially backward and the forward, it is worthwhile pursuing the cause of energy efficiency and conservation cutting across party and caste lines. Be it an officer or an organization they should be made accountable for the transgressions made in operation, implementation and planning levels that jeopardize not only the present economic, social welfare of mankind but also endanger the global environment times to come.

In the same vein, our political masters who in their over-enthusiastic populism do not budge to bestow any kind of favour on the vote banks as long as it suits their political convenience, should also be made answerable to environmental tribunals and ombudsmen for their indiscretions.

A case in point is the indiscriminate spread of fish and prawn farms across the coast of Andhra Pradesh which in the long run is sure not only to pollute the entire coastal region but may also end in a gigantic imbalance in the biotic system of the oceans. The prospect of all the fertile lands across the coast getting saline threatening serious food shortage in a not too far off future is lurking in the minds of conscientious environmentalists, whose voice any way goes unheeded by those at the helm.

The rampant corruption among the political and bureaucratic hierarchy has no mean role to play in the environmental disaster that is impending over the next century. The abject neglect of the most ecofriendly form of power generation, the hydropower in preference to the thermal alternative that has so many built-in hazards should be viewed in this perspective. The neglect of solar options and the other non-conventional sources such as the gobar-gas and wind power as also the energy efficient lighting to the traditional ones are acts of corrupt officials and their cohorts in the political hierarchy. Trade unions, officers associations should be chary of this pernicious nexus between the vested interests among businessmen and the greedy bureaucrats, if they are serious of protecting the environment.

Options

Indiscriminate distribution of precious power to villages at dirt cheap prices only squandered resources recklessly and it should be avoided at all costs. The rural tracts should be asked to depend on minihydel projects and bioenergy systems as far as possible. It would be better if the leaders show their preference and concern for the villages through sanctioning more wind and solar power projects for the villages. The bio-gas that is presently in a state of abject neglect could also be given political patronage through bringing constructive competition offering sops to such of those villages that successfully covert the entire gobar and organic waste within the precincts of their village into energy-efficient raw material than burning or dumping to add to the pollution.

World trends: In Sweden, hydro power contributes to the bulk of their energy, while it is about 21 per cent of the energy produced worldwide. But in India, it is a paltry 11 per cent of the total power produced. Solar collectors are a major source of hot water in Israel and wind power has taken hold firmly in California already. The Phillippines, a small and not very advanced country as yet, scientifically has made great strides in making geo-thermal energy their major source of electricity. Battery driven automobilies and electric trams as mass-transit are not uncommon in many nations small and big while we in India still harp on the obnoxious buses as the prime source of public transit even in our national capital.

If policy-makers do not grasp the link between energy-efficiency, renewable energy, and global warming, climatic stabilization will not be possible in the near forseeable future. Although governments around the world have supported these technologies and precepts for over a decade, their commitment has been inconsistent. A serious and lasting government commitment to the development and use of energy-efficient and renewable technologies is a prerequisite to stabilizing world climate. So too are the individual decisions about the kind of refrigerator to buy, the amount of home insulation to install and how much to drive a car, to possess a car at all in preference to public transport.

The international community should sit down to deliberate on how to raise resources to use photovoltaics rather than coal to electrify the Third World villages, if they are serious to spur the cause of sustainability.

We in India have to re-structure education at all levels by introducing the credit and semester system which will offer the kind of flexibility and choice for students to opt for particular subjects. This freedom to choose from a list of course offerings will give students a chance to learn many optional subjects and achieve all-round knowledge essential for a fulfilling life.

The vast variety of courses offered a t a college under the CSS will enable the student s to choose whatever course units they really like. For example, those who graduate in physical sciences today do not have any exposure to the arts or humanities, social sciences or even natural sciences. The biggest drawback of our present system is that most college graduates are unconnected with the socio-economic realities in the country and the world. They are not even aware of the problems of their locality. Their books and their annual exams will be followed in a dull and mechanical fashion. The CSS will give that flexibility essential for making higher education more up-to-date and relevant. It will reduce the tendency among scholars to learn by rote for selective learning from an examination angle.

Today's higher education of India is wholly exam-centred-annual-exam-centred, ehereas it ought to be divided into assimilable segments which are to be evaluate on a continous basis. Instead of the annual system, we should have the semester (half -yearly) system. Instead of taking a vst area of knowledge, logical sections of the area should be offered as course units. The instruction and evaluation in a particular course unit should be completed 14 or 15 weeks.

Each course unit is given credits depending on the number of hours of teaching; for example, a course that is taught for one hour a week for a semester of 14 or 15 weeks will be given a one-credit curse. A student who completes the requirements of a course offering through one hour of instruction a week for a semester of 14 or 15 weeks will get one credit. Most courses are 3-credit course.

Both the course instructor and the student will be on their toes throughout the semester because the method of instruction is different from that in the annual/ conventional system. Teachers are expected to guide the students to new knowledge thrugh constant updating. The students cannot depend solely on textbooks, lecture notes or the ubiquitous "guides", or bazaar notes. In the CSS, the teachers are the guides and not commercal notewriters. Since knowledge is constantly expanding, the market notes are not of much use to the students. Students have to depend more on their own library search and interactions with the teachers in and out of classrooms and seminars with fellow students and guest lecturers. Unfortunately this system does not find much favour withthe teachers in the present set-up.

Students get an opportunity to prove their worth by facing boldly what Jawaharlal Nehru called the 'adventure of ideas'. Gandhiji's hope that higher education should make them discover their own all-embracing personality can also be realized if colleges and all institutions of higher learning introduce the SCC.

But the biggest advantage is the freedom for the teachers to innovate and thereby help the students. The present system of teachers and students following a rigid three-subject and two-language pattern where instruction and evaluation do not go side by side has led to an insipid system of higher education. teachers depend on an outmoded syllabus (as old as their own college days, perhaps!) and students do not have read either at home or at the library and cut classes conveniently. (Even without such cutting, the average number of working days is below 100, certainly in Kerala, supposedly the most advanced state in India, educationally, as opposed to 200 or 180 days generally stipulated by the UGC and students can pass their annual exams.) If this is the case, why attend colleges? Why not depend solely on an outmoded exam system whose responsibility rests solely on the university—an anonymous exam-conducting body and nothing more? Precious working days are lost for strikes, bandhs, protests, sit-ins and what not? But working days, to be honest, are not working days, but non-working days. There are undeclared holidays in addition ot the large number of holidays declared by each State government in advance. Ours is a country that enjoys the largest number of holidays. Our young people are given the impression that they can become educated without any effort. Our teachers are setting a model for their young wards by coming to work late and leaving early. Where is the opportunity for them to sit in the library for at least an hour everyday to augment their own knowledge and thereby enhance the knowledge of their words. Are they endeavouring to transfer such newly acquired knowledge to their students?

It is very unfortunate that despite the tremendous growth in the number of colleges and universities in India, education that should conscientize the educated about their national socio-economic and political condition help liberate the nation from the shackles of old systems and ways of thinking is still a dream. Neither universalization of primary education nor vocatinoalization of primary education nor vocationalization of higher education has been achieved. It is sad that large sums of money spent on education (whether it be 3% or 6% of GNP) are not helping anyone to draw out the best in the educated (literally education means such drawing out).

The very basis of Gandhiji's educational vision was his belief that manual work was equal to mental work.

Dignity of labour was given a high place in his scheme. But what do we see today? the "educated" refuse to work with their hands. Those who have high degrees apply for lower level jobs and then refuse to work or offer unsatisfactory work.

Education introduced in the colonial period is still continuing in free India despite all the educational commissions and their recommendations. The Radhakrishnan Commission, the Kothari Commission, the Adiseshiah Commission, the Punnayya Commission and the host of UGC committees and special task forces have made many recommendations which, if implemented, would have raised the level of higher education. Unfortunatley these recommendations were not implemented, although newer commission and committees came into being. No structural changes were introduced and therefore the old systems continue even today with almost no basic change.

Universalization of education

There are more than 60 million youth out of schools and an additional 30 million youth in the age—group of 18 to 30 yearrs who had missed an educational opportunity. A large number of girls, children and youth from SC, ST and minority communities, specially from the rural areas, drop out of schools due to poor economic condition, social tabbos or their inability to cope up with the rigid demands of the formal education. These school drop—outs take to unskilled wage employment or become engaged in house—hold work. Only a flexible, life related programme of education delivered at the door steps can provide a fresh learning opportunity for them.

There has been a significant increase in the number of Secondary and increase in the number of Secondary and Senior Secondary schools and in enrolment during the period from 1987—88 to 1990—91. During this period enrolment at Secondary stage increased by 16.8 per cent and at the Senior Secondary stage by 17.6 per cent. The number of Secondary schools increased from 54,845 in 19987—88 to 59,468 in 1990—91; corresponding figures for Senior Secondary schools are 16,460 and 19,151 respectively. The ratio between Secondary schools and Primary schools had declined from 1:1.98 in 1987—88 to 1:1.86 in 1990—91.

Still there are unserved areas in the country where there is no school for 10 to 20 kms. like in some tribal areas, desert or hilly areas. An area may also be unserved due to geographical barriers like river or mountain. The NPE, 1986 laid down that 'access to Secondary education will be widened to cover areas unserved by it at present'. The target is by 2000 A.D. the unserved areas will be fully served.

Gender disparities in enrolments are significant. In 1990–91 girls accounted for 33.4 per cent of the enrolment at the Secondary stage and 32 per cent at the Senior Secondary stage. SCs accounted for 11.85 per cent at the Secondary stage and 9.7 per cent at the Secondary stage and 9.7 per cent at the Senior Secondary stage; corresponding figures for STs were 4.21 per cent and 3 per cent respectively. The girls, SCs and STs lag behind in enrolment to Secondary and Senior Secondary schools.

Inspite of spending an average of 22 per cent of the State budget on education, the formal schools can accomodate only about 35 per cent youth. Improvement in literacy rates has brought about a significant increase in enrolment in Elementary schools. A few years from now, the doors of Secondary schools too would be knocked. The States, even with an enhanced budget would not be able to expand the numbers of schools for the remaining 65 per cent. It is only open schooling then can serve marginalised groups, rural and urban poor and people in dispersed habitations. National Open Schooling (NOS) has been set up to design, develop and offer a flexible, life—oriented programme through distance education, in 1989 by the Government of India, Ministry of HRD, in pursuance of the NPE 1986, as an autonomous instituion. The task of NOS is universalization of education and special concern is the education of girls and women, rural youth, working men and women, SC and ST, handicapped and other disadvantaged groups.

The NOS provides the following programmes:

— Foundation programme—This course is for those who have discountinued education after 4 or 5 years of primary education. The course is equivalent to VIII standard and serves as a foundation or 'bridge' course for Secondary education. It comprises subjects such as Hindi, English, Mathematics, Science and Social Science.

- Secondary education programme—This course is offered to those who are desirous of completing 10th level education. The course comporises subjects like Hindi, English, Mathematics, science, Social Sciences Economics, Commerce, Home Science and Typewriting.
- Senior secondary education programme—This course is offered to those who like to complete 12th level education. It includes wide range of subjects such as Hndi, English, Mathemetics, Physics, Chemistry, Biology, History, Geography, Political Science, Economics, Commerce, Accountancy, Home Science, Typewriting, Stenography and Secretarial Practice.
- Vocational Education Programme—Several vocational courses such as Refrigeration & Air Conditioning, Electrical Technician, Radio & TV repairing, Plumbing, Library Science, Tailoring,

Beauty Culture either independently or in combination with the subjects in Secondary and Seniior Secondary courses.

- Life enrichment programmes—A few life enrichment programmes in Women's development, Community Health, Educational Technology, Institutional Management, Interactive Learning, Computor Applications, etc., are being planned to teachers, principals, executives in public and private sectors.

The distinctive feature of NOS are as follows:

- Students can learn at one's own speed and will have a period of 5 years and 9 chances to complete. He/she can also pass one subject at a time.
- Students can choose any subject combination like Science and Business Studies at Secondary level: History, Chemistry and Accountancy at Senior Secondary level.
- Student can earn credit collectively in all subjects for final certification.
- Student can know his/her continuous progress through Tutor Marked Assignments (TMAs).
- NOS offers programmes through distance education mode involving printed self learning materials, audio and video programmes, personal contact programmes in Accredited Institutions (AIs) or Study Centres.
- After the completion of NOS one can seek admission to the regular Colleges or Universities that have recognized its certificate. He/she can also take graduate course from open universities in Maharashtra, Andhra Pradesh, Rajasthan or IGNOU.
- Standard of education in NOS has been recognized by 12 State Boards okf Secondary Education. Its Senior Secondary Certificate is recognized by

Association of Indian Universities and 73 Universities including IITs and Agricultural Universities.

There are regional variations in NOS enrolment. From Delhi and other northern states, it is 65 per cent. The enrolment from the eastern region is about 18 per cent while from north—eastern states it is 7 per cent. The enrolment from western and southern regions are 7 per cent 3 per cent respectively.

Nearly 57 per cent of NOS students are from marginalised groups, of which 38 per cent are girls and women and 19 per cent are SCs and STs.

Admission is open to all, twice during the year. There is no upper age limit in NOS. There are 353 Study Centres/accredited Institutions (AIs) all over the country.

A student in NOS is a self–learner. For this specially printed self–instructional materials will be provided on different subjects. Also other support materials like audio cassettes, practical manuals, glossaries and study guides will be provided. Medium of instruction will be Hindi or English. Students are required to get pass marks is in 5 subjects with 1 or 2 languages for both Secondary and Senior Courses.

Contact sessions will be organised in the Accredited Institutions (AIs) on weekends and holidays. About 30 such contact sessions will be organized per subject in one academic year.

In these sessions students are expected to:

— Clear doubts and problems that they have faced while covering the syllabus.

— listen oto audio tapes;

— view video films;

— perform practicals in Science and other related subjects;
— get tutoring in specific and difficult concepts/areas;
— get assignments corrected by the AI teachers;
— discuss study problems, assignments with other students in groups; and
— meet other learners and form study groups.

The AIs will serve as study centre. Students have to go to AIs for—

— submitting application form with admission fees/ documents;
— receiving study materials and identity cards;
— attending contact classes;
— finding out the dates of payment of fees, examination date sheet;
— knowing results of public examination;
— collection of marksheet, pass certificate and migration certificate;
— change of subject(s) or additional subject;
— corrections in names, subjects and other particulars, etc.

NOS is authorized by; the Government of India to conduct Secondary and Senior Secondary examinations and issue certificates. The examinations are conducted twice a year in more than 250 centres spread all over the country.

Of the total 100 marks in each paper, 20 per cent weightage is given to continuous assessment in the form of Tutor Marked Assignments. Another 15 per cent marks are allotted to practical examinations in certain subjects. The remaining marks are for the end—of—the course public examinations.

Students are free to appear in one or more subjects at a time. The marks are retained in the computerized credit banks. He/she gets the certificate on earning the total requisite credit in 9 examinations over 5 years. NOS will also allow for improvement of performance in already passed subject, but only once.

Students pay a fees of Rs. 150, Rs. 650 and Rs. 775 to the Foundation, the Secondary and Senior Secondary courses respectively. To encourage education of girls, SC, ST and handicapped students a special concession is allowed. The fee includes the cost of the study materials, about 30 classes in each subject, audio and video programmes and a year's subscription to the magazine. When compared to the estimated cost of Rs. 3000 per student for Secondary and Senior Secondary courses in formal school, the education in NOS is cost effective. For every one student in the formal system, 4 to 5 students can be served by the open learning system.

NOS has an annual budget of more than ten crore. It generates about 95 per cent of its revenue through students' fees. The Government of India provides recurring cost (5 per cent) and full development cost. The Government share is about 30 per cent of the total budget compared to more than 90 per cent salary cost in formal education, the total administrative cost in NOS is about 15 per cent the rest is spent on academic activities.

In order to disseminate Foundation and Secondary education, it is necessary to impart education through regional languages. In a recent need assessment survey, 20 open schools have been suggested. These open schools have come up in A.P., Haryana, T.N., and Karnataka. Proposals from several other States are in active consideration. NOS will provide academic and technical support to such open schools.

NOS is a national apex institution in open learning.

A network of 20 to 25 State Open Schools along with NOS can provide education to 2.5 crore youth and adults. The multichannel learning, maintenance of quality of instructional process and the inherent flexibility make open schooling an acceptable complement to formal education, and a strategy in universalization of education. Open schooling would, thus, udoubtedly schooling would, thus, undoubtedly trigger new hopes in the lives of those who have lost hope.

Training institutions

Sainik schools prepare boys academically and physically for entry into National Defence Academy. There are 18 sainik schools in the country, one in each state, except in Nagaland, Meghalaya, Tripura, Sikkim, Arunachal Pradesh, Mizoram and Goa. These schools are affiliated to the Central Board of Secondary Education and follow the 10+2 pattern, in science stream.

Admission is made to class VI on the basis of an all-India entrance examination held every year in February, in which boys in the age group of 10-11 years are eligible to appear. From 1992-93 academic session lateral admission to class IX has also been started for which the boys have to be 13-14 years of age on 1st July of that year. Since its inception, a total of 4,647 boys from these schools were selected for admission to the National Defence Academy, Naval Academy, Armed Forces Medical College etc.

The National Defence Academy (NDA), Khadakwasla, is a Joint Services Training Institution which imparts academic as well as service training. The NDA has been brought in step with the national education format of 10+2+3. The syllabus of the Academy was reviewed to meet these requirements and has been approved by the Jawaharlal Nehru University for the grant of BA/B.Sc degree, at the time of passing out from

Academy. the first course commenced training on revised syllabi in January 1989. After passing out from the NDA, the cadets go to their respective service acadmies for further training before being commissioned as officers in the Armed Forces. The present authorised training strength of the Army, Navy and Air Force cadets at the Academy is 1,800. This includes cadets from Bhutan and other friendly countries on as required basis.

The Indian Military Academy (IMA), Dehra Dun caters for training of cadets for commission into the Army. Cadets join the Indian Military Academy as per the following modes of entry: (a) on passing out from NDA, (b) on graduation from the Army Cadet College which is a wing of the IMA itself, (c) Direct entry graduate cadets who join on qualifying at the Union Public Service Commission Examination and the Services Selection Board, and (d) Technical graduates and University Entry Scheme. The present authorised strength of trainees at the IMA is 1,200 which includes cadets from Bhutan, Shri Lanka, Maldives, Mauritius and Nepal. The authorised training strength of Army Cadet College is 450.

The Officers Training Academy (OTA), Madras imparts pre-commission training for the following type of courses, (a) Short Service Commission Course of 44 weeks for university graduates who quality in the Union Public Service Commission; (b) course of six months for lady cadets (Women Special Entry Scheme); (c) Permanent Commission on Special List (PC) (SL) to selected service candidates, who qualify after a training of four weeks and (d) Regimental Commission Course for selected service candidates, who qualify after a training of 13 weeks duration. Authorised training strength of the Academy is 500. So far 50 lady cadets have been granted Short Service Commission.

Education on public school lines is imparted at the Rashtriya Indian Military College (RIMC), Dehradun principally for the boys who subsequently desire to join the NDA with a view to obtaining a commission in the Armed Forces. The College runs classes from eighth to 10+2 class. Selection for the RIMC is through a written examination cum viva voce conducted through the state governments. Seats for the respective states are reserved, based on population. Intake into the RIMC is bi-annual.

Inaugurated by Pandit Nehru in 1960, the National Defence College is an Inter-Service Organisation functioning under the Ministry of Defence. The NDC is the highest defence institution in India imparting instructions on all elements of national security and strategy to officers due to become Major Generals and equivalent and attain similar status in the Civil Service. The aim is to equip these policy makers with the necessary background and understanding of the total system of economic, political, military, scientific, international relations, national organisational aspects and the planning necessary for national security, both in its internal dynamics as well as the external comulsions. The head of the College is the Commandant, with five faculty members from the Army, Navy, Air Force, IAS, IFS and an administrative staff.

Army Cadet College is a Wing of IMA which caters for the training of service cadets selected for commission. The academic format is similar to the NDA on the lines of 10+2+3, and the syllabus is common. On completion of the course these cadets also qualify for a BA/BSc degree recognised by the Jawaharlal Nehra University.

The College of Combat, Mhow conducts the higher command, senior command and junior command courses for Army officers. It also conducts a Combined Operational Review and Evaluation (CORE) programme for selected senior officers of the rank of Major General and equivalent of the three Services once every year. College of Military Engineering, Kirkee (Pune), imparts training to the officers and other ranks in all aspects of military engineering. Long courses of over two years duration are also conducted to train officers up to degree standards. Military College of Telecommunication Engineering, Mhow imparts basic and advanced technical training in telecommunications and signal tactics. Armoured Corps Centre and School, Ahmednagar, conducts training in tactical handling of armoured fighting vehicles, driving and maintenance. School of Artillery, Deolali, provides training in field branch artillery. The Air Defence Guided Missiles School at Gopalpuron-sea trains personnel of the Air Defence Artillery. The High Altitude Warfare School located at Gulmarg and Sonmarg train personnel in the art of mountain warfare including rock, snow and ice-craft. The Counter Insurgency and General Warfare School, Viairengate, trains officers and men in the art of combating insurgency.

Mechanised Infantry Regimental Centre conducts basic and technical training for recruits of mechanised infantry. In addition, it runs basic and instructor courses on anti-tank guided missiles for officers, JCOs and other ranks of mechanised infantry. It also carries out conversion training of units when they are converted to mechanised infantry or when change in equipment is involved. College of Materials Management, Jabalpur, imparts specialised training in materials management including ammunition and explosives and also in contemporary materials management techniques. Some of the other Army training centres and schools are Army Service Corps School, Bareilly; EME School, Vadodara; Military College of Electronics and Mechanical Engineering, Secunderabad; College of Defence

Management, Secunderabad; Remount and Veterinary Corps Centre and School, Meerut; Army Eucation Corps Training College and Centre, Pachmari; Army School Physical Training, Pune; Army/Air Transport School, Agra; Military Intelligence Training School and Depot, Pune; Army School of Mechanical Transport, Bangalore; Corps of Military Police Centre and School, Bangalore; Institute of Military Law, Kamptee; Armed Forces Medical College Pune; Institute of National Integration, Pune and Army Medical Corps Centre and School, Lucknow.

5

Scenario of Indian Education

An important element of post-independence educational policy has been to provide free and compulsory education to all children at least up to the elementary stage. The Directive Principles of State Policy as enunciated in our Constitution envisage that the State shall endeavour to provide free and compulsory education for children up to 14 years of age within a period of 10 years.

The constitutional directive has been spelt out unequivocally and emphatically in the National Policy on Education (NPE), 1986 and its Programme of Action (POA), 1992. The Policy envisages that free and compulsory education of satisfactory quality should be provided to all children up to the age of 14 years before the commencement of the twenty-first century.

In keeping with the policy objectives, the targets for the Ninth Five Year Plan have been fixed under three broad parameters-universal access, universal retention and universal achievement.

Universal access

— Universal enrolment of all children, including girls, disabled children and children belonging to Scheduled Castes (SCs) and scheduled Tribes (STs) in primary classes and provision of upper primary education for them.

— Provision of Non-formal Education (NFE) for school

drop-outs, working children and girls who cannot attend formal schools.

— Provision of early childhood care and education to children of 3-6 years of age.

Universal retention

Reduction of drop-out rate between Classes IV and I-VIII from the existing rate of 36.3 per cent and 56.5 per cent to 20 per cent and 40 per cent, respectively.

Universal achievement

— Expansion of Minimum Levels of Learning (MLLs) to all primary schools and extension of this concept to the upper primary stage.

— Substantial improvement in school infrastructure, teacher education and in quantity and quality of teaching-learning material.

— Promotion and extension of national curricular framework at the elementary stage which envisages a common core with adequate flexibility to relate it to the environment and the needs and interests of the learners.

Progress over the years

Improved performance of the UEE programmes over the years would be evident from the following:

Accessibility of schooling facilities is no longer a major problem. At the primary stage 94 per cent of the country's rural population now have schooling facilities within one km distance. At upper primary stage also 83.98 per cent of rural population have a school within 3 km distance. Enrolment ratio is 104 for Classes I-V and 67 for Classes VI-VIII.

While the gross enrolment ratio (GER) at the primary stage in the country as a whole and in most of its States exceed 100 per cent, there are quite a few States where the ratio is considerably lower. These include Uttar Pradesh, Bihar, Rajasthan, Haryana', Jammu and Kashmir and Meghalaya. At the upper primary stage, these States and in addition, Andhra Pradesh, Orissa and Sikkim have GER lower than the national average. In most of these States the literacy rates also are lower than the national average. There is thus a strong regional dimension of UEE.

Gender disparities

While Universalisation of Elementary Education is the ultimate goal, no strategy or programme of action can succeed without addressing itself to gender and regional dimensions specifically. Gender disparities are conspicuous in regard to enrolment and retention. Girls' enrolment has grown at primary stages from 5.4 million in 1950-51 to 47.4 million in 1997-98 and that at upper primary stages from 0.5 million to 15.87 million. The rate of growth of enrolment of girls has been higher than that of boys. But disparities still persist as girls still account for only 43.2 per cent of enrolment at primary stage and 39.0 per cent at upper primary stage. The drop-out rate of girls is much higher than that of boys at primary and upper primary stages.

Scheduled castes and scheduled tribes

According to the 1991 census, the population of Scheduled Castes (SCs) was 138.12 million (16.33%) and that of Scheduled Tribes (STs) was 67.8 million (8.01 %) of the country's population. The enrolment of SCs and STs has increased considerably at the primary stage because of the affirmative policies of the Government. The participation of SCs and STs is now more or less in proportion to their share in population at the primary level. Drop-outs, though declining over the years, are significantly large. Gender disparities are very conspicuous among SCs and STs also.

Strategy frame

In order to achieve Universalisation of Elementary Education by 2000 AD, following key strategies have been worked out in consultation with States and UTs:

— Overcome the problem of school drop-outs and lay emphasis on retention and achievement rather than on merely enrolment.

— Strengthen the alternatives of schooling, particularly, the Non-Formal Education system for working children, girls and children from other disadvantaged or marginalised sections of the society.

— Shift focus from educationally backward States to educationally backward districts.

— Adopt disaggregated approach with a focus on preparation of district-specific and population-specific plans.

— Provide universal access to schooling facilities particularly to girls, disaggregated groups and out-of-school children.

— Introduce Minimum Levels of Learning for enhancement of learners' achievement-, micro planning would provide the framework of universal access and universal participation while MLLs would be the strategy for universal achievement.

— Improve school effectiveness, teacher competence, training and motivation.

— Decentralisation of planning and management through Panchayati Raj Institutions (PRls)/ Village Education Committees (VECs) and stress on participative processes.

— Convergence of different schemes of elementary education and related services such as early childhood care and education and school health and nutrition programmes, etc.

Minimum levels of learning

India is one of the few developing countries which took initiative in 1991 to lay down Minimum Levels of Learning (MLLs) to be achieved at the primary stage. This new approach integrates various components of curriculum, classroom translation, evaluation and teacher orientation. The first phase of the programme was implemented through 18 voluntary agencies, research institutions, SCERTs, etc. The results of these projects show significant improvement in learning attainments of school children.

It has now been decided to upscale the MLL programme through institutional mechanism throughout the country. The national resource institutions like the National Council of Educational Research and Training (NCERT), Regional Institutes of Education [RIEs), State Councils of Educational Research and Training and District Institutes of Education and Training are being networked for this purpose. Curriculum revision, re-writing of textbooks to make them competency-based, enhancing their pedagogical value, training of teachers in the classroom processes are major activities undertaken.

The State Governments have introduced MLL in most of their primary schools including local body/private schools. The District Primary Education Programme (DPEP) has adopted MLL as a major strategy for improvement of quality of primary education. Non-formal education programme is also adopting MLLs wherever appropriate. Learning competencies for various subjects taught at the upper primary stage are under consideration.

Lok Jumbish

An innovative project called Lok Jumbish (People's Movement for Education for All) with assistance from the Swedish International Development Authority (SIDA) was undertaken in Rajasthan in 1992. The basic objective of the project is to achieve education for all through people's mobilisation and their participation.

Aims and objectives

— Providing access to primary education to all children up to 14 years of age.

— Ensuring that all enrolled children attend school/ NFE centres regularly and complete primary education.

— Creating necessary structures, and setting in motion processes which would empower women and make education an instrument of women's equality.

— Pursuing the goal of equity in education. Making necessary modifications in the content and process of education to better relate it to the environment.

— Effectively involving people in the planning and management of education.

The project is implemented by the Lok Jumbish Parishad (LJP), an autonomous society registered under the Societies Registration Act.

The first phase of the project was implemented between I June 1992 and 30 June 1994 and incurred an expenditure of Rs 14.03 crore shared in the ratio 3:2: 1 among SIDA, the Government of India and the Government of Rajasthan.

The second phase of the project was implemented between 1994 and 1998 with a revised outlay of Rs 95.65 crore shared in the ratio 3:2:1 In this phase, the project covered 75 blocks.

The LJP has undertaken environment building activities in 5,683 villages and has completed school mapping exercises in 4,006 villages. Three hundred eighty-three new schools have been opened while 227 primary schools have been upgraded.

The Lok Jumbish Project has made a positive contribution to quality improvement through the development of improved MLL-based textbooks from Classes I-IV, which have been mainstreamed in all schools of the Government of Rajasthan. Lok Jumbish has also set up vibrant block and cluster resource groups for providing academic supervision and regular training of primary school teachers. A renewed teacher training strategy in a cascade model is being implemented successfully.

An innovative and successful NFE programme launched by LJP has spread to more than 3,000 centres, called Sahaj Shiksha Centres. Catering to drop-outs and out-of school children, especially girls, the system has close linkages with the community and has shown to provide comparable learning achievement levels amongst students.

The LJP has been able to set up innovative management structures incorporating the principles of decentralisation and delegation of authority as well as build partnerships with local communities and the voluntary sector. Community mobilisation and school mapping exercises have shown good results and provide the bases for opening of new schools, Sahaj Shiksha Centres and community-centred building development programme.

New Initiatives

Based on the Report of the Committee of State Education Ministers, a proposal to amend the Constitution of India to make Right to Free and Compulsory Education for children from 6 to 14 years of age a Fundamental Right and also to make it a Fundamental Duty of parents to provide opportunities for education to children in 6 to 14 years age group was considered and approved by the Cabinet at its meeting held on 16 May 1997.

In pursuance of the decision of the Cabinet, the Constitution (Eighty-third Amendment) Bill, 1997 was introduced in the Rajya Sabha on 28 July 1997. The Bill was examined by the Department related Parliament Standing Committee on Human Resource Development. The matter is being further examined in the light of the report of the Parliamentary Standing Committee. It is felt that a wider public debate on the implications of the proposed legislation should be initiated.

National programme of media publicity

In order to build up public opinion and mobilise social support, a national programme of media publicity and advocacy for universalisation of elementary education is proposed to be launched in the Ninth Five Year Plan.

The programme will focus on four groups, namely

— Teachers and all those involved in education of children

— Students and parents of students, particularly non-literate parents

— Community opinion builders

— Policy makers and public representatives

It is envisaged that the programme would facilitate social mobilisation and environment building for operationalising the proposal to make elementary education a Fundamental Right.

National elementary education mission

The National Elementary Education Mission (NEEM) is proposed to have the central objective of mobilising all the resources—human, financial and institutional—necessary for achieving the goal of Universalisation of Elementary Education. The setting up of the Mission is expected to give a boost to the efforts being made by the Government and nongovernmental organisations to achieve Universalisation of Elementary Education.

Operation blackboard

In pursuance of the NPE 1986, the scheme of Operation Blackboard (OB) was launched in 1987-88 with the aim of improving the human and physical resources available in the primary schools of, the country existing as on, 30 September 1986. The scheme consisted of mainly three components:

— Provision of an additional teacher to single teacher primary schools.

— Providing at least two classrooms in each primary school.

— Providing teaching-learning equipment to all primary schools brought under the scheme. During the Eighth Plan, the scheme was revised in- 1993-94 and expanded to provide third classroom and third teacher to primary schools where enrolment exceeds 100 and extended to cover upper primary schools.

The scheme was intended to improve school publicity and advocacy for universalisation of environment, enhance retention and learning achievement of children by providing minimum essential facilities in all primary schools. Thus the scheme seeks to bring about both quantitative and qualitative improvement in primary education.

Hundred per cent central assistance is provided for appointment of an additional teacher in single teacher schools. Central assistance has been fully provided. The scheme is implemented through State Governments.

Construction of school building is the responsibility of the State Governments. However, in consultation with the Department of Education, the Ministry of Rural Areas and Employment has worked out a formula to make available the funds for construction of school buildings under Operation Blackboard scheme. According to this formula 48 per cent of the funds for construction are provided by the Ministry of Rural Areas and Employment under Jawahar Rozgar Yojana (JRY) if the States raise 40 per cent non-JRY and 12 per cent JRYs State share.

On the basis of past experience, observations of audit and evaluation reports it was observed that several States have unutilised funds sanctioned for teaching learning equipment under OB scheme. As such it was felt that to a large extent the above mentioned situation can be attributed to lack of sufficient flexibility and decentralised procurement and supply of teaching-learning equipment.

While indicating broad categories of teaching-learning equipment to be procured, the specific items under each category were left entirely to the discretion of the State Government who could decide the items to be procured as per local conditions.

The State Governments have also been advised that as far as possible, procurement of equipment should be decentralised and quality control scrupulously insisted upon. It was further suggested that involvement of representatives of Panchayati Raj Institutions, Village Education Committees and teachers/ headmasters in this process be ensured.

Flexibility in the selection of teaching learning equipments and their decentralized procurement has facilitated timely supply of quality materials in several States.

Teacher education

As envisaged in the National Policy on Education (NPE) and Programme of Action (POA) 1986, the Centrally Sponsored Scheme of Restructuring and Reorganisation of Teacher Education was taken up in 1987 to create a viable institutional infrastructure, academic and technical resource base for orientation, training and continuous upgradation of knowledge, competence and pedagogical skills of elementary school teachers in the country.

The scheme envisages setting up of DIETs in each district to provide academic and resource support to elementary education teachers and non-formal and adult education instructors. It also envisages establishment of CTEs/IASEs to organise pre-service and in-service training for secondary teachers and provide extension and resource support services to secondary schools, IASEs are expected to conduct programmes for preparation of elementary teacher educators, conduct in-service training for elementary and secondary teacher educators and principals of secondary schools, engage in advanced level fundamental and applied research especially of inter-disciplinary nature, and provide academic guidance to DIETs and support services to CTEs.

The scheme also envisages strengthening of SCERTs; orientation of primary teachers in the use of OB materials and implementation of MLL strategy with focus on teaching of languages, mathematics and environmental studies; and strengthening of Departments of Education in the universities through the UGC.

The Central Government provides financial assistance to States for setting up of DIETs/ CTEs/IASEs. DIETs are established by upgrading existing Elementary Teacher Education Institutions (ETEIs) or by setting up new institutions. The land for the purpose is provided by State Governments free of cost. CTEs are set up by upgrading existing Secondary Teacher Education Institutions (STEIs) offering B.Ed. courses, and IASEs by upgrading colleges and University Departments of Education offering M.Ed. courses.

DIETs have been playing an important role in the new educational initiatives like DPEP. These institutions have been identified as the principal technical and professional resource institutions in DPEP districts. The Department has recently advised State Governments to evolve appropriate mechanisms for effective coordination among

SCERTs, DIETs and DPEP project authorities for convergence and synergy of governmental efforts and strategies focused on the achievement of universalisation of elementary education.

The Department has prepared a National Action Plan (NAP) in collaboration with UNESCO and International Telecommunication Union (ITU) to utilise the latest communication technologies for training of teachers, teacher educators, educational supervisors and Panchayati Raj functionaries. The NAP would focus on integration of ongoing efforts under NCERT, DIETs and DPEP; capacity building; and mass training of above personnel at regular intervals without compromising on quality. It would also remove some of the weaknesses of the cascade model of face-to-face training of teachers, Interactive teleconferencing has been pilot tested for in-service training of 850 primary teachers in Karnataka and 1,450 teachers in Madhya Pradesh in 1996. In the light of the experience gained and the feedback furnished by implementing agencies and State Governments, it is proposed to launch a pilot project during the year to test the application of interactive television in distance education with a coverage of 8,000 teachers in Gujarat and Madhya Pradesh.

The progress of implementation of the scheme is being monitored through quarterly progress reports furnished by the States. Information received from States is analysed and they are suitably advised to take necessary action wherever warranted, for expediting construction of civil works, filling up of posts and organisation of pre-service and in-service training programmes for elementary school teachers. The pace and progress of implementation of the scheme was reviewed in the meeting of State Education Ministers and Secretaries held on 22-23 October 1998 at New Delhi. States were requested to take appropriate action to make all the DIETs fully operational as early as possible.

The task of assessing quantitative and qualitative progress made in implementation of the scheme has been assigned to NIEPA in 1997-98. The evaluation, which has been initiated, will also make a critical assessment of the performance of DIETs and recommend immediate and long-term measures needed for strengthening the capacity of these institutions.

The National Council for Teacher Education (NCTE) is responsible for achieving planned and co-ordinated development of the teacher education system throughout the country. It has initiated a process of consultation with the Principals of CTEs/IASEs/DIETs and Directors of SCERTs to understand various problems at the field level and suggest remedial steps for effective implementation of the Centrally Sponsored Scheme of Teacher Education. With this end in view, the NCTE has organised regional meetings of Principals of CTEs/IASEs and Directors of SCERTs. The NCTE has laid down norms and standards for pre-primary, elementary and secondary level teacher education institutions and for B.Ed. course through correspondence/distance education mode. Besides, a number of useful publications on teacher education have also been brought out by the NCTE.

National Council Teacher Education

The National Council for Teacher Education (NCTE) has been established as a national level statutory body by the Government of India vide its notification dated 17 August 1995. The main objectives of the Council are to achieve planned and co-ordinated development of the teacher education system, regulation and proper maintenance of norms and standards of teacher education. Some of the other major functions of the Council are laying down of norms for various teacher education courses, recognition of teacher education institutions, laying down of guidelines in respect of minimum qualification for appointment of teachers, surveys and studies, research and innovations, prevention of commercialisation of teacher education, etc. As per the provisions of the Act, four Regional Committees for the Northern, Southern, Eastern and Western Regions have been set up at Jaipur, Bangalore, Bhubaneswar and Bhopal, respectively. These Regional Committees consider the applications of the institutions of teacher education for recognition/ permission in accordance with the provisions of the Act.

During the last three years, the Council has been in existence, it has laid down norms and standards for pre-primary, elementary and secondary teacher education institutions and for B.Ed correspondence/ distance education mode. Norms for M.Ed and some other specialised areas of teacher education like physical education and special education have been prepared. On the basis of the recommendations of an Expert Committee, the NCTE has decided that education for the first degree/diploma should be through face-to face institutional course of teacher education of a minimum one year academic duration. The decision has been communicated to all the State Governments, Universities, Boards of Education, etc. However, with a view to provide avenues for professional growth of in-service teachers and to clear the backlog of untrained teachers in some regions of the country, B.Ed through correspondence/distance education is being continued on a limited scale. For this purpose, the NCTE has issued regulations laying down guidelines for the universities/ institutions running B.Ed through correspondence/ distance education.

The NCTE has published monographs, reports, self-learning modules for teacher educators and teachers, etc. Two documents on competency-based and commitment-oriented teacher education and nine units of self-learning modules on Human Rights and National Values have been brought out. The NCTE has organised two orientation programmes for elementary teacher educators in Science Education in Homi Bhabha Centre for Science Education, Mumbai.

Non-formal education

Objective

Despite considerable expansion of formal system of education, the achievement of UEE goals remain a distant dream as a large group of children remain outside the formal system due to various socio-economic constraints. In order to reach this large segment of marginalised children, the Department of Education has been running, since 1979-80, a programme of Non-Formal Education for children of 6-14 age group who remain outside the formal system due to various reasons. These include dropouts of the formal schools, children from habitations without schools, working children, children who assist in performing domestic chores like fetching fuel, fodder, water, attending to siblings, grazing cattle, etc. and girls who are unable to attend formal schools. The National Policy on Education, 1986 and the Programme of Action 1992 envisage a large systematic programme of NFE for those who cannot attend the full day schools. It assumes that if the essential requirements for running a good programme are fulfilled, NFE can result in provision of education comparable in quality with formal schooling. It visualises NFE as child-centred, environment-oriented system to meet the diverse needs of comparatively deprived sections of society. Decentralised community participation through Village Education Committees (VECs) in planning, running, and overseeing the NFE programme has been considered crucial for its success.

Coverage

Although the focus of the programme is on the educationally backward States, viz. Andhra Pradesh, Arunachal Pradesh, Assam, Bihar, Jammu and Kashmir,

Madhya Pradesh, Orissa, Rajasthan, Uttar Pradesh and West Bengal, it also covers urban slums, hilly, tribal and desert areas and projects for education of working children in other States/UTs as well. The programme at present, is in operation in 25 States/UTs.

Strategy

The strategy of NFE is as follows:

— Condensed course of about two years' duration.

— Part-time instructions at a time/place convenient to learners in small groups.

— Part-time honorary instructor /supervisor locally recruited and trained.

— Emphasis on flexibility and decentralisation of management.

— Use of curriculum and teaching-learning material comparable to the formal system and relevant to local environment and learner's needs.

— Testing and certification of NFE students to enable their entry into formal system.

The programme is implemented through State/ UT Governments as well as NGOs. The Central assistance to States/UTs is being provided on sharing basis between the Central Government and the State Governments in the ratio of 60:40 for co-educational centres and administrative resource support and 90: 10 for exclusively girls' centres. Hundred per cent Central assistance is being provided to NGOs for running NFE Centres and Experimental and Innovative Projects.

Monitoring and evaluation

The programme of NFE is being monitored through Quarterly Progress Reports (QPRs), periodic evaluations conducted by Joint Evaluation Teams (JETs) and field visits of Central and State Government officials. Moreover, seven external agencies evaluated the programme in eight

States, viz. Andhra Pradesh, Bihar, Gujarat, Madhya Pradesh, Orissa, Rajasthan, Uttar Pradesh and West Bengal. On the basis of the feedback received, remedial action is being taken for effective implementation of the programme. Operations Research Group (ORG), New Delhi has also been asked to develop tools for evaluation of the programme along with the schemes of Teacher Education and Operation Blackboard.

Ninth plan provisions

The emphasis during the Ninth Plan period would be on consolidation of the existing programme. Effort will be made to improve the quality, allow greater flexibility, re-location of NFE centres on the basis of micro-planning, area survey and promote more experimentation and innovation in the field of elementary education. Development and scaling up of NFE models that can help the learners to learn at their own pace will be a major thrust area. The cost parameters are being revised to make the scheme more acceptable and in keeping with socio-economic realities of the day.

Currently, 740 voluntary agencies are implementing NFE programme in 25 States/ UTs. Another 85 agencies have been sanctioned 9,485 NFE centres in the current year.

Revision of the NFE scheme

The scheme is under revision during the Ninth Plan. Effort to make the programme more meaningful is being taken up and experiences of successful NFE programme of organisations such as Lok Jumbish, Shiksha Karmi, etc. are being taken into consideration while revising the scheme.

Experimental/Innovative progammes of education under NFE

The overall aim of the scheme is to promote experimentation and innovation for the achievement of goals spelt out in the National Policy on Education. The scheme has been in operation from the year 1987-88. Under the scheme voluntary organisations are given 100 per cent grants for trying out innovative strategies that could be replicated/ disseminated in the formal stream. Main areas of experimentation and innovations have been: Action Research, Community Mobilisation, curriculum designing and preparation of need-based teaching-learning materials and aids, training of personnel and development of teaching techniques, new evaluation methods, linkage of school education with vocational education and alternative method of education for special target groups such as, disabled children, girls, working children, tribal children, etc.

Currently, 45 voluntary agencies are implementing the programme. Some of the leading agencies are MV Foundation, Secunderabad working on education of child labour, Deccan Development. Society working on vocational skills with scholastic studies, Agragamee, Orissa, working on education of tribal children and Eklavya, Bhopal, working on preparation of need-based teaching materials.

National Bal Bhavan

The National Bal Bhavan (formerly Bal Bhavan Society India), New Delhi was established by the Government of India in 1956 at the initiative of Pandit Jawahar Lal Nehru. An autonomous institution fully funded by the Department of Education, the National Bal Bhavan (NBB) has been contributing towards enhancing the creativity amongst children in the age-group 5-16 years especially from the weaker sections of the society. The children can pursue activities of their choice such as creative arts, performing arts, environment, astronomy, photography, integrated activities, physical activities, science-related activities, etc. in a joyful manner. The programmes are so designed as to explore the inner potential of a child and give him opportunities for expression of ideas through various media. Bal Bhavan thus aims at the all-round growth of a child in a free and happy atmosphere and helps them develop a scientific temper.

This year also summer programmes were organised by the National Bal Bhavan for the children wherein workshops on craft conservation, creative art, development of low-cost science games, models/toys, screen printing, videography, food preservation, mathematics and science through origamy, photography and aero modelling, etc. were arranged. A joint action programme of National Bal Bhavan and Centre for Environment Education on 'Building up Energies' for the teachers was organised in the month of April 1998. The Ambassador of Egypt in India distributed prizes to the winners of painting competition on 'Egypt in the Eyes of the Children of the World' in May 1998. Computer awareness programme, launching of a newspaper entitled Akkar-Bakkar Times by the children, organising literary camp, integrated environment projects and a workshop on how to make their own aquarium and how to maintain it are some of the other important activities undertaken during the year. The World Habitat Day was observed during September 1998.

National Bal Bhavan organised National Children's Assembly and Integration Camp 'Panchtatva' from 14 to 20 November 1998, which was inaugurated by the Hon'ble Prime Minister of India Shri Atal Bihari Vajpayee and the inaugural function was presided over by the Hon'ble Minister of Human Resource Development, Shri Murli Manohar Joshi.

Nutritional support to primary education

The programme of Nutritional Support to Primary Education, popularly known as the Mid-day Meals Scheme, was launched on 15 August 1995 on a nationwide scale. This programme intends to give a boost to the universalisation of primary education by increasing enrolment, retention and attendance and to improve the nutritional status of students in, the primary classes (I-V).

From 1997-98 onwards, the programme has covered all the children studying in primary classes in the Government, local body and government-aided schools. This is one of the largest school nutrition programmes in the world today. The total number of beneficiaries at present being covered is estimated to be 9.75 crore in nearly 6.88 lakh schools in all the blocks and urban areas in the country. The programme is much successful wherein cooked meals/processed food is being served.

The Central support under this programme is on:

— Provision of foodgrains free of cost to the implementing agencies for which economic cost is reimbursed to the Food Corporation of India.

— Reimbursement of transportation cost to district authorities for moving foodgrains from Food Corporation of India godowns to schools /villages.

Shiksha Karmi Project

Shiksha Karmi Project (SKP) was launched in 1987 on the basis of agreement signed between Swedish International Development Cooperation Agency (SIDA) and the Government of India. Phase I of the project was up to 30 June 1994. According to the specific agreement between the Government of India and the Government of Sweden, Phase II of the SKP was up to June 1997 which was subsequently extended to June 1998. During Phase I, SIDA and the Government of Rajasthan shared expenditure in the ratio of 9:1, respectively. During Phase II the cost-sharing between SIDA and the Government of Rajasthan was revised in the proportion of 50:50. Provision for the SIDA's share has been made in the Central Plan Budget which was subsequently reimbursable by SIDA on the basis of actual expenditure incurred by the Rajasthan Shiksha Karmi Board (RSKB) through which the Shiksha Karmi Project is being implemented.

The project aims at universalisation and qualitative improvement of primary education in remote and socio -economically backward villages in Rajasthan with primary attention given to girls. The project identifies teacher absenteeism as a major obstacle in achieving the goal of Universalisation of Elementary Education (UEE). It was realised that a primary school in remote villages, with the teacher not residing there, often tended to become dysfunctional, and parents as well as children failed to relate to such an institution, leading to high dropout rates. Under SKP, regular teachers are replaced by local teachers who are less qualified but specially trained. A Shiksha Karmi (SK) is a local person with minimum educational qualification of Class VIII for men and Class V for women. To overcome the basic lack of qualification, Shiksha Karmis are given intensive training through induction programme as well as periodic refresher courses. The project is being implemented by the Government of Rajasthan through Rajasthan Shiksha Karmi Board (RSKB) with the assistance of voluntary agencies. The RSKB has a Governing Council and an Executive Council. These bodies are represented through two representatives of this Department.

Non-Governmental Organisations (NGOs) and the community play a pivotal role in the implementation of the Shiksha Karmi Project. The Village Education Committees (VECs) have contributed to the improvement of school environment, augmentation of infrastructure and facilities, larger enrolment of children through school mapping and micro-planning in the Shiksha Karmi schools. Enrolment of girls, their attendance and retention in primary schools is one of the serious challenges in achieving Universalisation of Elementary Education in

Rajasthan. The SKP aims at addressing these through decentralised initiatives involving the community. At the grassroot level, Panchayat Samities, Shiksha Karmi Sahyogis, subject specialists of NGOs, Shiksha Karmis and the village community constantly interact with each other to achieve the aims of the project.

Prehar Pathshalas (PPs) (school of convenient timings) under the SKP provide educational programmes for out-of-school children who cannot attend regular day schools due to their preoccupation at home and in other work. In PPs condensed formal school curriculum and learning materials are followed. At present 22,359 girls who constitute 71 per cent of learners in PPs are benefiting from this facility.

Under the innovative and experimental activities, Angan Pathshalas have proved effective in attracting girls to primary schools. Mahila Sahyogis have confirmed their utility in motivating girls to attend schools/PPs in difficult areas. Integration of children with partial disabilities in day schools and PPs have been attempted on a pilot basis.

There is an in-built monitoring process at village, block, headquarter and state levels. There is a provision of Joint Biannual Reviews by SIDA, the Government of India and the Government of Rajasthan and independent evaluation by teams consisting of national and international experts. It has been the practice to conduct mid-term review/evaluation through extensive field trips, meetings, discussions and interactions with all functionaries and beneficiaries. Expert studies have revealed that academic attainments of primary school children in SKP areas are generally better than neighbouring schools managed by Panchayati Raj Institutions. The Shiksha Karmi Project has emerged as a unique instrument of human resource development.

It has enabled rural youth with inherent talent and potential to blossom into confident para-professlionals with self-respect and dignity. There has been six-fold increase in the enrolment of children in the schools taken over by the project. A significant number of children covered by the SK schools are from among SCs/STs.

The project now covers 2,697 villages in 146 blocks in Rajasthan. 6,285 Shiksha Karmis provide primary education to 2. 01 lakh children in day schools and PPs. The experience of SKP demonstrates that the motivation of Shiksha Karmis working in difficult conditions can be sustained over a long period of time by recurrent and effective training; sensitive nurturing, community support, regular participatory review; and problem solving. The success of SKP has attracted national and international recognition. The second phase of Shiksha Karmi Project has come to an end on 30 June 1998. The project document for the third phase is already with prospective donors, viz SIDA and DFID.

District Primary Education Programme

The District Primary Education Programme (DPEP) is a Centrally Sponsored Programme providing special thrust to achieve Universalisation of Primary Education (UPE). The programme takes a holistic view of primary education development and seeks to operationalise the strategy of UPE through district- specific planning with emphasis on decentralised management, participatory processes, empowerment and capacity building at all levels.

The programme is structured to provide additional inputs over and above the provision made by the State Governments for expenditure on elementary education. The programme fills in the existing gaps in the development of primary education and seeks to revitalise the existing system. The DPEP is contextual and has a marked gender focus. The programme components include construction of classrooms and new schools, opening of Non-formal/ Alternative Schooling Centres, appointment of new teachers, setting up of Block Resource Centres/Cluster Resource Centres, teacher training, development of teaching- learning material, research-based interventions, special interventions for education of girls, SC/ST, etc. The components of integrated education to children with disability and a distance education component for improving teacher training have also been incorporated in the programme.

Objectives

The programme mainly aims at providing access to primary education for all children, reducing primary dropout rates to less than 10 per cent, increasing learning achievement of primary school students by atleast 25 per cent, and reducing the gap among gender and social groups to less than 5 per cent.

District selection criteria

The district is the Unit of programme implementation and selected on the basis of twin criteria, viz. (a) educationally backward districts with female literacy below the national average, and (b) districts where Total Literacy Campaigns (TLCs) have been successful, leading to enhanced demand for elementary education.

Funding

The DPEP is a Centrally Sponsored Scheme. Eighty-five per cent of the project cost is shared by the Government of India and 15 per cent by State Government. Both the Central share and State share are passed on to State Implementation Societies directly as grant. The Government of India share is resourced by external funding. Several bilateral and multilateral agencies are providing financial assistance for the DPEP. The World

Bank has provided a credit amounting to US$ 260 million (approx. Rs 806 crores) under Phase I of DPEP (1994-2001). The European community has signed a financial agreement with the Government of India to provide a grant of 150 million ECU (approx. Rs 585 crores) as programme support for DPEP in Madhya Pradesh (1994-99). An agreement has been signed with International Development Agency (IDA) for a second credit amounting to US$425 million DPEP (1996-2002). The Government of Netherlands has provided a grant of US$ 25.8 million for DPEP in Gujarat. A grant of £42.5 million (Rs 220 crores) for DPEP in Andhra Pradesh and £31.7 million (Rs, 207 crores) for DPEP in West Bengal is available from Overseas Development Agency (ODA) (UK). IDA credit of US$ 152.4 million (Rs 530 crores) and a grant of US$ 10 million (Rs 36 crores) from UNICEF has been tied up for Phase III for DPEP in 27 Educational Districts of Bihar.

Coverage

The programme which was initially launched in 1994 in 42 districts of seven States has now been extended to cover 149 districts of 14 States, viz. Assam, Haryana, Karnataka, Kerala, Maharashtra, Tamil Nadu, Madhya Pradesh, Gujarat, Himachal Pradesh, Orissa, Andhra Pradesh, West Bengal, Uttar Pradesh and Bihar.

In-depth review of the programme

The first in-depth review conducted during September -October 1997 and the subsequent reviews have brought out that improvements are proceeding in the right direction and there are significant gains in access and retention. There has been a spurt in enrolment and increase in learning achievements. Increasing community involvement, improvement in classroom processes and concerted equity focus have emerged as key successes of the programme.

Secondary education

National Council of Educational Research and Training

The National Council of Educational Research and Training (NCERT) is an apex resource organisation to assist and advise the Central and the State Governments on academic matters related to school education. The Scheme is directly implemented by the Ministry of Human Resource Development. It provides academic and technical support for qualitative improvement of school education through its constituents, viz. (i) The National Institute of Education, New Delhi, (ii) Central Institute of Educational Technology, New Delhi, (iii) Pandit Sunderlal Sharma Central Institute of Vocational Education, Bhopal and (iv) Five Regional Institutes of Education located at Ajmer, Bhopal, Bhubaneswar, Mysore and Shillong.

The NCERT has been presented with Asia and the Pacific Centre for Educational Innovation for Development (ACEID) Excellence in Education Award for 1998 in recognition of its outstanding contribution to the work of UNESCO, ACEID and the APEID programme it administers. Highlights of the programmes conducted during 1998-99 are given below.

Early childhood education

In the area of Early Childhood Care and Education (ECE) the focus remained on training of ECE faculty of District Institutes of Education and Training (DIETs), strengthening of preschool education component of Integrated Child Development Scheme (ICDS), coordination of ECE project in 12 participating States, development of video and audio programmes for training package in ECE, documentation and dissemination of information through the newsletter Glimpses and *Aabhas*.

Elementary education

For promotion of elementary education instructional

materials in language (Hindi), mathematics, art and environment education were developed for Classes I and II. After getting feedback at the regional levels, the document The Primary Years was published. The Fourth International Seminar on the theme 'Researches in Learning Organisation, Community Participation and School Effectiveness at Primary Stage' was organised and follow-up action has been taken on action points drawn from the researches presented in earlier three International Research Seminars. Academic support to the DPEP States was provided to devise and implement instructional materials and training strategies for enhancing the competence of teachers to handle classroom situation. Resource support in the areas of Multigrade Teaching, Development of Diagnostic Tests in Language and Mathematics for primary classes, Evaluation of Primary Level Textbooks, Development of Training Modules for Key Persons and a study of classroom processes in relation to the Antecedent Factors and their Impact on the School Outcomes were some of the activities carried out under DPEP.

In addition, evaluation of Balika Shivir programme under Lok Jumbish in Rajasthan, continued. On the request from Uttar Pradesh Basic Education Project Board, Lucknow, Evaluation of Children was undertaken in the three districts of Varanasi, Sitapur and Nainital.

Non-formal education

The focus of Non-Formal Education (NFE) programmes remained on resource development in states and voluntary organisations. Training programmes were organised for Non-Formal Education faculty members of SCERTs/SRCs and State Level Key Persons in Non-Formal Education and Alternative Schooling (NFEAS) and for senior functionaries of voluntary agencies getting grant from the MHRD. Towards development of training package for District Resource Units (DRUs) of DIETs and voluntary agencies, the job analysis was done, required competencies have been culled out and a process-based manual has been developed. Studies on (i) status of NFE Programme at Upper Primary Stage in India (ii) status of SCERTs in the field of NFEAS, (iii) difficulties faced in teaching-learning of Hindi at primary level NFE centres and (iv) effectiveness of NFE for lower primary stage in Bihar, Haryana, Rajasthan and Uttar Pradesh are in progress.

Education of girls

Resource development and capacity-building received attention in the context of Education of Girl Child. A data bank of Women's Education and Development is being developed. A study of the impact of incentive schemes on the progress of education of girls from disadvantaged groups (SC/ST/ OBC /Minorities) of Madhya Pradesh continued. A national workshop was organised to develop a Curricular Framework for a Gender Sensitive Life Skills Programme. A handbook on Balika *Shiksha Mein Gram Shiksha Samiti Ka Sahyog—Ek Disha* for training of Village Education Committee (VEC) members was prepared and reviewed.

Education of SC/ST

In order to promote education of SC/ST children attitudinal issues among teachers towards SC children are being identified to develop a training package for changing the attitude of these teachers. The first draft of the conceptual paper on 'Changing Attitude of Tribal Area Teachers', has been completed. A textbook for Class I for Saora tribal children in Orissa, has been finalised. A training package is being developed on the content and methodology of tribal language training for non-tribal teachers in Tribal Area Schools in Orissa. A study to determine the efficacy of the Ashram schools is in progress. Under DPEP a conceptual workshop on Planning of Tribal Education was organised and technical inputs in the production of textbooks for tribal children have been provided during the National Debate on Bridge Language Issues organised by the Educational Consultants of India Ltd. (Ed.CIL.).

Education of minorities

For promotion of education of minorities a sample survey of the extent of educational benefits derived out of the Centrally Sponsored Schemes for minorities (Muslims) has been taken up. Under the study 'Analysis of Existing Curriculum in Government- aided Maktabs/ Madrasas' data has been collected. Analysis of data is in progress. A study of the educational needs of the minority-run institutions have also been initiated.

Special education

In the area of Special Education handbooks for primary school teachers—(i) of Low Vision Children and (ii) for teaching Hindi language to Hearing Impaired Children in Integrated Schools—and a guidebook regarding resource facilities in common schools for children with special needs have been developed and are under print. Handbooks for transaction of Mathematics Curriculum to Visually Impaired (Blind) Children and a source book for teachers in the area of Mental Retardation are also being developed. The NCERT has also undertaken the evaluation study for Integrated Education of the Disabled (IEDC). Teacher training has been undertaken for India-Australia Training and Capacity Building (IATCB) Project initiated by the Government of India and for primary school teachers from various Kendriya Vidyalayas.

Computer education

Under the area of Computer Education the activities

undertaken included establishment of the Computer Resource Centre at the NCERT headquarters, development of courseware on select topics in school curriculum, NCERT's Website on the Internet and training programmes for members of academic and administrative staff of the NCERT in the use of computers. A book on the Internet as an educational resource and computer courseware using multimedia technology is being developed.

Fabrication of Primary Science Kits, Integrated Science Kits and Mini Tool Kits for despatch to states and finalisation of teacher's handbooks of activities for Classes VI to VIII for integrated science kits are in progress. Thirty-two trainees from ITIs were trained in plastic moulding technology and seven apprentices in various trades are under training.

Vocational education

Major thrust of activities in the area of Vocational Education remained on training of personnel and development of materials. Orientation programmes for the key functionaries of the implementing States were conducted. Teacher training programmes in the area of Sericulture, Commercial Garment Designing and Making, Accounting and Auditing, Marketing and Salesmanship and Entrepreneurship Development and short-term training programmes for the key functionaries were organised. Working group meetings were held to develop a handbook on vocational guidance and counselling, development of national vocational qualifications in building maintenance area and to examine various provisions in Apprenticeship Act. Working Group Meetings are being organised to review existing curricula and for development of instructional material in Vocational Education.

The NCERT also organised a UNESCO-sponsored

In-country Training Workshop on the Development of the National System of Vocational Qualifications, three Golden Jubilee Regional Seminars on Vocational Education for Rural Development and four National Seminars in the area of Horticultural Vocational Courses, Food Preservation and Processing, Transport Sector and Work Experience/SUPW. Six video snippets of short duration were produced and Hindi translation of Curriculum and Instructional Materials was carried out.

Evaluation of vocational education programme in Tamil Nadu, Punjab, Haryana and Chandigarh is being undertaken. The work on development of Handbook of Vocational Guidance for the students of Secondary and Senior Secondary Schools, career conferences, one for each Lab. School of Bhopal, publication of Quarterly Bulletin, organisation of National Vocational Education Competition and exhibition and production of video programmes for popularisation of Vocational Education are in progress.

Talent search

In the context of Talent Search, the NCERT continued organising the National Talent Search Examination (NTSE) and interviews and disbursement of scholarships to existing awardees. An analysis of performance level of students at state and national level examinations in the NTSE and a follow-up study of NTS awardees of years 1987-90 is in progress.

Examination reform

Under technical/resource support to School Education Boards two workshops were organised for Haryana and Mizoram Boards of School Education. One issue of the Examination Reform Bulletin has been circulated and the other will be ready soon. Studies on (i) finding reasons for non-implementation of Continuous Comprehensive Evaluation (CCE) in schools at elementary level, (ii)

Analysis of evaluation practices in Chemistry practicals at +2 stage in various Education Boards in the country, (iii) critical analysis of question papers of various subjects at +2 stage in some Boards of School Education are in progress. Language exercises in English for Classes IV and V of KVs are being developed.

Educational psychology

The Post-Graduate Diploma in Guidance and Counselling 1998-99 is being conducted with 31 trainees. An enrichment course in Psychology of Teaching and Learning for DIETs personnel is scheduled to be organised in January 1999. Studies on (i) Analysis of the science textbooks of Secondary School stage with reference to the nature of science, attitudes, value towards science and its relevance for daily life. (ii) Predictive potential of selection procedure for performance in counsellor training programme and on-the-job performance, (iii) Critical analysis of educational psychology curriculum of elementary teacher training in India, (iv) Schooling in Mirambika, M Adolescent perception of social norms have been completed. The work on studies 'Guidance Research in India' and 'Counsellor in the Making: Status and Development', is in progress. The developmental activities like (I) Development of a curriculum in educational psychology for elementary teacher education, (ii) Counselling case management: Development of a practical guide, (iii) Teacher questioning in classroom: Development of resource material, (iv) Development of psychology curriculum at +2 stage, and (v) Development of popular psychology series are at various stages of completion. The enrichment of Guidance Laboratory, National Library of Educational and Psychological Tests and Career Information Centre is continuing.

Educational survey

The Sixth All India Educational Survey (AIES) with 30 September 1993 as the date of reference has been conducted jointly by the NCERT and NIC in collaboration with the State Governments. Studies on (i) Evolving Statewise Sampling Design for Sample Surveys in Education, (ii) Estimation of Single Age-wise Enrolment at Elementary stage, (iii) Enrolment of Non-formal education centres, Unrecognised Schools and Recognised Schools - A Sample Survey in Delhi, and (iv) Stagnation and Dropout at Primary Stage are in progress. The second Foundation Course in Qualitative Research Methods using Statistical Package for Social Science (SPSS) was conducted. The strategy for dissemination of data of the Sixth AIES is also being developed.

Educational research and innovations

Apart from the constituents of the NCERT undertaking research, the Educational Research and Innovations Committee (ERIC) of the NCERT provides financial assistance to outside institutions/ organisations for research in priority areas. A Researcher's Seminar to monitor the progress of ERIC-funded projects was organised. Two meetings regarding framing out priority areas for ERIC-sponsored research projects were held. Many projects were completed and reports received. Manuscripts of two issues of the Journal of Indian Education, three issues of Bhartiya Adhunik Shiksha and one issue of Indian Educational Review were prepared and printed. The fifth issue of Indian Educational Abstracts was brought out. All the chapters of abstracts of the second volume of Fifth Survey of Educational Research are under print.

Textual and supplementary materials

The work has been initiated for the reconsideration of the approaches to and framework of curriculum in social sciences, languages and art education. The linguistic competencies attained by students of Arunachal Pradesh in Hindi were evaluated. Textbooks in Sociology, an Atlas for the groups with special needs, a book on Human Rights Education, workbooks on practical aspects in Accountancy and a handbook in Economics were developed. Draft material of Sanskrit Grammar for Classes VI to VIII was reviewed. Second supplementary book for Class VIII was finalised. Songs of Freedom and Unity were selected. A training package for key persons for teaching of Hindi was tried out and 32 post-graduate teachers were trained on selected topics. Work relating to PSLE Project of Singapore was also completed. The promotion and publication of good quality children's literature continued by rewarding the authors and illustrators of children's literature in 19 languages. Comparative studies of school curriculum of some selected countries in Social Sciences, History, Geography, Economics, and Commerce are in progress.

In the field of Science and Mathematics, the task undertaken included (i) Curriculum revision, (ii) Nurturance of talent, (iii) Development of instructional materials for talented students and teachers, (iv) Popularisation of Science and Mathematics through state level and national level Science exhibitions, (v) Development of laboratory-oriented activities, low-cost experiments, laboratory skills and new courses in practicals, (vi) Activities for Mathematics laboratory, (vii) Bringing out School Science journal, and (viii) Training of Navodaya Vidyalaya PGTs in Physics, Chemistry and Mathematics. In view of major changes in the curriculum of Mathematics, 'supplements' for Classes XI and XII were developed. Popular Science books under the project 'Reading to Learn' are also being developed in new and applied areas of Science.

Teacher education

The NCERT extended all support to the Centrally Sponsored Scheme of Teacher Education, District Primary Education Programme (DPEP) and SCERTs/SIEs. The Regional Institutes of Education (RIEs) at Ajmer, Bhopal, Bhubaneswar and Mysore continued organising pre-service teacher education programmes, viz. (i) four-year integrated B.Sc. B.Ed. course and (ii) One-year M. Ed course with specialisation in Elementary Education. In order to meet the needs of in-service training of teachers and other educational personnel several programmes were undertaken by the RIEs as well as by other constituents of the NCERT. Training materials, packages in different subjects, and modules were developed by the RIEs for teachers/ teacher educators. The Centrally Sponsored Scheme of Special Orientation for Primary Teachers (SOPT) is being organised. Studies on (i) Operationalisation of the Scheme of DIETs, 00 Teaching Effectiveness of Primary Teachers in relation to their Educational and Professional Background, (iii) Evaluation of Implementation of SOPT Programme in Different States, (iv) Status of SCERTs/SIEs, (v) Fifty Years of Teacher Education in India: Appraisal, Future Perspectives, (vi) Innovation of Teacher Education and (vii) Case Studies of Autonomous SCERTs of Delhi and Kerala are in progress. A framework for participative and database system of Teacher Appraisal is being developed. Induction training programmes were organised for SCERT faculty, DIET's faculty and principals of DIETs. Competitions for school teachers and teacher educators were organised for Innovations in School Education.

Educational technology

In the area of Educational Technology, video and audio programmes supplemented curriculum development and curriculum transaction in school education and teacher education. Twenty-seven audio programmes comprising 8 for 'Umang' service, 9 for teaching of Sanskrit and 10 for teaching Indian languages were produced. Seventy ETV programmes were developed mainly on Low-Cost Teaching Aids and Measurements with an Interface with the computers. Studies on (i) Innovative Practices in Educational Technology, (ii) Audio Conferencing in Teacher Education, (iii) Need Assessment of Educational Media Programmes, (iv) Effect of Computer -Assisted Learning (CAL) on Hearing Impaired Children, (v) Research Implications for Media Production, (vi) Impact of TVs, and RCCPs, and (vii) Effectiveness of Radio Broadcast on Pre-School, are in progress. Development of multimedia packages and Media Support to SOPT is continuing. Training/orientation programmes in Educational Technology, through teleconferencing, video editing, evaluation of educational technology, materials and programmes etc. are being organised. The NCERT has been using DD-I and AIR (ten stations) network for primary, secondary and teacher education programmes.

Field services

The Field Advisers, NCERT continued liaison functions pertaining to implementation of programmes and activities undertaken by various constituents of the NCERT, MHRD and the State Education Departments, etc. They provided assistance to the Regional Institutes of Education in the context of identification of educational needs of the States requiring NCERT's inputs. The Field Advisers provided assistance to the State Education Departments in the context of selection of teachers for national awards, development of curricula and instructional materials, training of personnel and policy formulation, etc. Assistance was also provided to the MHRD in the context of (i) monitoring of implementation of the Centrally Sponsored Schemes in the states, (ii)

Presanction appraisal of NFE programmes, and (iii) assessment of functioning of the voluntary NFE agencies running NFE centres through the Joint Evaluation Teams.

Promotion of Hindi

A programme Hindi Pakhwara for promoting use of Hindi in official work of the NCERT was organised from I to 15 September 1998. Various competitions were organised during the period. A meeting of the NCERT's Official Language Implementation Committee was convened.

Publications

The NCERT continued publishing (i) school level textbooks, workbooks, prescribed supplementary readers, (ii) teachers' guides and other instructional materials, (iii) supplementary readers, (iv) research reports and monographs, and (v) educational journals. During April to October 1998, 272 titles under different categories were brought out.

National population education project

The National Population Education Project (NPEP) was launched in April 1980. Since its inception the project activities have been directed to attain the objective of institutionalising population education in school and non-formal education system. As an educational response to population issues, Population Education aims at making learners aware of the inter -relationship between population and developmental issues, developing in them rational attitude and responsible behaviour and promoting a positive value orientation so that they may take informed decisions on various population issues. In view of the paradigm shift in population and development reflected in the Programme of Action adopted at the International Conference on Population and Development (ICPD), 1994, the Framework of

Population Education was revised. In the light of the above framework of Population Education, a one-day workshop was organised at the Regional Institute of Education, Mysore to orient the facilitators for the Need Assessment Study on Adolescence Education under National Population Education Project (NPEP). An eleven-day training programme was held at the NIE Campus (NCERT), New Delhi from 26 October to 5 November 1998 to orient 29 project personnel of States and UTs.

Vocationalisation of secondary education

In accordance with the priority accorded to Vocationalisation of Education in the National Policy on Education, a Centrally Sponsored Scheme of Vocationalisation of Higher Secondary Education was introduced in February 1988. The main objectives of the scheme are to enhance individual employability, reduce the mismatch between demand and supply of skilled manpower and provide an alternative for those pursuing higher education without particular interest or purpose. A Centrally Sponsored Scheme of Prevocational Education at Lower Secondary Stage has also been introduced from the year 199394 primarily to impart training in simple marketable skills to the students of Classes IX and X, to develop vocational interests and to facilitate students in making a choice of Vocational courses at the higher secondary level.

The scheme is implemented through the State Governments /UT Administrations. So far, all States/UTs except Lakshadweep have joined the programme at the +2 level. Under the Prevocational Education Scheme, assistance has been provided to 11 States/ UTs for introduction of Pre-vocational courses in 652 schools. Assistance is also provided to non-governmental organisations for conducting innovative and non-formal programmes of Vocational Education. So far, 56 voluntary organisations have been assisted under the scheme.

The target laid down in the revised policy was to divert 10 per cent of higher secondary students to the vocational stream by 1995 and 25 per cent by 2000 AD. As against this, 18,719 Vocational sections have been sanctioned in 6,486 schools all over the country thereby creating capacity for diversion of about 9.35 lakh students to the vocational stream which is 11 per cent of the enrolment at the +2 stage. Following are the major steps taken to strengthen the programme:

— A Joint Council for Vocational Education (JCVE) was set up in April 1990 for policy formulation and co-ordination at the national level. Three meetings of JCVE and its Standing Committees are held at regular intervals.

— The Central Institute of Vocational Education (CIVE), set up at Bhopal in July 1993, provides technical and academic support to the programme in the country. This has been recognised by the UNESCO and is part of the UNEVOC chain.

— Of the 150 courses introduced under the scheme, 60 Vocational courses have been notified under the Apprenticeship Act and additional 34 courses have also been approved for covering under the Act.

— Collaborative arrangements have been made with some Government departments like Ministry of Railways, Ministry of Health, etc. Efforts are also being made to evolve need-based courses in the area of Textiles, Food Processing and Leather. A collaborative pilot project with the National Institute of Fashion Technology (NIFT) for introducing Fashion Designing courses in three schools in Vishakapatnam, Ludhiana and Indore has been started.

— The States have been advised to strengthen the

management structure at various levels, induct experts to infuse professionalism in the programme, introduce need-based courses and to strengthen linkages with the industry for on-the-job and apprenticeship training.

Consequent upon the meeting of the National Development Council (NDC), the matter of retention/ transfer of the scheme to the States was discussed in the internal meeting of the Planning Commission and it was proposed to categorise the scheme into distinct groups as follows:

— those to be retained as per the Approach Paper;
— those to be transferred with resources to be pooled and distributed among the States as per the Gadgil formula;
— those to be transferred with earmarking of funds; and
— those to be transferred in a phased manner.

The scheme falls under the category of the schemes to be transferred without earmarking of funds. Recently, the Planning Commission has given the go-ahead for continuation of the scheme till a final decision is taken by the NDC. Meanwhile, the pilot project with NIFT is being continued. Another pilot project is being finalised to set up industry-driven vocational courses in schools affiliated to CBSE in collaboration with FICCI/Confederation of Indian Industry.

The Department has also set up a Working Group to suggest modifications in the implementation of the programme in future. The Working Group has prepared a document entitled 'Vocational Education and Programmes—Issues and Implication for Future Planning'. It has been proposed to organise widespread consultation of the people concerned before the recommendations of the Working Group are operationalised.

Integrated education for disabled children

With the coming into force of the Persons with Disabilities Act, 1995 there is now a statutory responsibility on the Central, State and Local Governments to provide free education in an appropriate environment to all disabled children up to the age of 18 years.

The Department of Education has been implementing the scheme for Integrated Education of Disabled Children (IEDC) since 1974. The scheme aims at providing educational opportunities for moderately disabled children in the general school system so as to facilitate their retention and ultimate integration in this system. The scope of this scheme includes preschool training for disabled children and counselling of their parents. Under this scheme 100 per cent financial assistance is provided as per prescribed norms for facilities for disabled children like books and stationery, uniforms, transport and escort allowance for severely handicapped children, reader allowance for blind children and equipment which includes educational aids and assistive devices.

The IEDC scheme is presently being implemented in 26 States/UTs through nearly 15,000 schools and over 55,000 children are being benefited under this scheme. Efforts are being made to fund interventions for disabled children through various other schemes/ programmes being run by the Department of Education, viz. Adult Education, NFE and DPEP. Two polytechnics for disabled students have been set up at Mysore and Kanpur. The scheme also provides assistance to NGOs engaged in the field of integrated education.

The National Council for Teacher Education (NCTE) is engaged in developing curriculum for teacher training and orientation so that both general teachers as well as resource teachers are trained to handle disabled children. Multisite action and research programmes were launched in 23 DIETs and four Regional Institutes of Education. The NCERT has started the programme of training selected teachers (both general as well as resource) to make them Master Trainers who will in turn organise training programmes in their State under the guidance of experts provided by the NCERT or the Regional Institutes of Education. Considering that training of teachers is the most important aspect for the success of the scheme of IEDC, the Department of Education has tied up with Aus-Aid under the India-Australia Training and Capacity Building Project (IATCBP) under which about Rs 1.50 crore will be made available by the Australian Government for:

— intensive training of 10 teacher educators in Australia to turn them into Master Trainers,

— further training by the Master Trainers along with three Australian experts in various places in the country,

— a Study Tour of 6- 10 officers of the Government of India and State Governments as well as educational institutions to learn first-hand about the educational policy and its implementation by the Australian Government, and

— planning arrangements between institutions in India and those in Australia with a personnel and technology exchange programme to keep the system abreast of the latest advances in this field.

Promotion of yoga in schools

The NPE lays down that Yoga will receive special attention as a system which promotes the integrated development of the body and mind. The NPE also envisages the introduction of Yoga in all schools.

Based on an evaluation of an experimental programme of introduction of Yoga in KVs as also consultation with Yoga experts, a Centrally Sponsored Scheme for promotion of Yoga in schools was launched in 1989-90. This scheme was being implemented through the Education/ concerned Departments in the States/UTs as well as through Yoga Institutions of repute. Under this scheme, financial assistance was provided for training of teachers in Yoga and for building up of infrastructure necessary for the purpose. In addition institutions of all India character were given assistance for maintenance as well as developmental expenditure for promotion of basic research and teacher training programmes in various aspects of Yoga other than therapeutical aspects.

The Ministry of Finance recommended that efforts should be made to include Yoga as a subject in the school curriculum. Accordingly efforts are being made to include Yoga as a subject in school curriculum. The Department of Education is also engaged in formulating a fresh scheme for introduction of Yoga in schools which will have a widest scope, enhanced grants for teacher training and reduced assistance for infrastructure/ library facilities.

Central Board of Secondary Education

The Central Board of Secondary Education (CBSE), Delhi has been making constant endeavours to provide quality education and development of holistic individual. During the period under report, the following activities were undertaken by the Board.

Examinations

in all 2,36,795 candidates were registered for Senior School Certificate Examinations and 4,09,695 candidates were registered for Secondary School Examinations held in March April 1998. The CBSE regularly reviews its system and operational areas to bring out improvement, fairness and objectivity through the following procedure:

— Timely declaration of results
— Orientation of Head Examiners
— Marking Schemes
— Updating the outdated system
— E-mail service provided for the first time
— Marksheets sent along with results
— Sample Papers

All India pre-medical/pre-dental examination

1,41,597 candidates registered themselves for the All India Pre-Medical/Pre-Dental Examination this year.

Jawahar navodaya vidyalaya entrance test

The first examination for Jawahar Navodaya Vidyalaya selection test for admission to Class VI was conducted by the CBSE in two phases in the month of February and April. More than 5 lakh candidates registered and appeared at the examination which was held for summer and winter-bound schools.

Affiliation

The CBSE appoints the territorial study teams to conduct regular academic visits to the schools. This year 276 new schools have been added and the total number of affiliated schools stands at 5,119 located in different parts of India and in other countries like Bangladesh, Bahrain, Saudi Arabia, Kuwait, Russia, etc.

Academic curriculum design

The thrust of the curriculum design is upon providing knowledge, promoting psychomotor skills, developing logical thinking and scientific aptitude and strengthen value-based approach to life.

Vocational and technical education

The Board has provided 37 different courses which can be

offered depending upon the requirements and suitability of the students. The courses are defined in two categories:

— Job-oriented Courses

— Job-linked Vocational Courses

Generic vocational course

The CBSE is the first Board in the country to introduce Generic Vocational Course at the +2 level. This competency-based curriculum provides skills that cut across various vocations and prepare a learner for occupational role in general. The contents of this course include House Keeping to Automation and Robotics, Resource Management, Goal-setting, Work Culture, etc.

Consumer awareness

The publication printed by CBSE on Consumer Awareness educates teachers/ students about the theoretical aspects of consumer education and protection. The aim of the booklet is to create awareness in the minds of the students.

Environmental education

To familiarise the students with the growing concerns of environmental degradation, ecological imbalances and the global concerns on environmental issues, the Board has launched environmental education in schools.

International programmes

A delegation from Japan comprising primary, middle and secondary school teachers visited the CBSE to discuss and present their views on the education system in both the countries.

A team of senior level officers from South Africa led by the Superintendent General, Education Department, South Africa visited the CBSE. Detailed discussions were held about the pre- and post-examination procedures and actual conduct of examinations.

Kendriya vidyalayas

The Government of India approved the scheme of Kendriya Vidyalayas (KVs) in 1962 on the recommendations of the Second Central Pay Commission, with the idea of encouraging the growth of secondary schools with a common syllabus and medium of instruction for providing uninterrupted education to the children of Central Government employees who are liable to frequent transfers. Initially, 20 regimental schools in different States were taken over as Central Schools. In 1965, an autonomous body, called the Kendriya Vidyalaya Sangathan (KVS), was set up to run these Vidyalayas. Over the years, the number of Kendriya Vidyalayas increased to 875 as on 31 December 1998. As on 31 March 1998 the number of teaching staff is 36,030 while the number of non-teaching staff is 46,069.

Salient features

The salient features of Kendriya Vidyalayas are as follows:

— Kendriya Vidyalayas are fulfilling their commitment to cater to the educational needs of the wards of transferable Central Government employees to a large extent.

— Preference in admission is given to children whose parents have the largest number of transfers during the preceding seven years.

— All KVs are co-educational and composite.

— Common Textbooks with common curriculum and bilingual medium of instruction, i.e. English and Hindi are followed.

— All KVs are affiliated to the CBSE.

— Teaching of Sanskrit from Class V to IX is compulsory. However, the student can offer Sanskrit as an additional optional subject at Class X also.

— The quality of teaching is kept high by maintaining a proper teacher-pupil ratio. No tuition fee is charged from students up to Class VIII. The wards of staff of KVS, SC/ ST students, children of officers and men of the Armed Forces killed or disabled during hostilities in the wars of 1962, 1965 and 1971 against China and Pakistan and girl students are exempted from paying tuition fee up to Class XII.

KVS administration

The Minister for Human Resource Development is ex-officio Chairman of the Sangathan. The policies and guidelines issued by the Sangathan and its Board of Governors are executed by the Commissioner who is the executive head of the Sangathan. In order to execute all tasks and decisions about administrative and academic matters, the Commissioner is assisted by two Joint Commissioners and other officers and supporting staff at the KVS (Hq) and its 19 Regional Offices. The Regional Offices are headed by Assistant Commissioners. The main functions of the Regional Offices are to monitor and supervise the working of the Vidyalayas in the region, to carry out administrative work relating to service matters of both academic and general staff and to allot funds to Vidyalayas. At the Vidyalaya level, each Kendriya Vidyalaya is headed by a Principal/Vice-Principal assisted by a small group of administrative and other supporting staff, besides teaching personnel.

Opening of kendriya vidyalayas

Kendriya Vidyalayas are opened in the Civil Sector on the recommendations of various Ministries/ Departments of Central/State Government, or the Central Government Employees Welfare Association. Similarly, Vidyalayas are opened on the recommendations of the Ministry of Defence in the Defence Sector. The Kendriya Vidyalayas are also opened in Project Sector in the campuses of

Public Sector Undertakings (PSUs) and institutions of higher learning if the recurring and non-recurring expenditure is fully met by the sponsoring authorities.

In order to meet the increasing demands from the target groups (Civil and Defence Sectors), the Government approved in May 1993 opening of up to 20 Vidyalayas every year during the period 1993-94 to 1997-98 and as many as may be practicable, in view of suitable proposals, in the Project Sector.

Admissions

The main object of the Kendriya Vidyalayas is to provide uninterrupted educational facilities to the wards of Central Government employees who are transferred from one region to another and from one linguistic area to another. The main criterion for admission in Kendriya Vidyalayas is, therefore, the transferability of the parent, i.e. during the last seven years, immediately preceding the year of admission. Thereafter, the children of transferable employees of PSUs fully financed by the Government, followed by nontransferable employees are admitted. After meeting demands of the above categories, if vacancies are still available, admissions are also given to the floating population.

The Board of Governors has also approved certain exceptions for admission in Kendriya Vidyalayas over and above the class strength:

— The children and dependent grand-children of Members of Parliament, children of KVS/ NSG/SPG employees.

— Fifty seats for employees of Ministry of External Affairs and RAW.

— One hundred seats for the employees of the Department of Education.

— Children of Central Government employees who die in harness.

Reservations

Fifteen per cent and 7.5 per cent seats of fresh admissions are reserved for SC/ST candidates. After meeting the needs of the registered SC/ST candidates, the unfilled seats of one category can be transferred to another category to a maximum of 22.5 per cent of fresh admissions. There were about 7.52 lakh students studying in Kendriya Vidyalayas as on 1 April 1998.

Courses of study at +2 stage

Kendriya Vidyalayas provide Science, Commerce and Humanities streams mainly. Physical Education, Political Science, Fine Arts and Music have also been introduced in addition to Computer Science as elective subjects at the +2 stage.

Students belonging to SC/ST and those who have participated in Games and Sports Meets, Scouting and Guiding Camps/NCC/Adventure activities are given concession in admission at the +2 stage in Science and Commerce streams.

Academic performance

The academic performance of KVs at Class X and XII examinations conducted by the CBSE for 1998 is 76.80 per cent and 79.90 per cent, respectively.

Training of teachers

A well-chosen teaching staff and their periodical orientation in general and methodical areas by developing and building their competencies enable them to nurture the talents of the students fully. These regular training programmes, after a periodicity of six years, will improve with the establishment of five Zonal Institutes of Education and Training. The Government has already sanctioned Rs 3 crore for setting up of these institutes at the following places: Bolangir (Orissa), Gwalior (Madhya Pradesh), Karad (Maharashtra), Mysore (Karnataka), and Sirsa (Haryana).

These institutes are yet to be functional for want of sanction of posts.

Academic programmes

The following programmes and activities have been undertaken by KVS:

— A Project on Computer Literacy and Studies in Schools (CLASS) has been ongoing in 291 KVs.

— The revised CLASS Project has been introduced in 161 Kendriya Vidyalayas under UNIX Environment.

— The other activities like Youth Parliament. Associated Schools Project on National Integration and International Understanding, KVs Science Exhibition, Scouting and Guiding, Adventure Activities, NCC, NSS and Games and Sports, etc. are a part of the Curriculum of every Kendriya Vidyalaya.

— The project on Value Education as a pilot project, (ii) Strengthening of values through visual and performing arts, (iii) Students exchange programmes, (iv) Strengthening of primary education and (v) Celebration of 50th anniversary of Independence have been implemented.

— Fifty KVs have been identified as model Kendriya Vidyalayas which will be equipped with better infrastructure facilities for games and sports, library, senior and junior science laboratories and computers. These will act as resource centres for neighbouring Kendriya Vidyalayas.

Incentive awards for teachers

During the current year, 50 teachers were honoured with KVS Incentive Awards. Four KV teachers were awarded National Awards by the President of India in recognition of their meritorious services as teachers.

Navodaya vidyalayas

In order to provide high quality modern education including strong component of culture, inculcation of values, awareness of the environment, adventure activities and physical education to the talented children predominantly from the rural areas, without regard to their socio-economic conditions, the Government of India launched the scheme to establish, on an average, one Navodaya Vidyalaya (NV) in each district of the country. Navodaya Vidyalayas are fully residential, co-educational institutions providing education up to senior secondary stage. Education in NVs including boarding and lodging, textbooks, uniforms, etc. is free for all students.

Opening of navodaya vidyalayas

As on 31 December 1998, 397 schools have been sanctioned. It is expected to sanction 15 more new Navodaya Vidyalayas during 1998-99. The States of Tamil Nadu and West Bengal have not adopted the scheme as yet.

Admission

Admission to Navodaya Vidyalayas is made at the level of Class VI through a test conducted in the concerned district in which all children who have passed Class V from any of the recognised schools in the district are eligible to appear. The tests are designed and conducted by the NCERT. From the year 1998, JNVST is being conducted by CBSE.

Establishment of zonal training institutes

The Government has approved setting up of five Zonal Training Institutes for providing in-service training to the teachers of JNVs at various locations in the country.

Computer literacy programme

The existing Computer Literacy Programme (CLP) in 103 Navodaya Vidyalayas is being continued. It is proposed to extend this programme to more JNVs in a phased manner. The expansion of CLP to 100 more JNVs is expected to be finalised during this year.

Migration

As per migration policy of Navodaya Vidyalaya Samiti, 30 per cent migration of the students at Class IX level from 336 Vidyalayas has taken place during 1997-98. 4,683 students were proposed for migration against which 4,314 students have actually been migrated.

Allocation of streams

A total of 235 Navodaya Vidyalayas were upgraded to Senior Secondary stage during the period under report. Science, Commerce, Humanities and Vocational streams were introduced in these Vidyalayas. Various Vocational streams allocated to Vidyalayas, viz. Electrical Technology, Vocational Commerce and Hotel Management are functional in certain JNVs.

Sports and games

The NVS is actively taking part in sports/games. Judo and athletics teams have won third place and cash rewards in School Games Federation of India Competitions. It organised School Games Federation of India Competitions inviting teams from various States at Amravati, Maharashtra for the first time. The NVS National Games Group A and Group B national athletics were held during October -November 1998 at Delhi, Una and Vishakapatnam, respectively.

Training programmes

The Samiti organised a number of staff development programmes for the professional growth of teachers and Principals of JNVs. In this context it is also getting the help of agencies like CCRT, NCERT, NIEPA, SAI, etc. to update the knowledge of teachers and Principals. During the year 1998-99, the Samiti has organised 156 training programmes.

Education of SCs/STs/women

The Navodaya Vidyalayas are meant primarily for children from rural areas and admission of children from urban areas is restricted to a maximum of 25 per cent. The scheme also provides for reservation of SC/ST in proportion to their population in the concerned district subject to a maximum of 50 per cent provided that in any district such reservation will not be less than the national average.

Efforts are made to ensure that at least one-third of the students selected are girls. The percentage of SC/ST and girl students in JNVs during the academic session 1997-98 was 23 per cent, 14 per cent and 32 per cent, respectively.

Scout and guide and NCC

The Navodaya Vidyalaya Samiti is recognised as a State for Scouting and Guiding activities by Bharat Scouts and Guides. Various activities are being conducted in the Vidyalayas to make children imbibe the philosophy of Scouting and Guiding movement.

— Children of NVs participated in 13th national Jamboree of Bharat Scouts and Guides held at Khurda (Orissa) from 4 to 9 January 1998.

— NVS organised its first National Jamboree in Scouts and Guides as well as Rajya Puruskar Award function at Bangalore during April 1998; 209 Scouts and Guides, 27 Scouters anti Guiders of JNVs from all over India took part in the Jamboree.

— NVs children of Regional Office, Jaipur, Pune, Lucknow and Hyderabad attended President Scout and Guide testing camps. Important days like Sadbhawana Diwas, Anti Leprosy Day, Scout and Guide Foundation Day, etc. were celebrated by the Scout and Guide Unit in the Vidyalayas.

— NCC is being introduced in JNVs in a phased manner. The Samiti has a total of 7,950 cadet strength (6350 boys and 1600 girls). JNV cadets attended several NCC camps and excelled themselves. NCC cadets took part in Republic Day parade in several districts.

Exhibitions

Four science exhibits from Navodaya Vidyalayas Aurangabad, Muzaffarnagar, Sitapur and Kurnool were selected for Jawaharlal Nehru National Science Exhibition 1998, held at Amritsar.

National award presentation

National awards presentation function for the Navodaya toppers in the CBSE Public Examinations of March 1998 as well as to the outstanding teachers of the Navodaya Vidyalayas for their meritorious services was held on 3 December 1998 at New Delhi. Dr Murli Manohar Joshi, Minister for Human Resource Development and Chairman, NVS gave away the awards to the children and the teachers. While five children who are toppers in the Classes X and XII examinations of 1998 from NVs were given Director's Gold Medal and cash awards, 33 teachers from different JNVs were also honoured by presenting shawl, citation and cash awards.

National open school

Established as an autonomous institution under the Ministry of Human Resource Development, Government of India in 1989, the National Open School (NOS) mainly caters to the educational needs of the school dropouts and socially and economically backward learners. The focus of the NOS covers right from the elementary education to course at the pre-degree level, both academic and vocational. The NOS has shown a steady growth in student enrolment, number of courses and study centres.

Study centres

The number of study centres is increasing year after year and this year the number has touched 871. Special Accredited Institutes for Education of the Disadvantaged (SAIED) are being established by the NOS as special centres all over the country.

As a first step towards globalisation of its educational services, the NOS launched its study centres in the Middle East, i.e. Dubai and Abu Dhabi. The aim is to extend educational facilities through the open learning system to non-resident Indians and other nationals settled there. During the year under report, 116 Boards and Universities recognised the examination conducted by the NOS.

Audio-video production

Audio and Video programmes are one of the most important components of the multi-channel package offered by the NOS. These programmes developed by the Media Unit supplements and complements the other channels of learning such as self-learning print materials and personal contact programmes. The NOS has so far produced 35 audio programmes in Hindi and English languages and 56 video programmes each in Hindi and English language on different subjects of the secondary course.

Regional centres

Two more regional centres at Chandigarh and Cochin have been established during 1998-99. So far eight Regional Centres have been established to effectively implement and monitor the functioning of NOS programmes.

State open schooling and state centre for open schooling

Keeping in view its aims and objectives, the NOS is providing professional guidance for the establishment of

State Open Schools. Open Schools have already been established in Andhra Pradesh, Rajasthan, Haryana, Madhya Pradesh, Karnataka, West Bengal and Punjab. Similarly, the NOS has helped Himachal Pradesh and Assam in setting up State-Centre for Open Schooling.

Central Tibetan Schools Administration

The Central Tibetan Schools Administration (CTSA) was set up as an autonomous organisation by the Government of India. The main objectives of the CTSA are to run, manage and assist institutions for the education of Tibetan children in India. To keep the Tibetan community abreast with all aspects of modern education and development while retaining essentials of their traditional system and culture, schools have been opened all over the country, where there is concentration of Tibetans, mostly in hilly areas.

The Central Schools for Tibetans are affiliated to CBSE, Delhi and follow 10+2 system of education. They prepare students for the All India Secondary School and All India Senior School Certificate Examinations. The medium of instruction in the primary department is Tibetan whereas the medium of instruction from Class VI onwards is English. Up to Class VIII, the syllabi prepared by the NCERT are followed except in the case of Tibetan language which is designed by Central Tibetan Administration, Dharamsala. In Classes IX and X, the syllabi prescribed by the CBSE are followed.

At the +2 stage the Administration imparts education in Humanities, Science, Commerce and Vocational streams. Under Commerce-based Vocational streams, three courses have been in operation: Stenography (English), Accountancy and Auditing and Purchasing and Store Keeping.

The Administration runs 87 schools-eight senior secondary schools (six Residential and two Day Schools):

five Secondary Schools: nine Middle Schools: eight Primary Schools and 45 Pre-Primary Schools and 12 Grant-in-Aid Schools. 11,0 17 students are receiving education in these schools.

To ensure uniformity of academic standard, Common Annual Examination at the end of Class V, VIII, IX and XI are conducted by the Administration. Besides, these Physical and Health Education and SUPW form an integral part of the syllabus. Music and dance training is compulsory for all students up to Class X. Due stress is laid on National Core Curriculum, Value Education and Environmental Studies.

To encourage students to pursue further education, 15 Tibetan students are given scholarships for pursuing degree level courses and five students for diploma level courses. The Government of India has reserved some seats for Tibetan students in professional courses like Medical, Engineering, Teacher Education, pharmacy, etc. in diploma/degree level courses.

The CTSA has introduced some innovative schemes for achieving academic excellence. Remedial teaching for students of Classes X and XII is one such scheme to improve performance of students in the CBSE examination.

For professional development of teachers a number of in-service training courses are organised in collaboration with the NCERT and country, where there is concentration of CIIL, Mysore as well as with the Department of Education, MHRD and CTA, Dharamsala

Moreover, the CTSA has introduced a scheme of incentives to Indian teachers for acquiring proficiency in Tibetan language to promote closer interaction with the students.

National awards for teachers

The scheme of National Awards for Teachers was started in the year 1958-59 with the object to give public recognition to the meritorious teachers working in Primary, Middle and Higher Secondary schools. In 1967-68 the scope of the scheme was enlarged to cover the teachers of Sanskrit Pathshalas, Tolls, etc. run on traditional lines. In 1976 the scheme was further enlarged to cover Arabic/Persian teachers of Madrasas run on traditional lines. From 1993, the scheme has further been enlarged to cover teachers of Sainik Schools, Navodaya Vidyalayas and schools run by the Atomic Energy Education Society.

Each award carries a certificate of merit, cash award of Rs 10,000 and a silver medal. The number of awards have been increased from 296 to 302 from the year 1993.

Two hundred and sixty-one teachers were selected for the National Award for 1997. These awards were presented by the President of India on 5 September 1998 at a function organised at Vigyan Bhawan, New Delhi.

National Foundation for Teachers' Welfare

The National Foundation for Teachers' Welfare (NFTW) was set up in 1962 under the Charitable Endowments Act, 1890. The main objective of the Foundation is to promote the welfare of the school teachers, and to alleviate distress among them and their dependents in indigent circumstances through financial assistance.

The affairs of the organisation are managed through a General Committee under the Chairmanship of the Minister for Human Resource Development with Ministers in charge of School Education in the States/UTs as its Members. State level committees of the Foundation exist under the Chairmanship of the Education Ministers of States and Lt. Governors of Union Territories, respectively.

Annual contributions from Member States/ UTs and 10 per cent of the collections of donations on Teachers' Day constitute the corpus of the Foundation. The States/ UTs retain 90 per cent of the proceeds of donations. Funds of the Foundation at the Central level are invested in five-year time deposits through the Treasurer of Charitable Endowments for India (TCE).

Financial assistance is extended through the following schemes:

— Construction of Shikshak Sadans
— Subsidy for academic activities of teachers
— Paid holiday to the awardee teachers
— Support for professional education of children of school teachers
— Gratuitous relief in cases of serious accidents
— Grant of financial assistance to teachers for serious ailments.

The Foundation annually selects three teachers for the Prof. D.C. Sharma Memorial Award, instituted in 1970 in memory of the eminent educationist. Selections for 1994 and 1995 were made during the year under report.

Improvement of science education in schools

TO improve the quality of science education and promote scientific temper, as envisaged in the National Policy on Education 1986, a Centrally Sponsored Scheme 'Improvement of Science Education in Schools' has been operational since 1987-88. The scheme uses the resource and agency of the State Government and non-governmental organisations for achievement of these objectives.

Accordingly, 100 per cent assistance is provided to the States/Union Territories for provision of science kits to upper primary schools, upgradation of science laboratories and library facilities in Secondary/ Senior

Secondary schools and training of science and mathematics teachers. The scheme also provides for assistance to voluntary organisations for undertaking innovative projects in the field of science education.

Environmental orientation to school education

The National Policy on Education (NPE), 1986 provides that the protection of environment is a value which, along with certain other values, must form an integral part of curricula at all stages of education. Operationalisation of this novel objective requires that the mind and intellect of the students must be sensitised about the hazards inherent in over-exploiting the bounties of Nature, and to inculcate awareness and respect among them for the basic concepts relating to conservation of environment.

To this end, a Centrally Sponsored Scheme 'Environmental Orientation to School Education' was initiated in 1988-89. The scheme envisages assistance to State Governments/UT Administrations and voluntary agencies. The voluntary agencies are assisted for the conduct Of experimental and innovative programmes aimed at promoting integration of educational programmes in schools with local environmental conditions. The scheme envisages grants to States/UTs for various activities including review and development of curricula of various disciplines at primary, upper primary, secondary and senior secondary levels with a view to infusing environmental concepts therein; review and development of textbooks on 'Environmental Studies' at primary and upper primary levels: review of strategy for imparting environmental education at upper primary level; development of teaching-learning material: organisation of suitable innovative work experience activities. The scheme has been restricted to voluntary organisations only from 1996-97.

International science Olympiads

With a view to identifying and nurturing talent in Mathematics and Physics at school level, the International Mathematical Olympiad (IMO) and International Physics Olympiad (IPO) are held every year. India has been participating in these Olympiads since 1989 and 1998, respectively. Each participating country is required to send a team comprising not more than six secondary student contestants to IMO and five secondary student contestants to IPO apart from a leader and a deputy team leader.

As per the existing financial pattern, the host country pays for the food and accommodation and transportation of the participating teams during their stay in the host country, while the International travel cost is borne by the participating countries. Indian teams in the last Olympiads were jointly sponsored by the Department of Education, MHRD and the National Board for Higher Mathematics (NBHM) / Homi Bhabha Centre for Science Education (HBCSE), respectively. The cost of international travel was paid by the Department of Education while all other expenses on selection of students, internal travel, incidental expenses, etc. were borne by the NBHM/ HBSCE.

IMO-98 was held at Taipai, Taiwan in July 1998. Indian delegation participated in the event and won three gold and three silver medals. At IPO-98 held at Reyjavik (Iceland) during July 1998, Indian team won one silver and one bronze medals, while three contestants received honourable mentions.

Educational technology

This is a Centrally Sponsored Scheme combining certain elements of a Central Plan Scheme. This scheme seeks to provide the entire cost of radio-cum-cassette players in Primary Schools and 75 per cent cost of colour TVs in

Upper Primary Schools to provide access to quality education. To enable production of suitable programmes for these schools, six autonomous State Institutes of Educational Technology (SIETs) in Uttar Pradesh, Bihar, Orissa, Maharashtra, Gujarat and Andhra Pradesh, have also been funded under the scheme. The scheme also extends financial support to the Central Institute of Educational Technology (CIET) for producing programmes for the schools sector for telecast/ broadcasting through Doordarshan and Akashvani.

At present all the programmes for the schools sector for broadcasting through Akashvani and telecast through Doordarshan are produced by the CIET and SIETs.

So far 3,87,438 radio-cum-cassette players and 74,001 colour TVs have been sanctioned to States and UTs for installation in Primary/ Upper Primary Schools. During 1997-98, the CIET and SIET's have together produced 708 (169 audio and 539 video) programmes.

The Central Institute of Indian Languages (CIIEL), Mysore has been funded for production of cassettes for learning certain Indian languages at the school level.

Educational concessions

The Government of India and most of the States/ UTs offer educational concessions by way of reimbursement of tuition fees, boarding-lodging expenses, expenditure incurred on uniforms, textbooks, transport charges, etc. to the school students who are the wards of Armed Forces personnel killed or permanently disabled during Indo-China hostilities of 1962 and Indo-Pak hostilities of 1965 and 197 1. During 1988 these concessions were extended to the children of IPKF/CRPF personnel who were killed/disabled during action in Sri Lanka and to the children of Armed Forces personnel killed/disabled in action in Operation Meghdoot in Siachen area.

Computer literacy

Realising that children, who are the work-force of tomorrow, need to be exposed to utility and applications of computers, the Department of Electronics, in collaboration with the MHRD, initiated a pilot project Computer Literacy and Studies in Schools (CLASS) from the year 1984 85. The broad objectives of this pilot project included domestication of computers, and to provide hands-on experience.

The CLASS Project was modified and converted into a Centrally Sponsored Scheme from the year 1993-94. Under the revised scheme to be eligible for assistance the following conditions are to be satisfied by the States/UTs.

— The coverage of the scheme for new schools will be restricted to senior secondary schools.

— In selected schools, instructions in Computer Literacy will be compulsory for all students of Classes XI and XII.

The National Steering Committee under the Chairmanship of Education Secretary is responsible for monitoring and supervision of the project. At State/UT levels cells set up for the purpose will discharge the dual responsibility of monitoring and actual implementing agencies 2,371 schools have been covered under the revised CLASS scheme during the Eighth Five Year Plan.

Scheme hostel facilities

One of the main factors responsible for slow pace of growth of enrolment of adolescent girls of rural, tribal and other remote areas is the traditional, societal inhibitions against their movement outside the family precincts. Since the Secondary/ Higher Secondary Schools in such places are sparsely located, the girls remain particularly disadvantaged. In order to implement the recommendations in POA-1992 for formulating a special enabling plan to ensure increase in enrolment of girls in secondary education and the NPE directive for encouraging NGO participation in education, it was decided to launch the above-mentioned scheme during the Eighth Plan.

Under the Scheme for Strengthening of Boarding and Hostel Facilities for Girl Students of Secondary and Higher Secondary Schools, financial assistance is being given to the eligible voluntary organisations to improve the enrolment of adolescent girls belonging to rural areas and weaker sections. Preference in providing assistance is given to educationally backward districts, particularly those predominantly inhabited by SCs/STs and educationally backward minorities in the secondary and higher secondary schools.

The following types of grant are given under the scheme:

1. Rs 5000 per annum per girl boarder for food and salary of cook and warden if the hostel/boarding house accommodate atleast 25 girl boarders who are students of Classes IX-XII of recognised schools would get assistance under this scheme subject to an overall number of 50 boarders.
2. One time grant of Rs 1500 per girl boarders for purchase of furniture (including beds) and utensils and provision of basic recreational aids, particularly material for sports and games, reading room equipments and books.

Scheme culture and values in education

Education about India's common cultural heritage has been identified in the National Policy on Education as one of the core areas under the National System of Education. While spelling out the cultural perspective in education, the policy has stressed on the need to bridge the schism between the formal system of education and India's rich and varied cultural traditions.

In 1990, a decision was taken to review the earlier scheme of strengthening Culture/Art/ Values in Education to make it more purposeful. A reformulated scheme of Assistance for Strengthening Culture and Values in Education was introduced in the last quarter of 1992-93. The revised scheme has the following two broad components:

— Strengthening Cultural and Value Education inputs in the school and non formal education system.

— Strengthening the in-service training of art, craft, music and dance teachers.

The scheme has provided greater awareness among voluntary organisations and also the greater significance of value education.

Higher education

There has been a phenomenal proliferation of University and Higher Education in the country since Independence. At the dawn of Independence there were only 20 universities and 591 colleges, while up to November 1998, the number of universities has increased to 182 and the number of institutions deemed to be universities was 40 besides four institutions established under State Legislature Act.

Revision of pay scales of university

The Pay Review Committee set up by the UGC under the chairmanship of Prof. R.P. Rastogi, former Vice-Chancellor, Banaras Hindu University submitted its report on 28 May 1997. After taking into consideration the recommendations made by the Committee, comments of the UGC, representations received from various quarters and the outcome of the wide-ranging discussions, the government announced revised pay scales and other conditions of service of university and college teachers on 27.7.98 and with further modifications on 6.11.98. Consequently the UGC finalised and notified the scheme of revised scales and service conditions on 24 December 1998. The changed pay structure and conditions of services of teachers are aimed at attracting talents to teaching in University and Colleges, awarding merits and promoting excellence in the profession.

The State Governments have also been requested to adopt these scales for their university and college teachers. For this purpose the Centre has agreed to provide assistance to the extent of 80 per cent of the additional expenditure involved, for a period of five years.

Submission of report by the task force

The Government of India constituted a Task Force under the Chairmanship of Prof. Amrik Singh, former Vice-Chancellor of Punjabi University, Patiala to examine the relevant provisions of the UGC Act with a view to suggest amendments in order to provide suitable safeguards against the incidence of fake universities and to empower the Commission to cope with the emerging challenges with confidence and to strengthen and restructure the Commission. The Task Force deliberated for over four months and submitted its report on 15 February 1999. The important recommendations of the Task Force are (i) provision of five whole-time members in addition to the Chairperson; (ii) increase in the number of members to 15 and of the nominated category, at least one-third should be women; (iii) suitable punishment including a term of imprisonment fine ranging between one lakh and ten lakh rupees for contravening Sections 22 and 23 of the Act; (iv) opportunity for establishment of private or self-financing universities in the country, subject to observance of rules made by the Government for the establishment of such universities; and (v) the recognition of universities or institutions which may confer degrees including the operation of foreign universities /institutions in the country for running their courses and programme of studies.

World conference on higher education

India participated in the World Conference on Higher Education convened by UNESCO, in Paris, between 5-9 October 1998 with a high level delegation led by the Minister for Human Resource Development. The conference delebrated upon the needs and challenges of the higher education in the twenty-first century, "Vision and Action". The Indian delegation made significant contributions to the World Declaration by suggesting modifications and amendments, most of which were accepted; one such which received big applause was the world leaders of higher education reads as under:

> Ultimately, higher education should aim at the creation of a new society-nonviolent and non-exploitative-consisting of highly cultivated, motivated and integrated individuals, inspired by love for humanity and guided by wisdom.

The rapputeur of the conference observed that India's amendment was 'too beautiful to be rejected'.

University Grants Commission

The University Grants Commission (UGC), an apex body in the field of higher education is responsible for coordination, determination and maintenance of standards in higher education. It advises the Central and State Governments on the measures necessary for the improvement of university education besides framing regulations on various aspects of higher education. It also determines disbursement of funds for maintenance and development of Central/State Universities, and some colleges which qualify for such assistance. Some of the major thrust areas pursued by the UGC during the year under report are discussed below.

Ninth plan development schemes

The Commission's Policy for development of undergraduate and post-graduate education in the colleges during the Ninth Plan period will have the following main aims/objectives:

— Improvement of standards and quality of education.

— Removal of social disparities and regional imbalances in higher educational facilities. Restructuring of courses including developing career thrust in the courses.

— Grant of autonomous status to qualifying colleges.

To achieve these objectives, the Commission will provide assistance to the colleges which fulfil the minimum eligibility conditions and have the necessary viability and potential and are striving for better standards.

During the Ninth Plan, the UGC has launched many new schemes under the broad headings of (a) Relevance and Quality, (b) Access and Equity, (c) Extra Moral/ Adult, Continuing Education and Outreach and (d) Management of Education and Resource Mobilisation.

The Pay Review Committee submitted its report to the Commission on 28 May 1997. The report was sent to the Universities, Teachers' Associations and State Education Secretaries for higher education. The Commission had wide ranging discussions on the recommendations of the Pay Review Committee.

The UGC is finalising its notification on qualification and service conditions based on the Pay Committee Report in consultation with the MHRD.

Human resource development

The Commission has been striving to develop human resources and towards this end it provides assistance for various programmes which enable teachers and researchers to upgrade professional competence and keep abreast of the latest developments in their disciplines. Assistance for various types of Scholarships and Fellowships is provided to achieve this objective. Junior Research Fellowship is awarded to those research scholars who have qualified in the national level tests conducted by the UGC, CSIR, GATE, etc. Teachers in universities and colleges are given an opportunity to pursue research for a brief period of time without having to undertake full teaching responsibilities.

During the year under report, the Commission continued the scheme of Visiting Faculty in the universities so as to provide teaching/research assignments outside Kashmir to the teachers from Kashmir University and its affiliated colleges due to disturbed conditions there.

Studies in inter-disciplinary areas

Courses like Super -conductivity, Atmospheric 'Science, Environmental Education, Computer Application, etc. are included under this scheme.

The total number of universities supported under the Super-conductivity programme up to November 1998, was 35. It is supporting seven universities under the Atmospheric science programme. Courses in the emerging areas like computer application, functional Hindi, biotechnology, environment education, energy education, electronics, futurology, business administration, communication and remote sensing were being reviewed during the year under report.

Innovative programmes

The scheme aims at providing a framework for assistance to a limited number of innovative projects, not covered by other UGC schemes, within the available resources of the UGC. Some of the innovative programmes include Cognitive Science, Mathematical Modelling and

Designing through Computer graphics, Development of Microscale Experiments in Chemistry, setting up of Human Rights department in a university, development of Terracotta mural, etc.

The two programmes, viz. Courses in Emerging Areas and Innovative Programmes were integrated during the year and named Innovative Programmes for implementation during the Ninth Plan period. The Superconductivity R and D programme and the Atmospheric Science Programme are also now part of the Innovative Programmes.

Area studies programme

The Commission is providing assistance to centres identified as Area Study Centres for undertaking studies relating to problems and culture of a given area and developing interdisciplinary research and teaching within a comparative framework. The focus is on such countries and regions with which India has had close and direct contact. There were 20 such centres being funded in 17 universities.

Vocationalisation of education

The UGC launched the scheme of Career Orientation of Education at the first degree level in the universities and colleges in 199495, in conformity with the National Policy on Education. Under the scheme, universities/ colleges would introduce one to three vocational courses in 35 subjects identified by the Core Committee.

There are inbuilt training programmes for equipping teachers of the respective institutions for teaching the vocational subjects which are arranged for them through identified nodal institutions.

The UGC has identified areas to cater to the needs of under-developed and rural sectors specially women, tribal and hilly regions.

Subject panels

The UGC has panels of experts to advise it on measures to enhance the quality of teaching and research in various subjects, to prepare status reports regarding research and teaching facilities available in the universities, to indicate thrust areas, and to advise the Commission on other relevant matters. The recommendations of these panels contribute to updating and modernising courses and introducing new dimensions in teaching and research. There are 28 subject panels in various disciplines of Science, Humanities and Social Sciences. A major task taken up by these panels during the year was to revise the syllabus for the NET examination.

Autonomous colleges

The concept of autonomous colleges is aimed at providing academic freedom for potential colleges by way of designing their curricula, evolving new methods of teaching, research and learning, framing own rules for admission, prescribing own courses of study and conduct of examinations. Under the scheme of autonomous colleges, a college declared autonomous by its affiliating university is fully accountable for the content and quality of education it imparts. Such a college is also responsible for setting up its own examination papers and for the conduct of examinations. The college evaluates the students for the award of degrees which will be accepted by the parent university. Up to November 1998, 123 colleges were functioning as autonomous colleges spread over eight States, viz. Tamil Nadu, Andhra Pradesh, Madhya Pradesh, Orissa, Uttar Pradesh, Gujarat, Maharashtra and Himachal Pradesh.

Teacher recruitment

During the year, the Commission conducted qualifying test for determining the eligibility for lecturership and for award of Junior Research Fellowship in Humanities and

Social Sciences. Similar test in science subjects was conducted jointly by the UGC and the CSIR.

Teacher training

Under the Academic Staff Orientation Scheme for orientation of newly recruited and in-service college and university lecturers, the 45 Academic Staff Colleges identified by the Commission organised orientation programmes for new teachers and refresher courses for in-service teachers.

Improvement in efficiency

The Commission provided grants for setting up computer centres in 125 universities up to November 1998. Also, assistance was provided for upgradation of computer facilities in the computer centres of various universities. In addition, the Commission provided assistance to 3,137 colleges up to November 1998 for installing computer facilities. Universities were also assisted by the UGC for introducing Computer Application paper at PG level in all subjects wherever there was relevant need for it. As many as 13 universities were assisted under the scheme up to November 1998.

Development of engineering/technology

The UGC provides financial assistance to the universities / institutions for their Engineering and Technology Departments to enable them to carry out various programmes of higher education and research. Assistance was provided to 11 Technological Universities and 25 State/ Central/ Deemed to be Universities.

A new scheme 'Technology for Women' in women universities was introduced during 1998-99 for providing financial assistance for introduction of under-graduate courses in Engineering and Technology. Under the scheme, assistance would be provided for recurring and non-recurring items for a period of five years from the date of implementation of the course. To begin with, five women universities have been identified under the scheme during the Ninth Plan.

COSIST scheme

One hundred sixty-five departments have been assisted under the scheme of strengthening Infrastructure in Science and Technology Education (COSIST) and research till November 1998. Assistance under this programme is a one-time input. Departments supported under COSIST have been given functional autonomy. The infrastructural facilities extended through COSIST support have attracted additional funds not only from funding agencies in India but also from abroad and have improved teaching instructions both at the post-graduate and research level by enhancing the quality of teaching, particularly the experimental part of the courses.

Common facilities

The UGC assists a large number of centres as national facilities. There are six Inter University Centres and 11 other Centres as national facilities/ Information Centres assisted by the UGC. The Inter-University Centres are namely Nuclear Science Centre, Delhi, Inter-University Centre for Astronomy and Astro-physics, Pune, Inter-University Consortium for DAE Facilities, Indore, National Assessment and Accreditation Council, Bangalore, Information and Library Network (INFLIBNET), Ahmedabad and Consortium of Educational Communication, New Delhi.

Education international

Education International (EI), a commercial organisation, has been set up by the MHRD and the UGC under the overall supervision of CEC. El has a mandate to promote and sell educational programmes available with CEC, IGNOU, NCERT and NOS in the international market. It also markets CEC programmes nationwide.

Educational outreach activities

The guidelines for the scheme of Adult and Continuing Education, Extension and Field Outreach activities were revised for the Ninth Plan period.

The Ninth Plan guidelines involve the following programmes:

— Vocational/ career -oriented programmes
— Equivalency programme
— Quality of life improvement programme
— Leadership and human resource development programme
— Social and citizenship role awareness programme
— Individual interest programme.

The Commission deputes university/college teachers to work with Bharat Gyan Vigyan Samithi on wholetime basis for nationwide literacy movement. Fifteen Teacher Fellowships have also been provided for this purpose. Population Education programme, assisted by the UGC, is implemented by the universities as part of the United Nations Population Fund (UNPF)-UGC project through the Population Education Resource Centres (PERCs).

Facilities for weaker sections

In order to ensure effective implementation of reservation Policy for SCs and STs, the UGC provides assistance to universities/ deemed to be universities for the establishment of SC/ST Cells. The, Commission under this scheme provides some positions of staff for running these Cells. There is also a scheme of 'Remedial Coaching for Scheduled Castes and Scheduled Tribes' being implemented in universities and colleges which aims at improving the skills and linguistic proficiency of the students in various subjects and raising their level of comprehension in such subjects where quantitative techniques and laboratory work are involved. A significant policy decision taken during the year was to create a Central Pool Database in the UGC for SC/ST candidates to consider their candidature for teaching positions in universities and colleges.

The Commission also continued to provide assistance to identified centres and cells (in universities and colleges, respectively) for conducting coaching classes for the educationally backward among minority communities for preparing them for competitive examinations other than the higher Civil Services as also classes for preparing students and providing training in shorthand/ typing, computer literacy, strengthening knowledge of English and regional languages, etc. Under the scheme of Junior Research Fellowship, the Commission has reserved some positions for SC/ST candidates out of the total number of such fellowships instituted for various universities. This is in addition to 50 fellowships which the Commission is directly awarding to SC/ST candidates.

Also, the Commission has reserved 40 Research Associateships for SCs and STs. In order to provide opportunity to SC/ST teachers in affiliated colleges, 50 teacher fellowships have been earmarked for them to improve their qualifications by doing M.Phil/Ph.D. Relaxation has also been made in the criteria for financial assistance to colleges having SC/ ST enrolment and to those located in the backward regions.

In order to oversee the implementation of the reservation policy in Central Universities, the Commission has appointed a Monitoring Committee under the Chairmanship of the Secretary, UGC. A Standing Committee has also been constituted to consider various issues relating to the Reservation Policy for SC/ST candidates.

The UGC has also been implementing the scheme of

Integrated Education for Disabled Children with the initial financial support and sponsorship by the Department of Education, MHRD. The teachers and students trained under this programme are mainly placed in teaching general education to handicapped children in Integrated and Special Schools, Government Services, NGOs, research organisations, etc. as rehabilitation workers/ field workers to help the disabled community.

Women's studies

Assistance is provided by the UGC to universities and colleges for setting up Centres and Cells for Women's Studies. The Centres/ Cells are required to undertake research, develop curricula, and organise training and extension work in the areas of gender equity, economic self-reliance of women, girls' education, population issues, issues of human rights and social exploitation. These Centres/ Cells are not expected to be like other conventional departments of the universities, as they are not required to run courses that lead to under-graduate or a post-graduate degree.

Project on information and library network

This project was started by the UGC in the Seventh Plan with the aim of establishing a nationwide network of university libraries and information centres to organise library and information services based on sharing of library resources in the country and to promote academic interaction among academicians. The Centre is now an Inter-University Centre of the UGC. Main activities of the Centre include computerisation of libraries, upgrading the skill of existing library staff to work in the computerised library environment, establishment of networking facilities, creation of academic databases and organisation of information services. Various software packages required for library management services have been developed at this Centre. It has also developed an

Integrated Library Management Software (ILMS) for management of libraries in collaboration with DESIDOC, for use in university libraries.

Promotion and preservation of Indian culture, heritage and values

The Commission continued to provide assistance on cent per cent basis under Plan funds for the promotion of Gandhian, Buddhist and Nehru studies. The assistance is provided for setting up centres for these studies, conducting programmes to acquaint teachers and students with their philosophy and ideas and for the purchase of books and journals relating to these studies. It was also decided during the year to introduce the scheme of promotion of Ambedkar Studies. Proposals in this regard have been invited from universities. The Commission has also been providing assistance for value-oriented education in order to foster among students and teachers alike such values which are necessary for retaining national identity and sustaining a peaceful and harmonious society. As part of value-oriented education, the Commission is also promoting the programmes of National Integration in collaboration with the Association of Indian Universities.

Human rights scheme

The Commission has initiated the Human Rights Scheme and guidelines for the same were framed for introduction of Human Rights courses at the P.G. /Certificate levels and for organising seminars, symposia and workshops. These guidelines form part of the UGC Ninth Plan Approach to Promotion of Human Rights Education in Universities and Colleges, 1998.

Promotion of physical education and sports

The Commission continued to provide assistance to universities and colleges for running the three-year degree course in physical education, health education and sports.

Resource mobilisation by universities

The Commission approved the revised Ninth Plan guidelines to support universities for their resource mobilisation efforts. The main objectives of the scheme are to encourage universities to mobilise resources by participation/contribution of society in their development and to encourage and enhance the flow of resources coming from the society for university development.

University-elementary education linkages

The UGC has been pursuing the universities to take up extension activities in social and economic areas in their areas. Realising that the Universalisation of Elementary Education remains a national goal and challenge and the universities are in a pivotal situation to join the movement, the UGC initiated dialogues, during the year, with academicians, educationists, NGO representatives and Vice-Chancellor to bring out a policy strategy paper on university-elementary education linkages. The UGC paper encourages university academic community to take up research, evaluation, training, development, etc. to support and strengthen the elementary school system in the areas of their operation. One such pilot initiative was arrived by the Mumbai University in a meeting taken by the Chairperson in Mumbai. The Department of Education has committed to support the universities' initiative by funds also under its various schemes meant for the NGO's programme for elementary education indicating for the training ard research.

Jamia Millia Islamia

Jamia Millia islamia (JMI) which had been functioning as a Deemed to be University since 1962 acquired the status of a Central University in December 1988. The University imparts education from the Nursery stage to Post-graduate and Doctorate levels. It has six Faculties and eight Centres (excluding Balak Mata Centres). There has been a constant increase in the number of books and research journals in Dr Zakir Hussain Library of the University. The number of books in the Library rose from 2,61,247 (1996-97) to 2,64,292 (1997-98).

The A.J. Kidwai Mass Communication Research Centre of JMI is not only providing training at Post-graduate level in Mass Communication but it is also producing educational material on different educational aspects/ subjects for the UGC, INSAT programme. One live Video Conference was recorded between studios at the Centre and studios in Paris, France.

A residential Management Development Programme for University Administrators instituted with the approval and financial support of the UGC provides necessary training to Deputy and Assistant Registrars and equivalent posts enabling them to be eligible for placement in the next grade. The Centre has organised four programmes in 1997-98 and successfully provided training to 84 administrators from all India universities and institutions of higher learning.

Visva-Bharati

Visva-Bharati, an educational institution founded by Guru Rabindranath Tagore, was incorporated as a Central University by the Visva-Bharati Act, 195 1. The University imparts education from the Primary School level to Post-Graduate and Doctorate levels. It has 11 Institutes—eight at Santiniketan and three at Sriniketan. As on 31 March 1998, there were 6,336 students on the rolls of the University including its School Sections. The total strength of teaching and non-teaching staff was 506 and 1586, respectively. A few new courses, namely, B.A. (Vocational), functional course in Hindi, two-year post graduate course in Biotechnology and two-year M.Sc. (Agriculture) course in Horticulture have been introduced.

The library of the. University has a total collection of 3,59,601 books and 2,592 journals. In addition, 2,89,128 books are housed at 12 Sectional Libraries of the University. Implementation of the Information and Library Network programme started in January 1998 is in progress.

While the major focus of development was rightly pointed out towards modernisation of both academic institutions and administrative management, rural segment of Visva-Bharati, i.e. Sriniketan has been taken up with some priority with creation of CAREER (Centre for Advanced Rural Education, Extension and Research) and CSV (Centre for Science in Villages). The avenue for exploring the potential strength of the adjoining villages has been extended enormously. With the establishment of Nirman Bhavan (Building Centre), a project under the sponsorship of HUDCO for creating facilities in the housing technology in the rural area, with a possibility of replication, tremendous breakthrough is in the offing.

Aligarh Muslim university

Aligarh Muslim University (AMU), established in 1920 as a Central University, is one of the premier fully residential academic institutions of the country. The University has 92 Departments/ Institutions/ Centres grouped under 11 Faculties. The University also maintains four Hospitals, six Colleges (including Medical, Dental and Engineering Colleges), two Polytechnics and eight Schools. Admissions to BDS course in Dental College established in 1997-98 have been made during the current academic session, viz. 1998-99.

The University also offers six diploma courses exclusively for women, in the fields of Electronics

Engineering, Electronics (TV Technology), Computer Engineering, Costume Design and Garment Technology, Office Assistantship and Secretariat Practice, and General Nursing and Midwifery. Seven new courses namely, B.A/ LL.B (five-year integrated course), M.A. (Human Rights), P.G. Diploma (Human Rights), Bachelor of Fine Arts, Master of Fine Arts, B.A. (Hons.) in Communicative English and Master of Journalism and Mass Communication were introduced in the current session.

During the year under report, the University has on its roll a total of 18,562 students (including school strength). The total strength of teaching staff of AMU is 1,457 and that of non-teaching staff 5,899.

Each Department of the University has a Seminar Library for PG and Research Students. Colleges like J.N. Medical College, A.K. Tibbiya College, Z.H. College of Engineering and Technology and Women's College have separate libraries.

Academic Staff College of AMU has organised three Orientation Programmes, nine subject Refresher Courses and three Induction Training Programmes (sponsored by the All India Council for Technical Education). In addition, eight Programmes/ Courses are planned to be organised during the remaining part of the current academic session.

With a view to promoting sports and allied activities the University maintains ten clubs. namely, Riding Club, Hockey Club, Tennis Club, Hiking and Mountaineering Club, Swimming Club, Athletic Club, Cricket Club, Football Club, Gymkhana Club and Gymnasium Club. AMU is the only University in India which maintains (a) a Riding Club and (b) a covered swimming pool.

Assam university

Assam University, Silchar was established on 21.1.1994. It

is a teaching-cum-affiliating University with its jurisdiction over the districts of Cachar, Karimganj, Karhi, Anglong and Hailakandi in the State of Assam. The University has granted affiliation to 53 colleges. The University has all its departments and offices at Dorgakona where the Government of Assam had allotted 600 acres of land.

The University has 24 Departments under 8 schools of studies and in addition, it has 3 centres of studies. The total number of faculty members is 101. The University library has 32,400 volumes and has a subscription of 300 National and International journals. The University library is fully computerised.

Babasaheb Bhimrao Ambedkar University

Babasaheb Bhimrao Ambedkar University, Lucknow was established in 1994. The University was notified as a Central University on 10 January 1996. It aims to provide instructional and research facilities in new and frontier areas of learning and to launch academic programmes in these areas. The University has set up three schools and three centres: School of Ambedkar Studies, School for Information Science and Technology and School for Environmental Studies and Centre for Rural Technology, Centre for Vocational Studies and Centre for Human Rights. The academic programmes in these Schools and Centres have started with a faculty strength of 13 members and 118 students including 54 SC/ST candidates.

Banaras Hindu University

Banaras Hindu University (BHU) came into existence in 1916 as a teaching and residential University. The University consists of three Institutions-Institute of Medical Sciences, Institute of Technology and Institute of Agricultural Sciences-and 14 Faculties with 121 academic departments and four Interdisciplinary Schools. The

University also maintains a constituent Mahila Mahavidyalaya and three School level institutions. Four colleges in the city are admitted to its privileges. It also has a 1000-bedded Modern/Ayurvedic Medicine Hospital. The University has 14,812 students on its rolls. The strength of its teaching and non-teaching staff is 1, 162 and 7,088, respectively. During the current academic session, the University established a Centre for Advanced Studies in Sciences. The University also created the Malaya Centre for Peace Research as an Inter-disciplinary Centre under the Faculty of Social Sciences.

Seven endowment funds have been instituted by the University for various scholarships/ medals/cash prizes.

Delhi University

The University of Delhi is a premier university of the country which is known for its high standards in teaching and research and attracts a large number of students not only from all over India but also from several other countries. Established in February 1922 as a unitary and residential university with a nucleus of three colleges, two faculties and about 750 students, it has grown, over the years, into one of the largest universities in the country. At present it has 14 faculties, 82 teaching departments and 78 colleges spread all over Delhi.

There are about 2,49,400 students presently enrolled in the University. About 1,31,400 of the students are enrolled in non-formal education programmes offered by the School of Correspondence and Continuing Education, Non-Collegiate Women Education Board and the External Candidates Cell. There are about 337 Professors, 213 Readers, 143 Lecturers and 26 Research Associates making the total strength of 719 of the Faculty of the University.

In a special convocation on 13 December 1998, the University conferred Honorary degrees to various eminent persons: Dr Abdul Kalam, Dr R.A. Mashalkar, Dr M.S. Valiathan, Dr John Rawis, Dr Ikeda, Dr Edward Said, Dr Sarup Singh, Dr M.N. Srinivas, Dr Amartya Sen, Sardar Raunaq Singh, Sint. Gangubai Hangal, Ustad Amjad Ali Khan and Prof. K.N. Raj. The University has also accepted in principle, institution of about 13 new courses in various fields. The University has approved the proposal for the institution of scholarships, viz. Dr Virendra B. Mahesh Fellowship and Nupur Mathur Memorial Scholarship in Business Economics.

University of Hyderabad

The University of Hyderabad, established by an Act of Parliament in 1974, is a premier institution of post-graduate teaching and research in the country. The academic activities of the University are undertaken through its eight Schools of Studies. Besides, the Centre for Distance Education of the University offers post-graduate diplomae in five disciplines.

The University has a faculty strength of 215 consisting of 69 Professors, 86 Readers and 60 Lecturers during the year under report.

The faculty of the University has obtained research support from several funding agencies. Over 105 such research projects are currently under investigation by the faculty. Some projects for investigation by the faculty have been sponsored by foreign agencies such as Naval Research of USA, Volkswagen Foundation of Germany and Rockefeller Foundation of USA. Several faculty members have won National and International awards. The University has also entered into a few Memoranda, of Understanding with local industrialists. Several eminent scholars from India and abroad occupied the two prestigious chairs named after Shri Jawaharlal Nehru and Dr Sarvapalli Radhakrishnan.

Jawaharlal Nehru University

Jawaharlal Nehru University (JNU) came into existence in 1969. It is primarily concerned with Post-graduate Education and Research. The University has seven Schools consisting of 24 Centres of Studies. In addition, it has a separate Centre for Bio-Technology. The strength of its teaching and non-teaching staff is 370 and 1,350, respectively. The total enrolment in the University was 3,892 students with adequate representation of SCs., STs and other backward classes.

The Faculty members of the JNU produced 400 publications which include 55 books, contributed 10 chapters to books and 235 research articles in various national and international journals of repute. The Faculty has at present 174 on-going research projects sponsored by various funding agencies. A number of distinguished faculty members received honours/awards from various national and international organisations..

The University library acquired 5,321 volumes of various bound periodicals and newspapers in the year under report. The total collection of books and periodicals now stands at 6,67,993 volumes.

The JNU Academic Staff College set up by the UGC to impart refresher courses and orientation training to college and university teachers for their academic development and growth and organised 13 refresher courses during this period.

Indira Gandhi National Open University

Indira Gandhi National Open University (IGNOU) was established in 1985 for introduction and promotion of Open University and distance education system in the educational pattern of the country and for the coordination and the determination of standards in such systems. The major objectives of the IGNOU include widening of access to higher education by providing opportunities to large segments of the population, particularly the disadvantaged groups, organising programmes of continuing education and initiating special programmes of higher education for specific target groups like women, people living in backward regions, hilly areas, etc.

The University is offering 43 programmes. During 1998, the total number of students registered for various programmes was 1,63,000. The network of Students Supports Services in 1998 consist of 19 Regional Centres and 346 Study Centres. Three more Regional Centres are likely to be established during 1998-99 at Srinagar Valley, Dehradun and Chandigarh or Jalandhar.

The telecast of IGNOU programmes on the Doordarshan Network continued on every Monday, Wednesday and Friday up to September 1998. From October 1998 onwards IGNOU started telecast of its programmes for half an hour a day for six days from Monday to Saturday.

As part of its mandate for training of distance educational personnel, Staff Training and Research Institute in Distance Education (STRIDE) continued to organise workshops.

The IGNOU Act was amended in 1997 to allow the university to set up its Study Centre, outside the country with the approval of the Visitor.

The Distance Education Council (DEC) will assume the responsibility for development of correspondence education programmes offered by the traditional universities during the Ninth Plan. In the initial phase, the effort will be to transform the programmes into mainstream of distance education programmes. The DEC has finalised guidelines for providing development support to State Open Universities as well as the Directorates of Correspondence Education in the traditional universities.

Nagaland University

Nagaland University was established on 6 September 1994 by an Act of Parliament with headquarters at Lumami. It is an affiliating University with its jurisdiction over the whole of the State of Nagaland. Presently, the University is functioning from its campuses in Kohima, Lumami and Medziphema (School of Agricultural Sciences and Rural Development (SASRD). The University presently has 25 departments located in three campuses with 4 schools of studies. The total number of faculty members is 109. The University has 39 colleges affiliated to it. The University library, Kohima has 27,000 volumes and 139 periodicals/journals. The SASRD Library Campus has 18,000 volumes.

North-Eastern Hill University

The North-Eastern Hill university was established in 1973 at Shillong. It has a campus in Aizwal and a Centre in Tura. The University has 31 Post-graduate Departments and four Centres of Studies under its six Schools of Studies and an Under-graduate College. There are 58 Under-graduate Colleges and eight professional course colleges and North-Eastern Regional Institute of Science and Technology (NERIST) affiliated to it. The University also has Regional Sophisticated Instrumentation Centre (RSIC).

The University has an enrolment of 693 Post-graduate students and 65 research scholars, 19,716 Under-graduate students, and 2,274 professional course students during the year 1998-99.

The University Central Library has a collection of 1,61,737 books, 3,60,028 bound periodicals and a subscription of 316 foreign and 366 Indian journals. The Mizoram campus library has a total of 2,621 books and a subscription of 66 journals. The University has conducted various seminars/ conferences on such subjects as 'Role of Microbes in Environmental Protection', 'DNA Damage Repair and Radiation Calcinigenesis', and 'Anthropology and Allied Discipline in the North-East Region'.

Pondicherry University

Pondicherry University, established in 1985 as a teaching-cum-affiliating university, has its jurisdiction over the Union Territory of Pondicherry and Andaman and Nicobar Islands. As enshrined in the Act, Sri Aurobindo School of Eastern and Western Thought, Sri Subramaniya Bharathi School of Tamil Language and Literature have been established and given special attention. Pondicherry being the window of French Culture, French Studies is also given its due importance.

The University has six Schools, 16 Departments and 12 Centres and offers one Certificate, two P.G. Diploma and 27 Postgraduate courses, 17 M.Phil, 22 doctoral programmes and five-year integrated Master's Degree programme in two Aisciplines. The University has 22 affiliated institutions of which 13 are located in Pondicherry, three in Karaikal, two in Mahe, one in Yanam and three in Andaman and Nicobar Islands. The total students strength in these institutions is 16,374. The students enrolment in the University is 1257. The University has a faculty strength of 138 experienced teachers, 37 Professors, 42 Readers and 59 Lecturers. There are 566 non-teaching staff. There are five hostels, out of 650 hostel students, 208 are women and 120 are SC/ST students.

An innovative credit-based PG programme has been introduced since 1992-93 and this has attracted students from all over India. The credit system enables the students to construct their own curriculum and to complete the PG programme at their own pace. It also helps to develop academic networking with other universities institutions.

Pondicherry University had established the Centre for Pollution Control and Biowaste Energy in 1991 to give a renewed thrust to the University's efforts in providing advanced training, research, and consultancy facilities for regional as well as national benefit. During 1997-98 the Centre was further strengthened in terms of laboratory infrastructure and computational facilities which were procured mainly with the funds generated by the Centre through its industrial consultancy and R&D projects. As a consequence the Centre has taken rapid strides forward and is already beginning to be recognised as one of the foremost institutions of its type in India.

The University entered into a Memorandum of Understanding with the University of Rennes-2 (France); Poitiers University, France; University of Technology, Australia; and Marne la Vallee University, France in addition to five MOUs already entered with the IGNOU.

The Special Cell started in 1987 took all measures for the welfare of the SC/ST and physically handicapped students. Due reservations for SC/ST and physically handicapped candidates were given in admission as per Government of India orders. Out of the students admitted in the first year nearly 32 per cent teachers were women students. Of the 606 students on roll 84 were SC/ST. The number of women students on roll is 195.

Maulana Azad National Urdu University

Maulana Azad National Urdu University was established at Hyderabad mainly to promote and develop Urdu language and to impart vocational and technical education in Urdu medium through conventional and distance education system. The University Act was passed by the Parliament in 1997 and the University came into existence on 9 January 1998 with the enforcement of the Act.

Prof. Mohd. Shamim Jairajpuri and Dr M.S. Siddiqi

has been appointed as the first Vice-Chancellor and the first Registrar of the University, respectively, by the President of India in his capacity as the Visitor of the University. The first Executive Council of the University has also been constituted by the Visitor. As a gesture the Government of Andhra Pradesh has allotted 200 acres of land for the University free of cost.

The administrative office of the University has been set up at Hyderabad. Regional offices at Delhi, Patna and Bangalore have also been set up. The University organised two symposia to formulate its developmental proposal/layout. During the current academic session, the University has started B.A. course in Urdu medium through distance education mode.

Mahatma Gandhi Antar-rashtriya Hindi Vishwavidyalaya

Mahatma Gandhi Antarrashtriya Hindi Vishwavidyalaya Act, 1996 seeking establish the Mahatma Gandhi antarrashtriya Hindi Vishwavidyalaya at Wardha was passed by the Parliament in December 1996. The University has come into existence with effect from 29 December 1997. Dr Ashok Vajpeyi has been appointed as the first Vice-Chancellor by the President of India as the Visitor of the University.

Though the University will be located at Wardha, given the international character of the institution and initial preparatory responsibilities, the Vice-Chancellor shall have to function from Delhi for some time during the preparatory phase. The first Executive Council of the University has also been constituted by the President in his capacity as Visitor of the University. The Government of Maharashtra has agreed to allocate land for the University at Wardha.

Tezpur University

Tezpur University is a non-affiliated unitary Central

University set up in 1994. Its aim is to offer employment-oriented and interdisciplinary courses, mostly at post-graduate level, to meet the local and regional aspirations and the developmental needs of the region. The University has been offering courses and promoting research in emerging areas in Science and Technology. The total number of students enrolled during the year is 544. The total number of teachers is 67.

The University has 11 Departments under four Schools of Studies and six Centres of Studies. The first convocation of the University was held on 10 November 1998 wherein students of six Departments were awarded Post-graduate Degrees and Diplomas. Hon'ble President of India, the Visitor of the University, was the chief guest to the convocation. An International Conference on Disaster Management was held in April 1998.

Indian Institute of Advanced Study

The Indian Institute of Advanced Study (IIAS), set up in 1965, aims at free and creative enquiry into the fundamental themes and problems of life and thought. It is a residential centre for research and encourages promotion of creative thoughts in selected subjects like Humanities, Indian Culture, Comparative Religion, Social Sciences and Natural Sciences and in other areas as the Institute may from time to time decide. The Institute provides facilities for advanced consultation and collaboration besides exhaustive library and documentation facilities.

The IIAS awards fellowships for advanced research every year. The Institute holds three seminars each year on themes of national significance when outstanding scholars and experts are invited to join the members of the academic community of the Institute to examine theoretical issues and contemporary problems. Visiting Professors, both from India and abroad, are invited from time to time to deliver a series of lectures at the Institute.

Indian Council of Philosophical Research

Indian Council of Philosophical Research (ICPR) was set up by the Government to promote research in philosophy and allied disciplines. In order to achieve its aims and objects, the Council awards fellowships, organises seminars, conferences, workshops and refresher courses, provides financial support to organise seminars/ workshops, travel grant to scholars to present their papers at conferences/ seminars held aboard, sponsors major and minor projects and brings out publications and a triannual journal Journal of Indian Council of Philosophical Research. The ICPR offered four senior fellowships, 11 general fellowships, 17 junior research fellowships, four residual fellowships and one short-term fellowship during the year under report (up to November 1998).

Indian Council of Historical Research

The Indian Council of Historical Research (ICHR) was established in 1972 with a view to providing funds for historical research and to foster objective and scientific study of history. It has been promoting historical research including the history of art, literature and philosophy and allied subjects such as archaeology, numismatic, epigraphy, and the historical study of manuscripts. The Council awards fellowships, study-cum-travel grants and publication subsidies. It also endeavours to make available source material as well as result of historical research through an ambitious publication programme. It also brings out a journal The Indian Historical Review which includes interpretative papers and reviews. It organises seminars and academic conferences and gives financial assistance for travel within and outside the country for conducting historical research. The Council also maintains a large and continuously expanding library for the use of historians and researchers. Documentation services are also provided.

The most important function of the ICHR is to provide assistance to scholars/institutions for research and publications. National Fellowships are awarded to eminent historians who wish to work on projects of special historical importance.

Indian Council of Social Science Research

The Indian Council of Social Science Research (ICSSR) was established in 1969 with the objective to support and sponsor purposive and meaningful research in social sciences in India. The Council provides maintenance and development grants to 27 research institutes spread over the entire country. The Council has also established six Regional Centres for identification and development of talent through various programmes. During 1998-99, 130 new research projects are proposed to be sanctioned and 90 reports to be received for projects sanctioned earlier.

The Council will continue its Cultural Exchange Programmes (CEPs) with Russia, France, the Netherlands, China, South Korea and Vietnam in addition to new CEPs with Japan and SAARC. The Council has been actively participating in the activities of international organisations like ISSC, UNESCO, AASSREC, etc.

Indo-Dutch is one of the important bilateral programmes being implemented by the ICSSR in India and the Netherlands Organisation for International Cooperation in Higher Education in the. Netherlands. The collaborative programme has entered the fourth phase. Funding of the project will be continuing during 1999-2000.

The National Social Service Documentation Centre (NASSDOC) provides research information services to social scientists and researchers. It is currently involved in the development of a National Information Network in Social Sciences.

The data archives of the Council has been developed as a repository of primary data generated through research studies supported by the Council. It is also proposed to provide guidance and consultancy services in data processing to 60 scholars through 11 institutions. A major new initiative proposed in the Ninth Plan is to set up a network of socio-economic data bankers.

The ICSSR has been carrying out surveys of research in different social science disciplines. The first series of surveys in all the disciplines have been published. The Council is updating these surveys every five years.

Dr. Zakir Hussain Memorial College Trust

Dr Zakir Hussain Memorial College Trust, Delhi was established In 1973 to take over the responsibility of the management and maintenance of Zakir Hussain College (formerly Delhi College), which is one of the constituents of the University of Delhi. The maintenance expenditure of the college is shared between the UGC and the Trust in the ratio of 95:5. In addition, the UGC provides development grant to the College. The matching contribution of such development expenditure is required to be made by the Trust. Since the Trust has no resources of its own, grants are provided by the Department of Education, MHRD for meeting the above expenditure. Financial assistance is also provided for meeting the administrative expenditure of the Trust.

Association of Indian Universities

The Association of Indian Universities (AIU) is a voluntary organisation of Indian universities and is registered under the Societies Registration Act. It is also a forum for university administrators and academics to come together to exchange views and to discuss matters of common concern. It acts as a bureau of information in Higher Education and brings out a number of useful publications, research papers and a weekly journal known as University News.

The AIU is substantially financed from the annual subscription of the member universities. The Government of India 'sanctions grants for meeting a part of the maintenance and development expenditure including the Research Cell set up to undertake research activities concerning the university system. The Research Cell undertakes various activities including research studies, workshops, training programmes, question banks, tournament and databases, etc. The Evaluation Division of the AIU continued its work related to the grant of equivalence to foreign degrees and the recognition of institutions in India. The Students Information Services Division continued to serve the students, academics, parents, etc. by providing them information on the status of Indian higher education institutions and on the courses offered through regular/correspondence study by Indian universities and other institutions recognised by AICTE/ Government agencies.

Scheme of financial assistance

The scheme of financial assistance to all India Institute of Higher Education has been continuing from one plan period to the next plan period. Under the scheme, the MHRD has been providing financial assistance to some voluntary organisations / educational institutions. Assistance under the scheme is provided to institutions which are outside the university system and which are engaged in programme of innovative character. The institutions which have been receiving assistance from the Central Government are:

— Sri Aurobindo International Institute of Educational Research, Auroville, Tamil Nadu

— Sri Aurobindo International Centre of Education, Pondicherry

— Lok Bharati, Sanosra, Gujarat

— Mitraniketan, Vellanad, Kerala

Since assistance to the above institutions is being provided under the plan scheme, continuance of assistance from one plan period to the next plan period has to be decided at the end of every plan. In order to examine and to recommend the nature and quantum of assistance to be provided to these institutions during the Ninth Plan period, Visiting Committees were constituted by the MHRD to visit the institutions to make an on-the-spot assessment of their performance and to recommend nature and scope of future assistance during the Ninth Plan period.

International cooperation

The interest of foreigners in Higher Education is reflected in the large number of foreign scholars coming to India for doing research. Besides the research projects sponsored by the American Institute of Indian Studies, the United States Educational Foundation in India and the Shastri Indo-Canadian Institute, large number of scholars come for doing research either on self-funding basis or scholarships from their countries/other sources. During 1998-99, the number of research projects approved by the Ministry of Human Resource Development is 373. The Government has approved a number of bilateral agreements between Indian universities and their counterparts abroad. There has been significant increase in the number of bilateral international conferences/ symposia/seminars/workshops in collaboration with foreign universities. During the year 19 proposals for seminars/symposia/international conferences were approved on a variety of subjects under the aegis of universities, autonomous Organisations and Institutions of higher learning. The Government also approved 14 proposals of foreign scholars as visiting lecturers / professors in Indian universities in the country.

United States Educational Foundation in India

The United States Educational Foundation in India (USEFI) was established in February 1950 under a bilateral agreement as replaced by a new agreement in 1963 between the Government of India and the Government of United States of America to administer the Fullbright Educational Exchange Programme to promote mutual understanding between the people of the two countries by a wider exchange of knowledge and professional talents through educational contacts.

During 1998-99, 21 visiting lecturers, 15 research scholars and 40 student professionals were given Fullbright grants ranging from 3 to 12 months. One grant was given to an Indian fellow under National Institute of Drug Abuse Programme of the Hubert H. Humphrey Fellowship. The USEFI also administers the East West Centre (EWC) grants by conducting workshops/senlinars on various themes involving Indian scholars at many of the EWC Institutes.

The Foundation also administers research scholar grants, short-term group programmes for school/college teachers, workshops/seminars involving visiting American professors/eminent Indian faculty for Indian college/university teachers in various fields besides the regular exchange programme.

American Institute of Indian Studies

The American Institute of Indian Studies (AIIS), a consortium of about 50 major universities was established in 1960 with the approval of the Government of India to promote Indian studies, civilization and culture in the United States.

The Institute awards Research and Language Fellowships. Five Group Projects were undertaken during the year under report. Five publications have also been brought out by the Institute. The Archives and Research

Centre for Ethnomusiology continued its activities in computerising its library, field recordings and organising workshops.

The AIIS Centre for Art and Archaeology published a comprehensive Bibliography on Imperial Gupta. The Institute has already published nine volumes of the Encyclopaedia of Indian Temple Architecture and work on more volumes is in progress. Considering the AIIS contribution to the academic world, the Board of Directors of Encyclopaedia, Britannica has established an Editorial Board to proceed further on the Encyclopaedia project.

To celebrate the 50th year of India's Independence, the Institute brought out a volume entitled *Commemorating* the 50th Anniversary of India's Independence: India's World's and US Scholars. 1947-97.

Shastri Indo-Canadian Institute

A binational non-profit making organisation was established in 1968 by joint announcements of the Governments of India and Canada and signing a Memorandum of Understanding between the Government of India and the Shastri Indo-Canadian Institute for the operation of the Institute in India initially for a period of three years, which has been renewed from time to time. Action for renewal of agreement for a further period of five years, i.e. 1 April 1999 to 31 March 2004 is being initiated.

The India Studies Programme of the Institute funded by the MHRD provides fellowship to Canadian scholars and supplies Indian imprints to Canadian Universities. The Government of India has approved visit of 22 scholars during 1998-99 under this programme.

The Canadian Studies Programme funded by the Foreign Affairs and International Trade, Canada offers fellowship to Indian scholars for research in Canada and also for visiting lecturerships for Canadian academics. It also supplies Canadian imprints to Indian universities. During 1998-99, 19 Indian scholars have been selected for the fellowship.

The CIDI-SICI Project (CSP) funded by the Canadian International Development Agency runs the partnership programme, the journalism programme, the distinguished speaker programme and the summer programme in India. The partnership programme which proved to be a very popular component of the CSP has entered its second phase. The Institute is ready to start eleven partnership projects in the area of Development related to Environment, Gender, Social and Economic Reform and private sector development.

The Institute in its role as a mediator and catalyst in academic and non-academic collaborative initiatives between India and Canada was honoured by the Governor General of Canada on 31 March 1998 during his official visit to India.

National Council of Rural Institutes

The National Council of Rural Institutes (NCRI) was set up on 19 October 1995 at Hyderabad with the following aims and objectives to:

(i) promote rural higher education on the lines of Mahatma Gandhi's ideas on education so as to take up challenges of micro planning for transformation of rural areas,

(ii) consolidate network and develop institutions engaged in programmes of Gandhian Basic Education and Nai Talim;

(iii) encourage other educational institutions and voluntary agencies to develop in accordance with the Gandhian philosophy of education.

The NCRI is preparing an Action Plan for promotion/ revival of existing rural institutes as also to encourage new initiatives. It has encouraged the setting up of Swami Ramanand Tirth Rural Institute at Pochampalli for which the State Government has transferred 17 acres of land and has agreed to provide 15 per cent of annual expenditure. The Council has decided to start Rural Institutes in various parts of the country, namely Andhra Pradesh, Orissa, Bihar, Madhya Pradesh, Maharashtra, North-East India and two other states.

Technical education

Technical education has great potential for adding value to products and services for contributing to the national economy and for improving the quality of life of the people. Technical education is being improvised by modernisation and removal of obsolescence, promoting institution-industry interaction, providing continuing education for upgrading the skill and knowledge of technical personnel working In industry and service sectors, transfer of technology to the rural sector/setting up of Technology Development Missions to meet the emerging challenges in science and technology.

Indian Institutes of Technology

The six Indian Institutes of Technology (IITs), located at Mumbai, Delhi, Kanpur, Kharagpur, Chennai and Guwahati were set up by the Government of India as 'Institutions of National Importance'. The objective of these Institutes is to impart quality education, second to none in the world in various areas of pure and applied sciences and in engineering and technology at the under-graduate and postgraduate levels to further the advancement of knowledge through the conduct of basic and applied research in pure and applied sciences and in engineering and technology and to disseminate and transfer the knowledge so generated for the benefit of Indian industry and the other user sectors.

The IITs have been acting as leaders in technology innovation, training the necessary manpower and promoting generally advanced technology in the country. They have been effective in enhancing the country's techno-economic strength and technological self-reliance. The IITs have distinguished themselves by the excellence of their under-graduates, postgraduates and research programmes in Engineering/Technology and Science. Sponsored research for different funding agencies in the public and private sectors, industrial consultancy and continuing education programmes also are areas in which the IITs have made significant contributions over the years.

A special preparatory course of 10 months' duration was conducted to improve the intake of SC/ST students in the IITs. The SC/ST students were provided financial support by way of free messing, pocket allowance, loans and discretionary grants.

Indian Institute of Science, Bangalore

The Indian Institute of Science (IISc), Bangalore, was set up in 1909 with the objective of imparting post-graduate education and carrying out research in various areas of basic science and engineering and technology. Over the years, the IISc has earned global reputation as an inspiring centre of excellence in research in all its areas of specialisation. It was given a status of Deemed University in 1958. It has succeeded in encouraging creativity, nurturing excellence and boosting innovative Research and Development, Technology Transfer and support to industrial problems.

Several departments of the Institute have the dimensions of the best national laboratories in terms of productivity and linkages.

The Institute has taken up several new activities. It has introduced an integrated Ph.D. programme. Young students are admitted to Ph.D directly after their B.Sc. degree. The Institute offers an External Registration programme where active engineers and researchers working in industries and R&D organisations can register for a Ph.D degree at the Institute. There is a programme on Continuing Education involving a large number of technical personnel in and around Bangalore through its proficiency activities. The Institute has taken up a programme of technology development involving industries in the areas of Advanced Materials, Biotechnology, Information Processing and Food Processing Technologies.

The Institute has recently established a Society for Innovation and Development to channelise the technological development of activities carried out at the Institute. The Institute has also taken up an activity SUTRA (Sustainable Transformation of Rural Areas) under the aegis of ASTRA (Application of Science and technologies to Rural Areas) and in this programme, the Institute applies modern developments in technology to rural upliftment. The emphasis will be on biogasifiers, low-cost building, reappropriation of energy and water sources and such other activities.

The Institute has established a Super Computer Centre of national importance. It has microwave link with international terminals. The IISc has close links with the Department of Space and Defence Research and Development Organisation (DRDO). The Institute handles around 200 consultancy projects entrusted by industry every year. A recent assessment by UNESCO has placed Indian Institute of Science at the eighteenth rank among universities in the world and first in the Asia-Pacific region.

Technology development missions

A need was felt that institutions of excellence such as IITs and IISc should concentrate on technology assessment and forecast so that futuristic approaches could be reoriented to cope up with the emerging trends in science and technology. As a result of this innovative initiatives, projects in the following seven generic areas of strategic significance are being implemented in mission mode by five IITs and IISc, Bangalore:

— Food Processing Engineering (FPE)
— Integrated Design and Competitive Manufacturing (IDCM)
— Photonic Devices and Technologies (PDT)
— Energy Efficient Technologies (EET)
— Communication Networking and Intelligent Automation (CNIA)
— New Materials (NM)
— Genetic Engineering and Biotechnology (GEB)

One Indian Institute of Technology/Institute of Science is the lead Institute for each of the seven generic areas. There are up to three participating Institutes, apart from the participation of industries.

For implementation and coordination of the scheme, a National Steering Committee and Mission Management Boards have been constituted. Necessary directions have also been given to boost the activities of these projects.

In Mission Management Boards, the involvement of various participating agencies has been ensured. The scheme has earned wide acceptance of the Industry as is evident from the number of Memorandum of Understanding (MoU) signed by them for development of various technologies/products. The Mission approach adopted in the scheme has proved to be a lead example for establishment of Industry-Institute partnerships.

Indian Institutes of Management

Indian Institutes of Management (IIMs) located at Ahmedabad, Calcutta, Bangalore and Lucknow are institutions of excellence, established with the objectives of imparting high quality management education and training, conducting research and providing consultancy services in the field of management to various sectors of the Indian economy. Two more IIMs, one at Indore and the other at Calicut have also been recently established. While the IIM, Calicut has commenced its academic session from 199798, the IIM, Indore has started academic programme from 1998-99.

The IIMs conduct Post-graduate Diploma Programmes in Management (equivalent to MBA), Fellowship Programmes in Management (equivalent to Ph.D), Short-term Management Development and Organisa-tion-based Programmes as well as carry out Research and Consultancy for the industry.

These Institutes have established Research Centres to cater to the needs of non-corporate and under-managed sectors, viz. Agriculture, Rural. Development, Public Systems Management, Energy, Health Education, Habitat, etc.

IIMs play a leadership role in the nation's managerial manpower development and carry out research in new emerging areas. These Institutes are recognised as premier management institutions, comparable to the best in the world for teaching, research and interaction with industries. IIMs being Role Models have shared knowledge and skills with other institutions to improve their quality and standards in management education. IIMs have earned an international reputation for the quality of their alumni.

Regional Engineering Colleges

Regional Engineering Colleges (RECs) were established,

one each in the major States, to meet the country's growing requirement for trained technical manpower for various developmental projects. Each of the total 17 RECs, as existing today, is a joint and cooperative enterprise of the Central Government and the State Government of the concerned State in which the REC is situated. All the Colleges conduct under-graduate courses in various branches of Engineering and Technology. Barring three RECs, all other colleges have facilities for post-graduate and doctoral programmes in Engineering, Technology and Applied Sciences. The RECs are normally affiliated to the universities in the respective region where they are located. Some of the universities have however granted academic autonomy to the respective REC, affiliated to them.

The entire non-recurring expenditure and 50 per cent of the recurring expenditure on under-graduate courses run by the RECs are borne by the Government of India, the balance 50 per cent of the recurring expenditure is met by the respective State Governments. However, the entire expenditure for running PG courses in the RECs is borne by the Central Government.

The MHRD has taken a number of initiatives for developing curriculum in tune with the changing needs of the society and those of the industry to enable RECs to achieve excellence in education, research and development. A programme of Centres of Excellence' in RECs was initiated during 1993-94 to elevate the standards of teaching, research and other activities of RECs. Through this programme, the RECs capabilities in computer, library resources and R&D equipment have been enhanced. Such capability enhancements through improvement of infrastructural facilities would definitely pave the way for raising the academic standards of RECs as has been observed by the Monitoring Committee for RECs.

UK-India RECs project

An Indo-UK Technical Cooperation project to strengthen technical education in India through assistance to eight RECs in four technical themes-Design (RECs at Allahabad and Jaipur), Energy (RECs at Bhopal and Tiruchirapalli), Information Technology (RECs at Surathkal and Warangal) and Materials Engineering (RECs at Nagpur and Rourkela) commenced in April 1994 after a formal Memorandum of Understanding was signed between the Government of India and the UK on 12 January 1994.

The Indo-UK RECs Project has been useful to the RECs and the benefits accrued from the project are:

— Exposure to advanced technological aspects
— Exposure to improved teaching methodologies and updated curriculum at UG/PG level
— Stress on improved Industry- Institute interaction
— Procurement of equipment which will help in improving curriculum, consultancy, R&D, etc.
— Effective interaction /coordination among RECs
— Improvement of library facilities which will help not only students and staff in their R&D work but also to industries around the region.

Important committees

A high power committee constituted on 17 June 1996 under the Chairmanship of Dr R.A. Mashelkar, Director General and Secretary, DSIR, to review the 17 RECs has since completed its exercise and a final report is to be submitted shortly.

A committee under the Chairmanship of Prof. P.V. Indersen, Former Director, IIT, Chennai, was constituted to examine the issue of increase in student intake in Engineering disciplines in the RECs from the academic session 1998-99 and also to look into the additional requirement of equipment, lab space,- lecture room, additional hostel seats, etc. for the increased strength. On the basis of the committee's recommendations, student intake has been increased in various disciplines in 15 RECs.

All India Council for Technical Education

The All India Council for Technical Education (AICTE) was set up in 1945 as an advisory body in the Ministry. It was given a statutory status through an Act of Parliament in 1987. The main functions of the statutory AICTE include proper planning and coordinated development of technical education (including Architecture, Town Planning, Management and Pharmacy Education) in the country, qualitative improvement at all levels in relation to planned quantitative growth and regulations of the system and maintenance of norms and standards. The Council has laid down norms arid standards for diplomas, degrees and postgraduate courses in various fields.

The AICTE has also issued Regulations for granting approval to technical institutions, courses and programmes in the field of technical education. Under these Regulations, approvals are given to private unaided technical institutions also.

A number of statutory All India Boards have been set up by the AICTE for coordination and maintenance of standards in technical education. The AICTE has also set up a National Board of Accreditation to conduct evaluation of technical institutions and its programme.

The Regional Committees at Kanpur, Chennai, Bangalore, Mumbai and Calcutta have been activated as a support system to the AICTE. Two new Regional Committees at Bhopal and Chandigarh have also been established. In order to ensure planned growth of technical education, the Council has a scheme to generate database to monitor supply and demand of engineering and technical manpower to ensure planned development of technical education.

North Eastern Regional Institute of Science and Technology

The North Eastern Regional Institute of Science and Technology (NERIST), Itanagar (Arunachal Pradesh) was established in 1986 to generate skilled manpower in the field of Engineering and Technology as well as Applied Science streams for the development of the North Eastern Region. With effect from 1994-95, the Institute is being funded by the Department of Education. It was earlier funded through North Eastern Council (NEC).

The NERIST was conceived as a unique institute offering a sequence of modular programmes, each of two-year duration leading to six certificates, seven diplomas and seven degrees in technology and applied sciences. The modules provide linkages with occupational levels, i.e. technicians, supervisors and engineers. The base and diploma modules provide entry to next higher module, subject to required performance of the students in lower module(s) and with the provision to undergo certain bridge courses. Thus a certain percentage of students get siphoned out either voluntarily or compulsorily at the end of each module. The thrust of this modular and innovative academic programme is to encourage a policy for vocationalisation and to allow only motivated students to go for higher studies while permitting others to go for jobs or to develop their entrepreneurial skills.

The Institute also offers two PG courses—Information Technology, and Environmental Science and Technology. Provisional affiliation to the NERIST has been accorded by North Eastern Hill University.

Sant Longowal Institute of Engineering and Technology

The Sant Longowal Institute of Engineering and Technology (SLIET), village Longowal, District Sangrur,

Punjab is an autonomous Institute registered under the Societies Registration Act, established and fully funded by the Government of India with 500 acres of land provided by the State Government of Punjab. The courses are modular and terminal in nature of two-year duration each and are having bridge courses at appropriate levels. The Institute is offering 12 Certificate courses, 10 Diploma courses and eight Degree courses.

The academic pattern of the Institute is designed unconventionally on the pattern of the NERIST with vertical mobility and lateral entry introduced at different levels of courses in Engineering and Technology, namely Certificate, Diploma and Degree in an integrated manner. The educational programmes are non-conventional, cost effective, flexible, modular and credit-based having built-in entrepreneurship with stress on self-employment and continuity of education at various levels with provision for multipoint entry.

National Institute for Training in Industrial Engineering

The National Institute for Training in Industrial Engineering (NITIE), Mumbai is a national institute with the assistance of the UNDP. It is an autonomous organisation under the MHRD. It conducts long-term and short-term courses in Industrial Engineering and allied fields, industry-oriented programmes to suit the specific needs of an industry/ organisation, evolves syllabi, teaching materials, norms and standards and provides help to other institutions engaged in teaching Industrial Engineering and allied subjects. The Institute also carries out applied research, develops course material, adopts industrial engineering techniques to Indian requirements, collaborates with other institutions /organisations and professional bodies to promote industrial engineering and productivity techniques.

National Institute of Foundry and Forge Technology

The National Institute of Foundry and Forge Technology (NIFFT), Ranchi was established by the Government of India in collaboration with the UNDP in 1966 with the objectives to organise teaching in training programmes, conduct research and development activities in the frontier areas pertaining to Foundry, Forge and related technologies and provide technological consultancy guidance and documentation services to such industries. It offers (i) M.Tech courses in Foundry and Forge Technology and in Manufacturing Engineering, (ii) Four-year Integrated B.Tech. Degree courses in Manufacturing Engineering and Metallurgy and Materials Engineering, (iii) Post-graduate Diploma course in Manufacturing Engineering, (iv) Advanced Diploma course in Foundry and Forge Technology and organises short-term refresher courses.

School of planning and architecture

The School of Town and Country Planning, New Delhi was established by the Government of India in 1955 to provide facilities in education and training in the field of rural, urban and regional planning. This School was renamed as School of Planning and Architecture (SPA) after the Department of Architecture was included in 1959 to provide facilities for education in the discipline of Architecture also. In 1979, the SPA was conferred with the status of a Deemed University.

The SPA has been imparting undergraduate and Post-graduate programmes in architecture and planning disciplines. The School also organises short-term courses, seminars, workshops, special programmes, exhibitions. These are attended by senior/ middle level officers sponsored by State/ Central Government departments, town planning organisations, development authorities, housing boards, public and private undertakings as well as institutions.

An Overseas Research and Development Centre has been established by the School to extend education and research facilities to other developing centres in Africa, SAARC and South Asia and to support and participate in the external cultural programmes between India and other friendly countries in which the school is cited as an agency to participate in the specialised items of the cultural exchange programmes.

Technical Teachers Training Institutes

The Technical Teachers' Training Institutes (TTTIs) at Bhopal, Calcutta, Chandigarh and Chennai were established during the mid sixties. The objective of the Institutes is to impart training in polytechnic education. The duration of the training programme is 12 to 18 months and is offered to degree and diploma holding teachers of Polytechnics in addition to providing short-term training to teachers and introducing them to curriculum development and related activities. The Institutes at Bhopal and Chennai and more recently at Chandigarh also offer PG courses in technical teaching. Besides teachers' training, these Institutes also undertake activities such as resources development, extension work, consultancy and project formulation.

The TITIs have been involved in a big way with the planning and implementation of massive State sector project on technician education with World Bank assistance. The project also provides for strengthening of TTTIs to enable them to take on the added responsibility under the project for improvement of technician professionals on a continuing basis to enable the concerned educational authorities to plan area of growth in the fields of engineering-based requirements in the country.

Thrust Areas in Technical Education

Modernisation

High priority has been given to the modernisation and removal of obsolescence of Engineering and Technological Management, Pharmacy and Architecture Institutions in the country. Modernisation is undertaken to enhance functional efficiency of these Institutes for teaching, training and research purposes. The MHRD has been implementing this scheme for the Central Institutions including Regional Engineering Colleges since 1997-98.

Objectives

— Removal of obsolescence in workshop machinery and equipment of laboratories for Engineering and Technological Management, Pharmacy and Architecture courses in the Central Institutions including Regional Colleges.

— Modernisation of laboratories and workshops by addition of new equipments. Augmentation of the library facilities.

— Support for projects involving new innovations in classroom technology, laboratory instructions, instructional materials and charts, development of appropriate technology.

— Training and retraining for the teaching and supporting technical staff.

— Upgradation of computing and networking facilities.

Research and development

The Research and Development (R&D) activities have been considered as an essential component of higher education because of its role in creating new knowledge and insight and imparting excitement and dynamism to the educational process. The MHRD had initiated a scheme in 1987-88 for promoting and augmentation of R&D activities with the following objectives:

— Creating and updating the infrastructure for R&D effort.

— Supporting sponsored/joint research projects in Engineering and Technology, Pharmacy, Architecture and Management. The joint research projects with other Technological Institutions, research laboratories and industries of repute will be preferred.

Thrust areas

The scheme provides project-based financial support for creation of infrastructural facilities in terms of laboratories and quality manpower in the emerging areas. The Ministry has been implementing the scheme in respect of the Central Institutions including Regional Engineering Colleges with the following objectives:

— To develop the infrastructure in terms of modern laboratories in the thrust areas.

— To develop a strong base for advance level work by identifying programmes and courses by institutions taking into account the vastness of the country and regional needs with special attention to the rural society and disadvantaged sections.

— To develop horizontal and vertical linkages with other institutions, research laboratories, industry and user agencies through multiplicity of programmes including consultancy.

Reservation of seats in technical courses

The MHRD extends the facilities of technical education to all States/UTs in view of national integration and for their socio-economic developments, by reserving seats in degree/ diploma level technical courses in Engineering Technology/ Pharmacy/Architecture in the Institutions approved by the AICTE for those States/UTs which either do not have proper facilities for technical education or which lack in facility for training in some specific fields of technical education depending upon the availability of seats offered by contributing States/UTs and keeping in view the demand of seats of lacking States/UTs. Nomination of candidates against these seats are made directly by the State/UT Government.

The reservation is also extended to the Ministry of External Affairs in view of the international commitment, for self-financing and' foreign recipients at the Indian Council for Cultural Relation Scholarship (in Government-funded institutions), and for the wards of the Government employees posted in Indian Mission abroad as well as to the Indian Council for Child Welfare, for the recipients of Children Bravery Award on the occasion of Republic Day and to the Central Tibetan Schools Administration. However, no seat is reserved in IITs, RECs, etc. under the scheme. Further, there is no discretionary quota of seats in this Ministry for nominating/ granting admission to an individual in any institution.

Facilities to self-financing foreign students

Post-graduate level technical course

Self-financing foreign students who intend to pursue studies in post-graduate programme in technical subjects (except concerning health and medical subjects) in institutions in India are issued No Objection Certificate (NOC) by this Ministry on receipt of clearance from the Ministry of External Affairs.

Under-graduate level technical course

Self-financing foreign students/Non- Resident Indians can take direct admission in Undergraduate course offered by unaided private and All India Council for Technical Education approved institutions in India upto five per cent of its sanctioned intake (allowed as per Supreme Court judgement). The Department of Education, MHRD is issuing NOC to the Heads of the Institutions for such admissions on their applications.

Board of assessment for educational qualifications

The Board of Assessment for Educational Qualifications was set up by the Government of India for the purpose of recognition of academic and professional qualifications (except concerning Health and Medical subjects) for employment to posts and services under the Central Government. The Chairman/Member, UPSC is the Chairman of this Board and the Secretariat of the Board is functioning from the Technical Education Bureau, Department of Education. The Board held its 23rd meeting on 24 November 1997. The term of the last Board expired on 18 June 1996. The present Board is to function for the period from 19 June 1996 to 18 June 1999.

Apprenticeship training

The National Scheme of Apprenticeship Training provides opportunities for practical training to graduate engineers, diploma holders (technicians) and 10+2 vocational pass-outs in different industrial establishments and other organisations as per the Apprentices Act 1961, as amended from time to time and as per policies and guidelines laid down by the Central Apprenticeship Council (CAC).

The four Regional Boards of Apprenticeship/ Practical Training located at Mumbai, Calcutta, Kanpur and Chennai are fully funded autonomous organisations of the MHRD which have been authorised in their respective regions to implement the Apprenticeship Act. The period of Apprenticeship training under the Act is one year in three categories of apprentices. During this training period the apprentices are paid monthly stipend which is shared between the Central Government and the employer on 50:50 basis.

Community polytechnics

The scheme of Community Polytechnics (CPs) aims at sustainable community development without environmental degradation by way of S&T applications for socio-economic upliftment and improvement in the quality of life of the common man through micro level planning and people's participation at the grassroots level. The scheme lays stress on poverty alleviation, employment generation and removal of drudgery for the women through location-culture-specific non-formal, need-based, short-term training in skill-oriented technical/vocational trades with no precondition of age, sex or qualification.

The training is specially geared to the needs of the unemployed/underemployed youth/school/college dropouts, the under-privileged and disadvantaged including women, minorities and the weaker sections of the society. These polytechnics also undertake, activities like technology transfer, technical support and S&T awareness for the community.

As on 31 March 1998, 442 CPs are functioning all over the country out of which 83 are exclusively for women. All the identified minority concentration districts (41 in number) in the country have been covered under the scheme. The Technical Teachers' Training Institutes located at Bhopal, Calcutta, Chandigarh and Chennai act as Resource Centres to provide necessary academic, technical and managerial support. About 100 technical / vocational trades relevant to respective local socio-economic conditions have been identified for imparting skill development training oriented towards employment generation.

Community Polytechnics have made significant contribution towards promoting transfer of a large number of tested and approved items of technology to the rural areas including windmills, smokeless chulhas, rural latrines, solar appliances, agricultural implements, etc. These institutions have been able to establish proper linkages and effective collaboration and coordination with a number of Government and non-Government agencies.

World bank-assisted technician education project.

As a follow-up of the National Policy on Education, the Government of India initiated a massive effort for strengthening technician education and improving the quality of polytechnic pass-outs in the country. The project was launched with the assistance of the World Bank as State Sector Project in two phases. The first phase commenced from December 1990 and ended in September 1998, for integrated development of polytechnics and the state systems of polytechnic education in 17 States and two Union Territories. The objectives of this project are classified into three major target sectors, viz. Capacity Expansion, Quality Improvement and Efficiency Enhancement of Technician Education System in the country.

Enhancing participation of women students in polytechnics is one of the thrust areas under the World Bank-assisted Technician Education Project. The overall percentage of women students has improved from 11 per cent in 1990 to 28 per cent in 1998. Twenty-six new co-educational polytechnics and 30 new women's polytechnics, besides 10 Wings for women have been established. To facilitate participation of women in Technician Education in co-educational polytechnics, hostels for women have also been constructed. Moreover, two special polytechnics have been set up for imparting Technician Education to the handicapped.

Educational consultants India limited

Educational Consultants India Limited was conceived and incorporated as a Public Sector Undertaking by the

Government of India in 1981 under the Department of Education to offer educational consultancy and technical services in different aspects of education and human resource development not only in India but also on global basis.

Asian Institute of Technology Bangkok

The Asian Institute of Technology (AIT), Bangkok is an autonomous international Graduate Institute providing advanced education in Engineering, Science and allied fields. It enrolls about 600 students from more than twenty countries and h as international faculty members. The Institute is governed by an International Board of Trustees, whose members come from different countries along with those from India. The faculty members from India are selected by the MHRD.

Canada-India Institutional Co-operation Project

The Canada-India Institutional Cooperation Project (CIICP) is a technical education project mandated by a Memorandum of Understanding between the Governments of Canada and India, and funded by the Canadian International Development Agency (CIDA). The Canadian Executing Agency is the Association of Canadian Community Colleges (ACCC). This is the first major project supported by the Government of Canada in the technical education sector in India. The overall project direction is provided by the MHRD. The focus is on human resource development with special emphasis on skill development in the following areas:

— Strategic Planning
— Staff Development
— Industry-Institute Interaction
— Continuing Education
— Management Development

— Management Information Systems
— Women in Development
— Environment Development
— Student Services
— Equipment Repair Facility

The project is designed to foster links among the Indian and Canadian partner institutions comprising (i) the Indian Society for Technical Education (ISTE), New Delhi, (ii) Technical Teachers' Training Institute (TTI), Chennai, (i ii) Directorates of Technical Education (DTEs) of Karnataka, Kerala and Tamil Nadu, (iv) 13 polytechnics in these states, (v) Association of Canadian Community Colleges (ACCC) and (vi) selected Canadian Colleges and Institutes.

Phase I of the Project (1991-96) was completed by March 1996. The project has been extended for three years (1996-99) to achieve sustainability and transfer of responsibility to Indian partners and, accordingly, considerable inputs are being provided to strengthen the DTEs in the respective States. Twelve new polytechnics from the Project States have been added in the extended period of the Project for replication of the Project outcomes.

The DTEs are developing appropriate systems and procedures to provide continued support and encouragement to the project polytechnics in all CIICP activities. In the replication polytechnics, the entire staff is showing a high level of commitment and interest in the replication process with the result that, in many instances, targets are being achieved much faster than planned or expected. Moreover, a sense of belonging, ownership and team spirit is prevailing in all Project polytechnics with respect to all Project initiatives. An abundance of good resource material and well-trained and committed resource persons on HRD-related areas are already available. The ISTE and TTTI, Chennai have been suitably strengthened. The linkages and coordination between the Indian partner institutes and organisations like MHRD, Directorates, ISTE, TTTI and the Project polytechnics are now stronger than ever before.

Technical education in union territories

The Department of Education, MHRD renders all help, support, assistance, co-operation and guidance to the UT Governments/Administrations as well as to the individual Degree/Diploma level Technical Institutions in the respective Union Territories for governance and for proper planning, monitoring and implementation of Academic/Technical activities in each of these institutions.

At present, facilities for Degree/Diploma level technical education are available in 28 technical institutions functioning under the administrative control of the respective Union Territory administrations of (i) A&N Islands, (ii) Chandigarh, (iii) Dadra and Nagar Haveli, (iv) Daman & Diu, (v) Delhi and (vi) Pondicherry. The Department of Education apart from providing necessary academic, administrative and technical help, support and guidance to the UT Administrations also extends its fullest co-operation to help and decide on all issues concerning academic, administrative, financial and personnel aspects associated with the individual technical institutions in the respective Union Territories.

Meetings

To finalise the recruitment qualifications for Group 'A' teaching posts of the Chandigarh College of Architecture, Chandigarh, a meeting of the concerned agencies involved, viz. (i) Chandigarh College of Architecture, (ii) Chandigarh Administration, (iii) Union Public Service

Commission, (iv) Council of Architecture, (v) All India Council for Technical Education and (vi) Department of Education, MHRD was organised by the Department of Education in Shastri Bhawan, New Delhi on 1 July 1998.

Special projects for eradication of illiteracy

The uniqueness of the literacy campaign lies in the fact that it is delivered through voluntarism. Literacy campaigns are implemented by the Zilla Saksharata Samitis (ZSSs) which create a fusion between the district administration headed by the Collector on the one hand, and volunteer groups, panchayats, and social activists on the other. The literacy campaigns are implemented by funding ZSSs through the Central and State Governments in the ratio of 2:1 (4:1 for districts in the Tribal Sub-Plan areas).

The initiation of the TLC begins with the process of consultation and consensus involving political parties, teachers and cultural groups.

This gives rise to the organisational structure of the Zila Saksharta Samiti. The Zila Saksharta Samiti conducts a survey to identify the nonliterate population as well as the potential volunteer teachers. Mass mobilisation takes place during the literacy campaigns through a multi-faceted communication strategy which includes Kala Jathas, Nukkad Nataks, wall writings, Padyatras, literacy songs, posters, banners, etc. Locally relevant teaching-learning materials are developed using an innovative pedagogy called Improved Pace and Content of Learning (IPCL). Primer-specific training is imparted to trainers in the literacy campaigns. The environment building activities as well as monitoring and supervision continues throughout the actual teaching-learning process which takes 200 hours and is spread over a period of 6 to 9 months. Monitoring and supervision of Total Literacy Campaigns (TLCs) is done through a periodic system of reporting as well as through concurrent and external evaluations which are conducted by evaluation agencies identified by State Directorates of Adult Education and the NLM.

The Total Literacy Campaign is followed by the Post Literacy Campaign which aims to consolidate the gains accrued during the basic literacy stage. It also takes care of the dropouts and left-outs of the Total Literacy Campaigns through a process of mopping up. It is during the post-literacy stage that convergence with other development programmes, and skill upgradation of neo-literates is sought.

So far 450 districts have been covered under TLC in the States of Andhra Pradesh, Assam, Bihar, Delhi, Goa, Gujarat, Haryana, Himachal Pradesh, Jammu & Kashmir, Karnataka, Maharashtra, Madhya Pradesh and West Bengal and Union Territories of Chandigarh, Daman & Diu, Dadra and Nagar Haveli and Pondicherry. Of these, 250 campaign's have moved into Post-Literacy and 65 to the Continuing Education stage.

The campaigns cover an estimated 148 million persons, among whom 121 million learners were identified through survey. Of the 94 million persons enrolled, 72.55 million persons have been made literate (learners having completed level III) so far.

Keeping in view the way the Mission has moved, the following new strategies have evolved:

— Preparation of time-bound action plans for TLC coverage of uncovered districts in the States of Bihar, Punjab, Jammu & Kashmir and north-eastern States.

— Non-cash incentives for motivating volunteers so as not to defeat their spirit.

— Instituting linkages between literacy campaigns and Panchayati Raj Institutions. Linking literacy schemes and other development programmes.

— Regular and systematic monitoring by holding state-level monthly meetings.

— Compilation and dissemination of accurate field-level data.

— Concurrent and final evaluations of campaigns by independent social research agencies with proven track record.

— Decentralisation and delegation of authority for implementation of literacy programmes to State governments by establishing State Literacy Mission Authorities (SLMAs).

— Strengthening State Directorates of Adult Education to act as nodal agencies of monitoring and evaluation.

— Augmenting State Resource Centres (SRCs) for providing improved techno-pedagogic and training support to literacy programmes.

Shramik Vidyapeeths

The scheme of Shramik Vidyapeeths (SVPs) is a programme of Polyvalent (multi-faceted) Adult Education for workers and their family members in urban and industrial areas. The programme was evolved to respond to educational and vocational training needs of numerous groups of adults and young people living in urban and industrial areas and for persons who have been migrating from rural to urban settings.

The first Shramik Vidyapeeth was established in Mumbai (Worli) in the year 1967 and gradually the number 4 Vidyapeeths has increased to 58 in 16 States and 1 Union Territory in 1997.

Hitherto, the scheme of SVP has been restricted to urban/ semi-urban areas. During the Ninth Five Year Plan period the scheme will expand its area of operation. In the changed scenario, the main task of SVP will be to act as district level resource support agency, especially, in regard to organisation of vocational training and skill development programmes for the neo-literates and other target groups under the scheme of Continuing Education for neo-literates.

The Shramik Vidyapeeths are registered under the Societies Registration Act 1860 with its own Memorandum of Association and Rules and Regulations.

Annual assistance to the extent of Rs 12.30 lakh to Shramik Vidyapeeths that have completed five years and Rs 8.00 lakh along with one time grant of Rs 3.00 lakh to those that are yet to complete five years is given by the Ministry of Human Resource Development, Department of Education. The grant is likely to be increased substantially during the Ninth Five Year Plan to help strengthen their infrastructure.

Shramik Vidyapeeths offer around 225 different vocational training programmes right from candle and agarbatti making to computer courses.

National Literacy Resource Centre

The National Literacy Resource Centre (NLRC) was set up by the NLM at the Lal Bahadur Shastri Academy of Administration, Mussoorie. The most important activity of the NLRC is to organise training and orientation workshops for District Mission leaders and various district functionaries of Zilla Saksharata Samitis and Panchayati Raj Institutions, apart from preparing various case studies and video documentations. After the initial period of two years, the Centre at Mussoorie has been approved for a period of five years from 1998-99 to 2000-2003.

In the years 1997-98, NLRC organised training workshops for various functionaries of Uttar Pradesh, Rajasthan, Haryana and Madhya Pradesh. In addition, regional workshops for preparing training materials have also been organised at Chennai (Tamil Nadu) and Dumka (Bihar). The NLRC continues to build human resources for literacy promotion.

Continuing education programme

Continuing Education is perceived as an indispensable aspect of the strategy of human resource development and of the goal of creation of learning society. Continuing Education provides a second chance to those deprived section of the society who missed formal education.

The scheme of Continuing Education is being implemented since 1996-97. Around 62 Districts spreading in 12 States and I Union Territory have been covered till December 1998 under the scheme. Around 38,000 Continuing Education Centres and 4,800 nodal Continuing Education Centres are being set up in these Districts. The Continuing Education Centre serves as the focal point for providing learning opportunities such as literacy classes, library, reading room, learning centre, training centre, cultural centre, sport centre and other individual interest promotion programme centres.

The scheme of Continuing Education also provides the opportunity to undertake diverse activities involving alternative and innovative approaches to cater to the need of the learners.

Taking into account the local conditions and the resource availability, various target-specific activities such as Equivalency Programmes (EPs), Quality of Life Improvement Programmes (QLIPs), Income Generating Programmes (IGPs) and Individual Interest Promotion Programmes (IIPPs) are also organised for specific groups of beneficiaries. The programme of continuing education is being implemented under the aegis of Zilla Saksharata Samiti. Zilla Saksharata Samitis along with Districts, Blocks and Gram Panchayat Level Committees are responsible for overseeing the programme in the entire district. Component of flexibility in implementational strategy, sustainable of the programme in the long run, community participation, non-duplication efforts and integration of development activities are broader approaches on which the Continuing Education Programme is being implemented.

Strengthening of Administrative Structures

The scheme of Strengthening of Administrative Structure (SAS) was introduced in 1978-79 to create necessary supportive administrative structures at the State, Union Territory and District levels for implementing adult education programmes. In the scheme of SAS the Central Government bore the financial burden of the sanctioned posts in the States and UTs. Seed money was also provided to six State Literacy Mission Authorities (SLMAs) for strengthening of their infrastructure.

During the current year financial allocation of Rs 4.67 crores were released against committed liabilities of previous years to nine States/UTs (Himachal Pradesh, Karnataka, MP, Maharashtra, Manipur, UP, Andaman & Nicobar Islands), The Central assistance under the scheme of SAS has been discontinued after 31 March 1998. The State Governments and Union Territories are expected to bear the financial burden from their own sources.

Rural functional literacy project

Launched in 1978 as the main Centrally Sponsored Scheme under the National Adult Education Programme (NAEP), Rural Functional Literacy Project (RFLP) was to cover 100 million non-literates in five years. The strengths of RFLP were high participation of women and weaker sections, and production of good quality teaching and learning materials. However, reviews indicated that RFLP in its original form did not have the expected impact. A revised RFLP was initiated to be implemented during the Eighth Five Year Plan in Jammu & Kashmir, Sikkim, the North Eastern States, border districts of Rajasthan., and Dadra & Nagar Haveli. Today the scheme is operational in Jammu & Kashmir, States of the North-East and Sikkim.

During the current financial year an amount of Rs 60.00 lakhs has been released to J&K Government till December 1998. The scheme of RFLP is proposed to be subsumed with TLC/PLC scheme in the Ninth Five Year Plan.

Assistance to voluntary agencies

During the year under report voluntary agencies continued to implement total and post literacy projects. Fresh total literacy projects were funded in North East (Manipur) and J&K.

With the sanctioning of Continuing Education projects to more than 60 districts in thirteen States in the country, focus has been on changing techno-pedagogic needs for these programmes.

A Regional Workshop on Role of Resource Centres in Continuing Education was organised in Hyderabad from 15 to 17 June 1998. The workshop deliberated on:

— Strategy and Policy formulation of Project Proposal of CE
— Redesigning training for new requirements
— Development of materials
— Methodology and format of Monitoring and
— Evaluation
— Training of staff of Resource Centres.

The Resource Centres during this year have taken up projects in their annual action plan to establish at least one nodal Continuing Education Centre in the area of jurisdiction. These centres will become the models for implementation of the CE scheme at a larger scale.

Four Voluntary agencies have been involved in the project 'Training and Cooperation Literacy in India-Plan of Operation' executed jointly by the National Literacy Mission and the UNESCO. The studies undertaken were

— Planning and management of literacy campaigns.
— The implementation of literacy and continuing education activities for out-of school girls and women.
— Improving the training of literacy personnel and their social status in the context of literacy work.
— The role of social mobilisation for literacy through decentralisation and community involvement.

Directorate of Adult Education

The Directorate of Adult Education (DAE), a subordinate office of the Department of Education has been functioning as the national resource centre for adult education and literacy programmes in the country. It is the functional arm of the National Literacy Mission which is responsible for monitoring and evaluation of various schemes launched under the aegis of NLM. The highlights of various units of the DAE during the year 1997-98 are as under.

The Monitoring Unit maintained a close look at the literacy campaigns launched in about 450 districts spread over 26 States and UTs through its Management Information System. The receipt of monthly reports in the prescribed formats developed by DAE from various States were ensured and based on these reports periodical and annual reports for the use of planners, administrators and policy makers in various levels were generated, The Unit has been developed as a data bank relating to all relevant information about basic literacy, post-literacy and continuing education in the country.

The Evaluation Unit received 19 concurrent evaluation and 49 final evaluation reports of the TLCs during the year which were critically examined and follow-up action taken to streamline the campaigns. The Unit also prepared the guidelines for mid-term and final evaluation of post-literacy programmes through a series of regional and national workshops and circulated these guidelines amongst all concerned. The Unit organised two orientation workshops for the empanelled evaluating agencies in which representatives of NLM, State DAE and SRCs and RRCs participated. It also organised two workshops on identifying the priority areas in research in the field of adult education.

The Materials Unit brought out the policy guidelines on production, selection and purchase of neo-literate materials for continuing education centres. It also finalised a set of Improved Pace and Content of Learning (IPCL) primers for industrial workers under the scheme 'Literacy in Workplace'. Two regional workshops for orientation of writers in designing IPCL primers and preparation of sample materials in languages and tribal dialects of North East States including Nepali, Limba, Lipcha, Bhutia and 16 tribal dialects of Manipur were organised during the year. Four regional workshops, including two for Urdu language, were also organised to orient the writers in the art of designing neo-literate materials.

The Media Unit undertook 19 new productions with 137 episodes in different languages through different producers. Intensive media campaign on literacy was also launched through telecast of literacy spots over Doordarshan, twice a week telecast of literacy programmes of Doordarshan and through Closed Circuit TV (CCTV) at selected railway stations throughout the country. One of the video productions of DAE titled Manoj Ki Kahani won a prize at the Eighth Audio Visual festival held at Hyderabad.

The Publications Unit brought out more than 20 publications related to literacy. These included the prestigious publication A Decade of Literacy published on the occasion of the International Literacy Day on 8 September 1998 by the SRC, Delhi on behalf of the National Literacy Mission and the UNESCO. It also produced another prestigious publication entitled Outreach in collaboration with the Indian Navy, Ministry of Social Justice and Empowerment and Confederation of Indian Industries which was released by the Hon'ble Prime Minister of India on the occasion of Navy Day on 4 December 1998. Besides this, the Unit also assisted in producing hundreds of reports generated through various workshops and seminars organised by the NLM and the DAE during the year. It was instrumental in putting up an impressive display exhibition on literacy on the social development fair at Pragati Maidan, New Delhi.

The Urban Unit of the Directorate finalised the new, guidelines for the Shramik Vidyapeeths renamed as Jana Sikshan Sansthan (Institute of People's Education) keeping in view their enhanced role in the Ninth Five Year Plan. While providing guidance to the 58 Shramik Vidyapeeths now under operation in various parts of the country, it also conducted feasibility study with six voluntary agencies which have applied for establishing Shramik Vidyapeeths. The Unit prepared a report titled 'Facts at a Glance' containing the details of the achievements of SVPs during the Eighth Five Year Plan and also the annual report for SVPs for the year 1997-98.

The Directorate is implementing the UNFPA-funded 'Population Education Project in Adult Literacy' through the technical resource support of 21 States and Regional Resource Centres across the country. During the year 1997-98, the third phase of the project has begun which aims at infusing population and development education in post-literacy and continuing education.

The Unit commissioned four evaluation/impact studies on population and development education and received final reports which have been circulated amongst SRCs, RRCs, Ministry of Health and Family Welfare and UNFPA, etc. It also conducted two inter-state comparative studies. A three-day orientation programme on population education was organised for the Director and Programme Officers of SRCs and RRCs at Bhubaneswar while two national level workshops were held at Hyderabad and Jaipur. The Directorate prepared a directory of publications developed and produced by SRC. Regional workshops on continuing education were organised at Chennai, Hyderabad and Udaipur while a five-day orientation programme of training of trainers of SRCs was held at Pune.